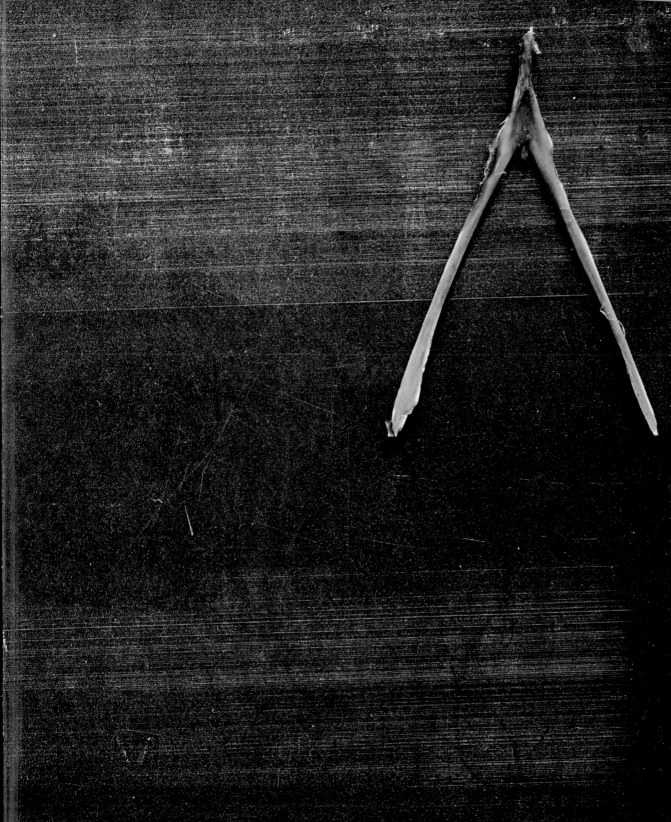

BRINGING IT
home

ALSO BY GAIL SIMMONS

Talking with My Mouth Full:
My Life as a Professional Eater

BRINGING IT *home*

Favorite
Recipes from
a Life of
Adventurous
Eating

GAIL SIMMONS

WITH **MINDY FOX**

FOREWORD BY
TOM COLICCHIO

PHOTOGRAPHS BY
JOHNNY MILLER

GRAND CENTRAL
Life & Style
NEW YORK BOSTON

Grand Central Life & Style

Hachette Book Group

1290 Avenue of the Americas, New York, NY 10104

grandcentrallifeandstyle.com

twitter.com/grandcentralpub

First Edition: October 2017

Grand Central Life & Style is an imprint of Grand Central Publishing.
The Grand Central Life & Style name and logo are trademarks of
Hachette Book Group, Inc.

The publisher is not responsible for websites (or their content)
that are not owned by the publisher.

The Hachette Speakers Bureau provides a wide range of authors for
speaking events. To find out more, go to www.hachettespeakersbureau.com
or call (866) 376-6591.

Photo of the Food & Wine Classic in Aspen on page xix by Huge Galdones.
Courtesy of *Food & Wine.*

Food styling by Rebecca Jurkevich

Prop styling by Bette Blau

Library of Congress Cataloging-in-Publication Data

Names: Simmons, Gail, author. | Fox, Mindy (Mindy Miller), author.
Title: Bringing it home : favorite recipes from a life of adventurous eating /
    Gail Simmons with Mindy Fox ; foreword by Tom Colicchio ; photographs
    by Johnny Miller.
Description: New York : Life & Style, [2017] | Includes bibliographical
    references and index.
Identifiers: LCCN 2017020073| ISBN 978-1-4555-4220-8 (hardcover) |
    ISBN 978-1-4555-4221-5 (ebook)
Subjects: LCSH: Cooking. | LCGFT: Cookbooks.
Classification: LCC TX714 .S5757 2017 | DDC 641.5/1—dc23
LC record available at https://lccn.loc.gov/2017020073

ISBNs: 978-1-4555-4220-8 (hardcover); 978-1-4555-4221-5 (ebook)

Printed in the United States of America

Q-MA

10 9 8 7 6 5 4 3 2 1

Contents

FOREWORD

by Tom Colicchio

◆

Gail Simmons eats her way through life. Sounds simple
enough—we all do, right? Nope. Not like this.

Food is not just Gail's job. It's what fires her up and sets her in motion (well, that and chasing her three-year-old, Dahlia).

Most of us eat at regular intervals in our lives; Gail eats her way through life. These are different things. When Gail is not eating, she's thinking about what she ate last night, writing about what she ate this morning, planning what she's going to eat tomorrow, etc. Whereas most people eat while enjoying life's experiences—for Gail the food itself is the experience.

For a normal person this would seem compulsive, even borderline obsessive. Fear not: Gail is one of the healthiest, most upbeat, thoroughly honest, balanced, and charming people on the planet. She doesn't need therapy to deal with her food obsession. She just needs more food.

I first met Gail when she was working with Jeffrey Steingarten on an article about the perfect steak. I don't remember too much about the encounter other than those eyes, that smile, that intellect, and the genuine hunger to plumb, to taste, and to catalog everything there was to know about steak. Aging, marbling, grilling…this wasn't just a job for Gail, it was a mission. When it was all done, most researchers would have sworn off beef for a few months; Gail probably went out for a burger.

In the years that we've worked together on *Top Chef*, I've come to see Gail as more than a co-judge. For one, she's become a great friend. She shares my passion for beef jerky and licorice (the real kind, not the red stuff). She is always reassuringly seated to my left which makes me feel good, as I know it means we can expect a serious food discussion (as in seriously informed and passionate, not serious-boring). Gail's opinions about food come directly from her own encyclopedic experiences as an eater. At the Judges' Table, that leads us to richer discussions and deeper, more meaningful debate. When the future of an aspiring chef is at stake, that's a good thing.

Top Chef has taken us eating around the world. For years now, I have been blessedly freed from the rigors of travel research because Gail has the list. On our days off from filming, Gail has anywhere from eight to twelve off-the-beaten-track food options only the locals have heard of, thanks to her personal network of fellow food obsessives who know exactly which hawker stand in Singapore or strip mall in Vegas we must visit that minute. And while most of us enjoy these exotic tastes and move on, Gail files the flavors and techniques away in the vivid hard drive of her memory and then mines them later in her own home kitchen for the people she loves.

This book is your chance to experience this for yourself—the world as seen through the eyes of a passionate eater, brined in Jewish common sense, leavened with Canadian decency and good humor, then distilled into achievable recipes for the home cook. It's your invitation to join Gail for dinner, for the pleasure of the food and the wonderful stories and singular point of view that only she could bring. Cheers!

INTRODUCTION

◆

"Do you cook at home?"

I've been asked this question more times than there are grains of salt in a shaker. It's easy to understand. Fans of *Top Chef,* the show I've been on for over a decade, don't see me at dawn padding around the kitchen in my pajamas, plotting the first meal of the day, or standing at my stove after work, eager to cook dinner for my family. They don't see the stacks of syrupy Sunday morning pancakes I make with my daughter, Dahlia, or the happy chaos that ensues (and gives our home kitchen that truly lived-in feel) when my husband, Jeremy, and I invite friends for dinner. Instead, they see the discerning critic in a cocktail dress, with styled hair and polished makeup, hyperanalyzing ingredients and cooking techniques.

The truth is, my delicious dual-decade career in the food industry didn't begin with a bespoke seat at the *Top Chef* Judges' Table, or with any of the many twists and turns that guided my professional path up until that point. Instead, it began with four words hollered by my mother to my two brothers and me each and every day of our young lives: "Alan! Eric! Gail!…SUPPER!"

My mom, a freelance food writer and part-time cooking teacher, was a natural at the stove. Her call to the family dinner table—seven nights a week, no excuses—got us kids up and running, no matter what we were doing. She made it clear, both by her words and the heartfelt effort she made to shop for and prepare great meals, that our nightly time together truly mattered. It didn't hurt to know that the dishes she put down in front of us would be utterly delicious.

In addition to her emphasis on cooking for family and friends, my mom's ease and spontaneity in the kitchen, as well as her drive to continually expand her food knowledge, made an impression on me at any early age. She would cull the great markets of our home city of Toronto, filling her shopping bags with ingredients that were exotic at the time: Chinese bok choy and Vietnamese *rambutans;* Portuguese *churrasco* and Greek sheep's milk cheeses; sweet Indian *ras malai* and tart Middle Eastern sumac. I have vivid memories of so many of her dishes and now clearly see her influence on my own passions in the kitchen—my liberal use of dill and penchant for zucchini; my obsession with pickles; the thrill I get when challenged by an unfamiliar cut of meat; my craving for tandoori chicken, served just as my mom was taught to make it by her close friend from Pakistan.

Above: *Mom and Dad, newly engaged, 1966*

My parents loved to travel. My mom, a native Montrealer, had attended graduate school in Belgium and spent a year exploring pockets of Europe and the Middle East before moving back to Canada and settling in Toronto, where soon after, she met my dad—a dashing chemical engineer who had made his way to the city from his homeland of South Africa via London. They were passionate explorers and often took my brothers and me along on their adventures. We traveled often to South Africa to visit family and took vacations to faraway places like Costa Rica, Israel, England, and Mexico. No trip was complete without time set aside to explore local markets, where we'd learn about and taste new foods and collect first-hand intel on the best down-home eateries and cafés.

When I began college at McGill University in Montreal, I had a chance to put my own knack for exploring to the test. The city offered an endless array of ethnic restaurants that lured food-loving locals and budget-conscious students alike. My friends and I slurped noodles from fragrant, brothy bowls of Vietnamese pho. At BYOB Greek restaurants, we shared plates of stuffed grape leaves, *taramasalata*, *saganaki*, and other mesmerizing *meze*, all washed down with bottles of store-bought boxed wine and Québec-made microbrews. We frequented the old Jewish delis of the Plateau for delectably fatty smoked meat and fresh warm bagels. At Portuguese rotisseries, we squeezed fresh lemon wedges over plates of spit-roasted chickens and potatoes slick with their delicious drippings, and ate it all up with abandon.

Late night post-bar bites included piping hot slices of thin crust pizza and, of course, poutine—the gut-busting French-Canadian junk-food specialty of French fries and cheese curds covered in a rich brown gravy—but also more exotic eats, like Lebanese-Canadian chicken shawarma sandwiches (called *shish taouk*) packed with pickled turnips, fresh cucumber, and tomato salad, generously drizzled with a creamy garlic sauce, and served with French fries.

Paging through the *McGill Tribune* one day during my senior year, I noticed there wasn't any food or local dining coverage. I was eager to do some creative writing outside of the requirements for my anthropology and Spanish studies, so I pitched the editor on a few restaurant reviews. There was no budget for the work, but she was happy to give me the page space to fill. I wrote about cheese fondue and Peruvian ceviche, delighting in the chance to relay my foodie exploits in what felt like a somewhat professional way.

Around that time, I began cooking for myself, too, calling my mom at all hours of the day and night to get her recipes for easy basics, like roast chicken and homemade tomato sauce. After winter break, I lugged her extra food processor back to school, using it to puree fresh herbs into pestos and make ricotta cheese fillings for pasta. I bought my first kitchen "bible," a second-hand copy of Mollie Katzen's *The Moosewood Cookbook*, and happily splattered its pages with oil and spices, sauces and soups, as I cooked my way through.

When we graduated, all of my close girlfriends seemed to have their career plans sorted. I did not. No one, not even my parents, had suggested I think through next steps. I had loved and excelled at my schoolwork, which included a junior year abroad in Seville, after which I traveled through Spain, France, Italy, Switzerland, Belgium, Holland, London, Prague, and Morocco. I had spent a summer living and working on a kibbutz in Israel, and another bartending in Australia and backpacking in New Zealand. My worldview had expanded exponentially through those unique and thrilling experiences, but I hadn't taken any time to chart out my future.

Moving back home from college, I felt a little deflated. I knew I loved to write and cook, but (despite my mother's own work in the field) it didn't occur to me that those interests could be parlayed into a means of gainful employment until a family friend sat me down and pointed out that if what I loved most to do was to eat, write, travel, and cook, then that's what I should pursue. Before I knew it, I was off and running.

A four-month internship at *Toronto Life* magazine led to a job as an editorial assistant in the lifestyle section of a new Canadian newspaper called the *National Post*. My work largely entailed research and fact-checking, but I took on any opportunity to write, no matter how small. Short pieces on subjects like mayonnaise taste tests and regional McDonald's specialties around the world (did you know they used to offer lamb burgers in India?) were among my first bylines, and they made me infinitely proud. I became buddies with the food critic, who often took me along to restaurants, and the food editor, who ultimately gave me an invaluable piece of advice on how to pursue a career in food media: If I wanted to become a bona fide food writer, he told me, I needed to go to culinary school. I needed to learn how to cook, and how to eat.

I enrolled in Peter Kump's cooking school (now known as the Institute of Culinary Education) in New York City, where I had always dreamed of living. For the final part of my coursework, I did an apprenticeship at the grande dame of the city's classic French restaurants, Le Cirque 2000, where I had the chance not only to work with luxe ingredients like foie gras, caviar, and truffles, but also to begin to understand the level of efficiency and meticulousness (among many other traits) that a chef must possess in order to excel in the high-pressured environment of a professional kitchen. I went on to cook at Jean-Georges Vongerichten's then-groundbreaking restaurant, Vong, where French and Thai techniques and flavors met in the form of dishes like crispy duck spring rolls and poached lobster served with paper-thin slices of daikon radish and a rosemary-ginger vinaigrette.

After 12- to 14-hour shifts at the restaurant, my fellow line cooks often went out drinking. Me? I worked myself down from the fever pitch of restaurant life by going home and reading late into the night. One book recommended to me by a friend was

The Man Who Ate Everything, by *Vogue* magazine's food critic, Jeffrey Steingarten, which I devoured in two post-work sittings. Jeffrey's impassioned, authoritative and hilarious writing not only taught me innumerable food facts and kept me in stitches, it inspired my move back to media. It wasn't ever my long-term plan to be a chef; restaurant cooking was a means to an end. Reading Jeffrey's words made me realize I was ready to bring my hard-earned food knowledge back into the world of publishing. In true NYC-dream-story fashion, I discovered Jeffrey was looking for a new assistant and hustled my way into the job.

Working for Jeffrey was a whirlwind. No two days were ever alike, which was exactly as I had hoped. One day I'd be at the New York Public Library, researching Parisian menus from the turn of the century. The next, I'd be scouring the Asian markets and restaurant supply stores of New York's Chinatown and the Bowery, hunting for the perfect oversized mortar and pestle and a laundry list of rare chilies and spices, galangal, and lemongrass, which Jeffrey would use to make Thai jungle curry.

We once visited nearly every restaurant in the city that had a wood-burning pizza oven, collecting data on the internal temperature of each fiery inferno with a Raytek infrared thermometer, then tested dozens of recipes for pizza dough to see whether or not we could successfully make an authentic Neapolitan pie at home. (The answer: It is entirely possible to produce a very tasty *amateur* version in a home oven at 500 degrees, but it will never be as ethereally crisp and perfectly burnt in spots as a pizza baked for 5 minutes at 850 degrees.)

To perfect a recipe for *real* coq au vin, I was tasked with finding a poultry farmer who could supply enough old roosters for us to test and re-test the classic stew every day for over a month. (Using a tough, mature male bird, as opposed to a standard chicken, is a key factor to turning out an authentic version of the dish, I learned!) Then there was the time we fine-tuned the ultimate technique for the perfect grilled steak—a feat that took over 97 days, requiring interviews with 40-some butchers and steakhouse chefs; the dry-aging of 50-plus porterhouse steaks in Jeffrey's makeshift "aging refrigerator"; and over a dozen tastings prepared for us by a young chef named Alex Guarnaschelli and a rising star named Tom Colicchio.

Through Jeffrey, I met all of the major players in the food world—everyone from pastry master Pierre Hermé to food science guru Harold McGee, plus Ruth Reichl, Alice Waters, Martha Stewart, and chef Daniel Boulud, who—when I was ready to leave Jeffrey—offered me my next job. At the time, Daniel's public relations and marketing team needed help, which included working on new restaurant openings, cookbooks, and events. It was a bit of a detour from my journalism track, but the opportunity to work for the most acclaimed French chef in New York, and learn the business side of restaurants, was too exciting to pass up. I now think back on my time with Daniel as my "restaurant MBA."

Three years into the job with Daniel's restaurant group, I was approached by *Food & Wine* magazine about a position on their marketing team. I jumped at the chance to put all of the food and chef knowledge I had acquired into working for a publication I

Opposite, clockwise from top left: *Early days, enjoying food to the fullest; Me and mom (and a cookie); Mom with my 3ʳᵈ birthday cake, made by Aunt Sue; Once a gourmet, always a gourmet*

Above, from left to right: *Alan, Eric, and me, with popsicles, 1978; Summer days on Lake Ontario*

had always loved and admired. Within a year I took over the management of the Food & Wine Classic in Aspen—the industry's most prestigious annual food festival, celebrating great chefs and winemakers from all over the world. Around the same time, Bravo came to the magazine with an idea for a new reality competition show, which would give viewers a revolutionary, behind-the-scenes look at the world of professional chefs. Having done a little on-camera work for the magazine, covering recipes and food trends, I was chosen to represent *Food & Wine* on the show. Reality TV was in its infancy and I had no idea what to expect, but before I could give it much thought I was on my way to San Francisco to shoot Season 1 of *Top Chef.*

Although I had done a fair bit of international travel growing up, I'd visited relatively little of North America before my days on *Top Chef.* Cities like Chicago, Charleston, New Orleans, and Austin were all new to me, not to mention places like Singapore and Hawaii. Since then—now twelve years later—my food perspective has greatly broadened, not just by spending time exploring all of these great food cultures, but also by cooking and traveling with the many great chefs and food personalities I've been so lucky to befriend along the way. Together, we've had no shortage of adventures. I've fly-fished in Alaska with Emeril Lagasse, Hugh Acheson, and Tom Colicchio; prepared holiday meals with Marcus Samuelsson; baked birthday cakes with Christina Tosi; and

filled my belly with "smothered, covered and peppered" hash browns, late night at the Waffle House with Dominique Ansel. With these friends and more, I've taken pilgrimages to ramshackle food stalls and four-star restaurants in equal measure, and done deep dives into a wide array of cuisines, ingredients, and dishes—from refreshingly simple to wonderfully complex.

Every industry has a vocabulary, a jargon—doctors, lawyers, scientists, landscapers. Chefs are no different. After more than a decade at the Judges' Table, I've found my role on *Top Chef* to be that of a translator, gathering recipes, tips, and tricks, then boiling it all down into accessible information for home cooks and food enthusiasts alike. These lessons, along with my own life experiences and travels, are my starting point for creating do-able recipes and deliciously approachable meals for my own family and friends. And that's where this book comes in.

A noodle dish I make for my daughter, Dahlia, is a perfect example: During *Top Chef*'s Season 7 finale, I spent a day touring Singapore's famed hawker centers—rowdy outdoor food courts brimming with what is arguably the best street food in the world. Along with Tom Colicchio, chef David Chang, and former *Food & Wine* editor in chief Dana Cowin, I was led through the city's magnificent maze of dining options by food guru KF Seetoh, creator of the Asian culinary guide, *Makansutra*. Despite dozens of food stalls and the dizzying array of things we tasted that day, one dish grabbed my attention above the rest: hokkien noodles. They were made by a man who had learned his craft from his father, who had worked in the very same stall. I was mesmerized by the graceful rhythm of his cooking. Into a blazing hot wok went a beaten egg, then two types of noodles: thin rice sticks called *bee hoon*, and thicker, chewy udon-like wheat noodles, along with a little shrimp stock, garlic, a splash of fish sauce and soy sauce, then fresh shrimp and squid, and just a pinch of salty, fatty pork belly. The dish came together in what felt like an instant—layers of flavor, yet so simple, savory, and bright.

Back home and haunted by this irresistible combination, I failed to find an equivalent. So I made it myself using common supermarket rice noodles and an easy shrimp stock fortified with store-bought clam juice. In place of calamansi, an Asian citrus not often found in the U.S., I blended fresh lime and orange juices until I found the perfect sweet-sour balance. *Bringing it home to my own kitchen table.* It's now a family favorite (and you can find it on page 93).

After years spent working in other people's kitchens, and watching countless young chefs toil at their craft, I have found a cooking style I can now call my own: curious, adventurous, fresh, and easygoing. In my home kitchen, food is a celebration; a "welcome to the table" to try something new. There's often a story or point of origin that grounds my recipes and lets my love of exploration and discovery shine through.

Over the years and especially since having a family of my own, I find myself faced with the same issues as any home cook. Most nights, like most people, I want to put a nourishing meal on the table in as little time as possible. What I've learned is, with a little planning, a trip to a good market or the savvy navigation of my local grocery store, and the fairly simple upkeep of a smartly stocked pantry, I can usually ace this goal. The results of my efforts are flavor-packed dishes that are accessible and delicious; a hint of the familiar, but definitely not the same old skipping-record repertoire.

In the pages that follow, you'll find over one hundred of my favorite personal recipes. From the perfect bagel brunch with beet-cured salmon and savory cream cheese mix-ins to a recipe for eggs baked in potato skins, inspired by beach-house summers with my husband's family; killer fish tacos with a lime crema created in homage to my favorite tortilla chip; and a sticky maple pudding cake born out of many a blustery Canadian winter. There's my holiday brisket fried rice and my Balinese shrimp and grapefruit salad packed with chilies and herbs; a blow-your-mind spaghetti pie (see page 89!); and Mishmosh—a fully-loaded barley and matzo ball soup seasoned with lemon and dill, a remix of the great soups I learned from the many Jewish mothers in my life. And while I've made it a mission to stockpile my larder with finds from my treks the world over, I also share unique uses for basic pantry ingredients, like nut butters, coconut flakes, canned tomatoes, and common pantry spices, that will elevate your everyday cooking game.

Above, from left to right:
Fly fishing in Alaska, with Emeril, Hugh, and Tom during Top Chef's Season 10 finale; Celebrating at the 2017 Food & Wine Classic in Aspen

Alongside recipes, I've also included useful information on ingredients and techniques in Kitchen Wisdom tips to help you shop and cook with confidence, as well as tidbits of trivia that I call Snippets (a nod to a family nickname I've had since childhood)—fun facts that give you a broader understanding behind an ingredient or dish. Sprinkled throughout the book you'll also find easy how-tos for professional techniques, like how to spatchcock a chicken or flash-cool potatoes to get the crispiest skins. I call them Chef Techs.

I do my best cooking at home when I approach the stove with a lighthearted state of mind and realistic expectations. When I cook at home, I'm like everyone else: I run out of ingredients (or time!); I often need to improvise, adapting as necessary when things don't go quite as planned. At home, there's no judging, no critical analysis. It's just about creating easy and satisfying food for the people I love. I know that even as a confident cook it's often trial and error when you're cooking alone. With this in mind, I hope you'll take this book into your kitchen and use it not only for the recipes and to learn a few new tricks, but also to help guide and encourage you to cook more often, with less of a focus on making food perfect and more on making it memorable. Along the way, may your own adventures inspire you to turn your favorite food memories into beloved dishes to bring home to your family table. Let's dig in, together.

FAVORITE KITCHEN TOOLS

There are hundreds of kitchen gadgets and tools on the market (most of them quite useful; many less so), and few things are more fun for chefs and avid cooks to shop for and collect. While not an exhaustive list, here are some of my favorites and the ones I turn to most in my day-to-day cooking. They all can be found at kitchenware shops or online, unless otherwise indicated.

Baking sheets: I rely on standard 13 x 18-inch rimmed baking sheets (known in restaurant kitchens as half-sheet pans), for everything from making cookies to roasting vegetables, baking chicken and fish, toasting nuts, and making candies (like Chocolate Honeycomb Crunch, page 235). The smaller-sized quarter-sheet pans (which fit into some larger toaster ovens) come in handy for small-batch toasting and roasting. Opt for good-quality commercial-grade aluminum or stainless steel pans; they heat evenly, stand the test of time, and don't tend to warp. Avoid nonstick and dark-coated baking sheets, which cause excessive browning, and sometimes burning, before food is properly cooked.

A good blender (or two): A good-quality **countertop blender** is perfect for pureeing everything from fresh juices to sauces, salad dressings, and more. But for hot dishes, I tend to reach for my **immersion (aka stick) blender,** which allows me to blitz soups while they're still in the pot, instead of having to transfer the hot mixture to a countertop blender and then back into the pot for reheating.

Cast iron skillet: This classic pan goes from stovetop to oven, which is a huge part of its draw. It's an incredibly durable pan and retains heat better than most other skillet types. A wide range of sizes is available. If you're just starting your collection, begin with a 10-inch, which is great for searing steaks, frying chicken, and baking egg dishes, buttery cornbread, and my favorite upside-down cake (page 225).

Wire cooling racks: Cooling racks come in many shapes and sizes. The ones that fit snugly into rimmed baking sheets are optimal. Use them on their own to cool cakes and cookies, or in tandem with baking sheets to elevate items, like crispy Ginger-Chili Chicken Wings (page 132), for increased air circulation during cooking. The same "rack in pan" setup is also perfect for catching excess glaze when drizzling chocolate, icing, or caramel over cakes or candies.

Cutting boards: Every home cook needs a few good cutting boards in a variety of sizes. Little ones are great for slicing small fruits and chopping onions and garlic, while bigger boards help you get through multi-ingredient dishes and work with larger items, like whole chickens, with ease. Boards with rubber edges stay put while you cut, though you can also do as chefs do and spread a damp dishtowel under your board to keep it in place. Materials vary from plastic to glass, bamboo, and wood. I tend to favor the latter two; they're gentlest on knife blades and look great. I also recommend having one or two plastic boards that can be cleaned easily or run through the dishwasher after use with raw meats and fish. Since most cutting boards, even after washing, naturally absorb a touch of garlic and onion odor, I also keep a "fruit-only" board. These can be

inconspicuously marked with a permanent marker (a small dot or "F" in one corner usually does the trick) or purchased in a different finish, color, or shape to keep track. I also advise having at least one board that has a juice groove to collect liquids that seep out from citrus, roasted beets, cooked meats, and other juicy ingredients.

Dutch oven or wide, heavy pot with lid: Like a cast iron skillet, this workhorse goes from stovetop to oven. It's great for poaching chicken, browning and braising meats, making soups, stews, and other one-pot meals, boiling water for cooking vegetables or pasta, and even baking no-knead bread. Dutch ovens and good-quality wide, heavy pots conduct and retain heat well. A 6- to 8-quart size will tackle most recipes that yield 4 to 8 servings.

Electric mixer: As far as these guys go, there are two types: **stand mixers** and **hand-held mixers**. The former, while significantly more expensive and space hogging, is more powerful, and thus faster for some tasks, and allows you to work hands-free. With its multiple attachments, it can also knead bread dough and cream butter and sugar, which is impossible with the latter. For those who love to bake and have ample countertop or storage space, a stand mixer is a worthy investment. Otherwise, a hand mixer is perfectly suited for beating eggs, whipping cream, and mixing simple cake batters.

Fine-mesh sieve: Great for rinsing berries and straining homemade sauces, pureed soups and pulpy juices (page 179), this multipurpose tool also makes a great sifter for flour and other dry baking ingredients, and is perfect for dusting confectioners' sugar over brownies, cakes, and more.

Fish spatula: This thin, flexible beauty is designed to slip effortlessly under and carefully turn delicate fish fillets, but it's also surprisingly terrific for anything that's a bit stuck to a skillet or baking sheet (think roasted vegetables, pan-fried chicken, pork cutlets, fried eggs, and cookies or scones), especially when said food has a crispy crust or golden bits that you want to keep intact.

Grill pan: Having a ridged stovetop pan makes indoor grilling possible all year long. These come in various sizes and styles, including high-sided skillets and single or double-sided griddles, the flat side of which can be used to cook pancakes, French toast, eggs, and grilled cheese or other toasted sandwiches. Grill pans can be made of cast iron, stainless steel, or nonstick aluminum. Cast iron, which is the best of the three at retaining heat, delivers the deepest char. In addition to grilling meat, fish, and vegetables, these pans also give a toasty warm-up to sliced bread and muffins.

Heat-resistant rubber spatula: Terrific for maneuvering omelets and clearing scrambled eggs from pan edges while cooking, a heat-resistant rubber spatula also allows you to scrape every drop of liquid, dough, and more from bowls, and gently fold ingredients together. The mini size is perfect for getting into small pans, jars, and bowls.

Kitchen tongs: In professional kitchens, no chef is ever without his or her tongs, which are indispensable for lifting, turning, flipping, and moving everything from shrimp, sausages, and steak to firm vegetables like potatoes, asparagus, and corn. It doesn't take long to become comfortable using this tool; you'll soon feel as though it's an extension of your hand. Spring-loaded, stainless steel models are generally easy to maneuver and durable. Lengths vary from about 5 to 22 inches. I find 12 inches most comfortable for all-purpose cooking in the kitchen, and 16 inches, which gives you a bit more distance from the fire, perfect for grilling. Avoid using tongs with delicate ingredients like salad greens, fish fillets, and tomatoes.

Knives: Good-quality knives can last a lifetime, so buy the best you can afford and keep them razor sharp, either by learning how to sharpen on your own, or bringing them to an expert for service when needed. A key factor in buying the right knife is personal comfort. Some kitchen stores offer a cutting board and a vegetable or two, so you can try before you buy. While there are many types of knives to invest in, at the end of the day, you can tackle nearly every cooking task with these four:

- A **chef's knife** is the one you'll use to slice and chop most meat, fish, vegetables, fruit, and fresh herbs. Comfort is key, so purchase this knife in a size and with a blade and handle style that feels best in your own grip. Though sizes range from 5 to 10 inches, the 10-inch length can feel unwieldy for many cooks; a 6- to 8-inch length is a good place to start.

- With an average blade length of 3½ inches, a **paring knife** gives you more control with small items, and is particularly suited for detail-oriented tasks like coring and peeling fruit, hulling strawberries, and cutting zest, rind, and segments from citrus.

- Known as the go-to for slicing bread, a **serrated knife** is also terrific for sawing through sandwiches and cutting cakes as well as tomatoes and other tender fruit. This knife is made in three styles: offset, flat, and curved. With the blade positioned 1 to 2 inches below the handle, the offset is designed to allow for ample knuckle clearance, which to me is most comfortable and allows for maximum control. Blades are either scalloped or pointed. Pointed is the most common and wins my vote; it's the better of the two at filling multipurpose needs and for slicing crusty bread.

- Though not essential, the thin, flexible **boning knife** makes quick, easy, and clean work of tasks like spatchcocking whole chickens (page 126), filleting fish, butchering meat, and removing silver skin from tenderloins.

Oven thermometer: All ovens, no matter the price point, fall out of calibration from time to time, meaning that while your temperature setting may indicate one level, the actual temperature might be higher or lower, perhaps significantly enough to affect the outcome of a recipe. The easiest way to track calibration is to keep an oven thermometer in your oven, positioning it on the center rack. You can then simply adjust your dial accordingly to fit your desired temperature. Oven thermometers are inexpensive and

available at kitchenware shops and most hardware stores. With use, they become splattered with grease and other stuck-on foods, which come off easily with a scouring pad, a household powdered cleanser, and a little elbow grease. Replace oven thermometers once a year for best accuracy.

Rasp grater: While a multiblade food processor and good box grater are both terrific tools for grating cheddar and other soft cheeses, as well as large vegetables like carrots and potatoes, the grater I turn to most frequently is the rasp-style model. This hand-held tool gives you optimal control for grating small items like garlic, whole nutmeg, and fresh ginger. It's also perfect for grating citrus zest, Parmesan, and other hard cheeses directly into mixing bowls or over pastas, salads, and other dishes just before serving, and makes beautiful chocolate shavings for desserts.

Spice grinder: While ground spices are convenient, there is nothing like the aroma and intensity of freshly toasted and ground whole spices. The quickest and easiest way to grind whole spices is to use a spice or coffee grinder (note that it's ideal to have one grinder to use exclusively for spices and another for coffee, to keep spice flavors from contaminating your morning roast and vice versa). A tablespoon or so of raw white rice, pulverized to a fine powder, does a great job of cleaning grinders between jobs and absorbing oils and aromas, but you can also use a good-quality spice- or coffee-grinder cleaning brush or cloth. Try toasting and grinding your own spices when you make my Moroccan Lentil & Chickpea Soup (page 69).

FAVORITE PANTRY BOOSTERS

Most chefs and avid home cooks have a list of go-to ingredients they can't live without. I call mine "pantry boosters." These are items I keep well-stocked in my pantry and fridge—the utility players I count on, whether I'm putting together one of my favorite recipes or a quick weeknight meal on the fly. While not an all-inclusive list of pantry ingredients, these are the ones you'll see recurring in this book in a variety of ways. Try keeping at least a few of them on hand in your kitchen. I bet they'll soon become your favorites, too!

Anchovies: These versatile little fish are packed with flavor and easy to find in just about any sort of food market. Known for their saline funkiness, good-quality anchovies, in moderation, add a unique complexity to dishes that is often surprisingly subtle. Use them to top toasts, cook into pasta sauces, and blend into salad dressings or savory butters to spread on bread or melt and drizzle over grilled or roasted vegetables (page 53). The highest-quality anchovies come packed in salt and need to be soaked, rinsed, and removed from the bone before using, but there are many less fussy high-quality oil-packed versions that are equally delicious. Look for oil-packed anchovies (canned or jarred) imported from Spain, Italy, or Morocco. After opening, transfer unused canned portions into a small jar and cover with olive oil. Anchovies keep, covered and refrigerated, for many months. Once you've eaten the anchovies, use their oil for salad dressings or drizzle it over pasta. It's also packed with salty, savory flavor.

Canned whole tomatoes: When fresh tomatoes are in season, I can't get enough. The rest of the year I opt for canned versions, which I count on for convenience and quality. Use them to make quick weeknight sauces for pastas, as a delicious base for soups or baked eggs, or to simmer chicken or fish in (I often add olives and sprigs of fresh herbs). When available, I choose DOP-certified San Marzano tomatoes, which, cultivated especially for cooking, are prized for their sweetness and low acidity. DOP stands for *denominazione di origine protteta*, signifying that a product comes from a particular region and is produced in accordance with regulated standards.

Capers: Bright, tangy, and floral, capers add a great pop of salty, pungent flavor to pastas, tuna and potato salads, chicken, salmon, and other fish dishes. They're also great in flavored butters, essential for a bagel brunch (page 24), and a key element in the totally addictive sauce for My Kinda Burger (page 149). Capers are sold packed in brine or salt. The latter tend to be plumper, firmer, sharper, and purer in flavor (they're also more expensive); I prefer them, especially for fresh applications, but I rely equally on the brine-packed version. Rinse capers in several changes of water before using to remove excess salt or brine.

Citrus: A little bit of citrus goes a long way in adding bright flavor to savory and sweet dishes. I use it in practically everything—as both an easy way to enhance the flavor of a dish or as its driving force—and love experimenting with all sorts of varieties, including grapefruits, lemons, limes, blood oranges, and mandarins. You'll find citrus used throughout this book, including in drinks and salad dressings; and squeezed over cooked meat and fish dishes, and into finished soups. The zest alone is great for making simple sauces (page 105) or sprinkling over savory dishes or desserts (page 216). Citrus juices can be blended and used in sauces, drinks, or sweets. One of my favorite techniques is to char citrus before squeezing it, which is a great way to add a smoky note to drinks and dressings and helps get every ounce of juice out of the fruit (pages 190, 46).

Coconut flakes, chips, and oil: I keep a plethora of all things coconut on hand, because I love the flavor in all sorts of dishes from breakfast to dessert, and even drinks (page 176). Toasting coconut flakes and chips before using adds a nutty quality and intensifies the sweet, tropical flavor.

Fish sauce: This pungent amber-colored liquid adds a deep savoriness to dipping sauces, slaws, and salad dressings, sauces for shrimp or fish, and even Asian omelets (page 19). It's also a great seasoning for Asian broths, roasted vegetables, and fried rice. Most fish sauce sold in the U.S. comes from Vietnam and Thailand, where it is called *nuoc mam* and *nam pla*, respectively. I prefer the slightly milder Vietnamese version, though they are equally good. Add fish sauce to dishes little by little, as it's a powerful flavor agent.

Harissa: This North African paste, made up of chili peppers, garlic, and aromatic spices, like coriander, cumin, and mint, is one of my favorite condiments, not only for its heat but also for its complex blend of flavors. I use it in salad dressings (page 59), sauces, shakshuka, and other baked egg dishes; as a rub for roast chicken or fish; and as an all-purpose hot sauce for cooked meats and more.

Horseradish: I fold this earthy, sinus-clearing root vegetable (which is actually a member of the cabbage family) into cream cheeses for bagels, mayo for sandwiches, and yogurt or sour cream to use as a dip. I also whisk it into warm sauces and salad dressings, add it to soups and stews, and use it to make a piquant crust for salmon or brisket (page 140). Horseradish is sold both fresh and jarred (aka "prepared"). The best prepared types are refrigerated, and are most often simply horseradish, vinegar, and salt. The shelf-stable ones contain added ingredients, like preservatives, sugars, oils, and artificial flavorings, and don't taste nearly as pure or delicious. When shopping for fresh horseradish, look for plump, firm roots. Fresh horseradish should be peeled before grating, and grated in a well-ventilated space.

Malt vinegar: Made from fermented malted barley or sour unhopped beer, this robust, savory vinegar is the British go-to for fish and chips, and the Canadian choice for dressing French fries. At home, I use it on crispy roasted smashed potatoes (page 54); roasted vegetables; and in simple marinades for chicken or steak.

Miso: I use miso (fermented soy paste) to up the ante in glazes for meats and fish, flavored butters, salad dressings, broths, and soups. For my Grilled Corn with Miso-Chili Butter and lots more miso info, see page 49.

Mustard: My number one favorite condiment of all time is mustard. I keep at least three varieties in my fridge, including Dijon, grainy mustard, and even the golden yellow "ballpark" type. For me, no sandwich is complete without mustard (even my egg sandwich on page 11). I also use it in dressings and sauces, under the skin of chicken before roasting, and as a dip for French fries. It's no wonder my favorite breakfast is Welsh rarebit (toast smothered in a sauce made from sharp cheddar, beer, and mustard from Wales) with an egg on top, the recipe for which I shared in my first book, *Talking with My Mouth Full*.

Nuts and seeds: These little guys pack a lot of unexpected punch, adding crunch, flavor, and dimension to all sorts of dishes. You'll find them liberally sprinkled throughout this book, in everything from warm breakfast cereals (page 9) to soups, salads, roasted vegetable and fish dishes, and of course sweets. Toasting whole nuts and seeds before using intensifies their flavor.

Parmesan cheese: It's worth buying good-quality Parmesan cheese (look for the Italian import *Parmigiano-Reggiano* at good supermarkets and cheese shops) and keeping a hunk in your fridge to grate or shave over pastas, baked eggs, salads, and even soups (page 67), but also to use in salad dressings and sweet or savory doughs, mix with breadcrumbs to make crusts for meat or fish (page 123), or make a crispy Italian snack, called *frico*. The rinds can be saved—they keep forever, sealed in an airtight plastic bag and stored in the freezer—to enhance broths and soups (add them at the beginning of the recipe, then remove and discard before serving). To grate Parmesan, use a box or rasp grater; to shave it, try a vegetable peeler, or very thinly slice with a sharp chef's knife. Parmesan, like all cheeses, keeps best tightly wrapped in cheese paper or in parchment or wax paper, then with foil or plastic wrap. When you take Parmesan out of the fridge, let it stand uncovered for 15 minutes before using, to allow moisture lost by refrigeration to reabsorb into the cheese.

Pickles: These briny, crunchy, sharp, salty, vinegary bites are EVERYTHING to me. I love making my own pickled vegetables and fruits (page 158). I also keep a collection of store-bought types on hand to serve as snacks, slip into sandwiches, or batter and fry (page 161). Pickles are a great counterpoint to rich or fatty dishes, like burgers, egg sandwiches, and my mom's amazing chopped liver (page 163). Putting them in boozy cocktails might even keep you young (page 197).

Scallions: These unassuming immature onions are well known in Asian and Mexican cuisines and add dimension to many dishes. They're great chopped and sprinkled over salads; added to dressings or sauces; folded into or used as a garnish for rice, noodles and egg dishes; or broiled, grilled, or roasted, which brings out their sweetness. Both the whites and greens are edible; the greens are milder, and perfect both for cooking and using raw, without the intense bite that other onions might add.

Spices and spice blends: Keeping good-quality spices on hand means you can dress up a piece of meat or fish and all sorts of vegetables in infinitely exciting ways before

grilling, roasting, or pan-cooking. Spices are also great for seasoning and using in baked goods. It's always fun to experiment with blends, devising your own mixes to suit your personal taste. As you will quickly come to know through this book, my favorite spices and spice blends include Aleppo pepper, caraway, cardamom, cayenne, chile powder, cinnamon, coriander, cumin, dukkah, ginger, sumac, turmeric, and za'taar. In my kitchen, I have a dedicated spice grinder for grinding whole spices, but you can also crush them with a mortar and pestle or the bottom of a heavy saucepan. Toasting spices before grinding brings out their aroma and flavor; use low heat and keep your eye on the pan, as spices can quickly burn. Keep spices in a drawer or pantry, away from sunlight and heat. Refresh ground spices every six to twelve months, as their potency tends to diminish with time. Whole spices keep a little longer.

Tahini: A thick, creamy paste made from ground and often hulled and toasted sesame seeds, tahini is a staple ingredient used in many cuisines, especially Mediterranean and Middle Eastern. A primary component in hummus (page 167), baba ghanoush, salad dressings (page 34), dips, and desserts, it can also be thinned out with a little water, seasoned with salt, and simply drizzled over falafel, roasted vegetables, or even French fries. Tahini is available in most large supermarkets (look for preservative-free varieties in the nut butter and/or ethnic foods aisle), specialty markets, and online. It has a nutty, earthy flavor, and a high fat content, which can cause it to separate in the jar so you'll want to give it a good stir before each use. Tahini keeps, covered and refrigerated, for up to two years.

CHEF LESSONS WORTH BRINGING HOME

◆

I've been lucky enough to sit at the *Top Chef* Judges' Table for fifteen seasons and six drama-filled spinoffs. Through the triumphant victories and heartbreaking defeats of our chef contestants (aka cheftestants), and from many of the world's greatest chefs who have appeared as guest judges, I've gleaned invaluable cooking tips and techniques. Adopting this insider intel can help ensure success in the home kitchen, too. Here are my most valuable takeaways.

1. Mise-en-Place Is Everything

If there's one mantra that all professional cooks live by, it's the term, *mise-en-place*. French for "put in place," it refers to having your ingredients prepped and your tools and equipment at the ready *before* you begin cooking, so that when the literal and proverbial heat is on you can move fluidly from step one of a recipe straight through to the end, without missing an ingredient or a beat. In other words, be organized. At home, practice mise-en-place like this:

- Carefully read through a recipe in its entirety before shopping and again before you begin cooking, to account for and organize your ingredients and tools.

- Clear counter space (as best you can) *before* you begin prepping, and clean as you work to maintain an uncluttered space.

- Prep your ingredients as indicated in the ingredient list before you begin cooking (e.g., slice your onion, cube that bell pepper, grate your ginger, measure out your flour, etc.), then organize them in small bowls near your stove or work area so you can easily see and reach for them as you cook through the recipe step by step. Ingredients that are added in the same step of a recipe can often be combined into one bowl to further streamline your effort.

Mise-en-place is an important practice to employ for any dish, but especially for those that come together quickly once the cooking is underway, like my Singapore-Style Hokkien Noodles (page 93) or Chocolate Honeycomb Crunch (page 235).

2. Use the Best, But Stay Flex

Use the best quality ingredients you can access and afford, keeping in mind that making modifications to a recipe or even veering off your roadmap when necessary is the surest way to clinch a kitchen win. Cheftestants often learn the hard way that if an ingredient isn't top quality, or a first attempt at a dish doesn't quite cut it, it's wisest to find a substitute or go with a Plan B rather than serve something subpar. Case in point: Say you're making my Peppery Greens with Tahini Dressing (page 33), and mustard greens aren't available, or the arugula isn't first-rate. Take a look around at the other hearty and/or peppery greens on offer, like spinach, watercress, or mizuna, and choose whichever single green or combo is the most gorgeous and fresh. While good swaps or last-minute detours aren't always easy, as you expand your knowledge of ingredients and cooking techniques, you'll find that making adjustments with ease eventually becomes second nature.

3. The Clock Is Always Ticking

On *Top Chef*, contestants are always in a race against the clock. While real life isn't usually that dramatic, we all face time constraints. I'm always thrilled when I have several hours or even a whole day to tackle a recipe project. More often than not, though, my time in the kitchen is limited to an hour or less at the end of the day. Even so, with a little advance planning I can still cook something fresh, healthy, and delicious for my family. Here are a few strategies that help:

- Start a collection of favorite fast dishes (this book is filled with them), tagging them or keeping a running list so you can quickly turn to the ones that best fit your time constraints on any given day.

- Set aside time to shop for and cook multiple recipes at once. Getting ahead by preparing soups, stews, roast meats, or even salad dressings in advance will make for quick work (or no work!) when you need a meal after a busy day of work or play. You can also make a double batch of one or more recipes and freeze some for later.

- Practice smart shortcuts by using ingredients like shredded rotisserie chicken (instead of roasting a bird from scratch) in a salad or soup, as I do in my Cold Soba Noodle Salad with Shredded Chicken (page 90), or by making my Hummus with Harissa Oil, Toasted Fennel Seeds, & Mint (page 167) with canned chickpeas instead of soaking and cooking the dried version.

4. Have a Salt Strategy

I can't overstate the importance of salt in cooking; it can be the key to achieving the perfect balance in a dish or the single element that ruins it. Salt softens bitter notes while enhancing both sweet and savory ones, as well as aromas—all of which have a significant effect on how we taste our food. To salt wisely, keep these tips in mind:

- There are myriad types of salts to explore. I recommend keeping at least two on hand: a kosher salt for all-purpose seasoning (it's inexpensive, dissolves easily and quickly, and has a neutral flavor) and a flaky salt, like Maldon, to season and add a pop of flavor and texture to fresh foods like salads and cooked dishes just before serving (a technique known as "finishing"). Add specialty salts, like fleur de sel, smoked sea salt, seasoned salts, and more, as you like (see Sources, page 241).

- Season throughout the cooking process and taste as you go. An incremental seasoning strategy makes it less likely to under- or over-season a dish. This is why a good soup recipe, for example, might instruct you to season a sauté of onions and other vegetables at the start of the dish, then season again after adding liquid, and finally taste and season accordingly a third time just before serving. Try your hand at incremental seasoning with my Za'atar Chicken Schnitzel (page 130).

- Multicomponent recipes taste best when each element is seasoned individually, which helps bring a dish into balance. When you make pasta, for example, season the sauce as well as the pasta cooking water, which seasons the noodles as they cook. You'll see multicomponent seasoning in action when you make dishes like my Warm Farro Bowls with Roasted Cauliflower & Kale (page 35) and many more.

- Salty ingredients, like capers, Parmesan cheese, olives, and pickles, add both flavor and seasoning to a dish. When you're using these ingredients, taste first before adding extra salt.

- Have you ever noticed a chef lift their hand 8 to 12 inches above a piece of meat or a plate of vegetables to season from above? This move is not for show. Working this way helps to evenly disperse salt and other seasonings. Try seasoning from above with my Shaved Zucchini Salad (page 58).

5. Know When a Dish Needs Acid

On *Top Chef*, we judges often talk about acid when we're evaluating a dish. But what does *needing acid* actually mean? Like salt, acid can be a key component in balancing flavor. Acidic ingredients like fresh citrus juice, vinegars, fermented foods, and wine, lend not only flavor and complexity, but also a brightness that helps balance sugar, salt, and fat. Though wine is often added during the cooking process as a layering element and to pull together flavors, vinegars and fresh citrus are often best used as a final touch ("at the finish," in chef speak) and not cooked, to make flavors pop. When you add a squeeze of fresh lemon juice to my Mishmosh Soup (page 67), you'll see exactly what I mean. Acid also helps keep delicate fruits, once cut, from oxidizing and browning (apples, pears, and artichokes, for example). The term *acidulated water* is simply cold water with a bit of acid added (usually lemon juice or distilled vinegar) and is used to prevent discoloration while an ingredient is being prepped. Note that if you happen to add too much acid to a salad dressing or sauce, it can often be counterbalanced by adding more of the fat (e.g., olive oil or butter) that is already present in the dish.

6. Texture Matters

Whether smooth and silky, chewy, crispy, creamy, or crunchy, texture is an important part of our tasting experience and another way to add dimension to a dish. Understanding how this works allows you to cook with textural components in a thoughtful manner. When you're first experimenting with texture, keep it simple—even just one added element can make an impact. By sprinkling toasted nuts and seeds over a cooked cereal, for example—as I do in my Quinoa Cereal with Stone Fruit Jam (page 9)—you create a satisfying contrast of soft and crunchy. Keep textural elements within the context of the dish as a whole (potato chips are also crunchy, but in most cases won't work well over breakfast porridge!). Textural contrast can come not only from ingredients, but by way of cooking method, too. Techniques like searing or high-heat roasting can caramelize and create a delectably crispy crust on fish, meats, and vegetables, while gentler approaches, like braising and poaching, produce a meltingly tender result. Some of the many texture-enhancing ingredients you'll find throughout this book include nuts and seeds, flaky sea salt, turbinado sugar, dried fruits, and whipped cream. You'll see these at play in my Roasted Zucchini with Coriander Vinaigrette (page 60), Campfire Sundae (page 232), and more.

7. Always Rest Your Meat

Top Chef fans have heard me and some of the other judges say time and again that it's essential to let your meat rest before slicing and serving it. As cooked meat rests its muscle fibers relax, allowing it to hold onto most of its precious, flavor-packed juices once sliced. Cut it too soon and those juices wind up not in the meat but lost to your cutting board or plate, and your meat is tough instead of tender. While resting, meat also continues to cook for several minutes. This "carryover cook time" is the reason that meat is taken off the heat when its internal temperature, taken with a meat thermometer inserted into the thickest part of a cut and not touching bone, measures five to 10 degrees lower than the desired doneness. (Most recipes account for carryover cooking, but when you're cooking on your own, remember to keep it in mind.) Resting time varies by cut or type of meat. If a recipe doesn't specify resting time, wait until the internal temperature drops to 120°F before slicing. Most steaks and chops require 10 minutes or so, but a prime rib or whole turkey will require 30 to 45 minutes, so plan accordingly. Try resting meat before digging in when you make my Hanger Steak with Arugula-Mint Chimichurri (page 136) or Piri Piri Roast Chicken (page 126).

8. Simple Doesn't Mean Boring

Coco Chanel was famous for her sage advice when it came to dressing with accessories: "Before you leave the house, look in the mirror and take one thing off." Great chefs use a similar culinary intelligence when crafting a new dish, by incorporating layers of flavor and texture while maintaining a measure of restraint. Think of the dishes that have stood the test of time because of their understated elegance, like spaghetti with fresh tomato sauce and basil, or a perfectly roasted chicken with lemon and thyme. On *Top Chef*, there are times when cheftestants—whether they are still honing this skill or forget its importance in the heat of the moment—overload a dish with ingredients and techniques; the result is often muddled and unfocused. To avoid this fate, focus on the quality of the ingredients in a single dish, rather than the quantity, and keep techniques relatively straightforward. Start by practicing with simple snacks and breakfast dishes, then build from there. Crunchy Fruit & Veg with Chili & Sumac (page 154) is a great example of an uncomplicated yet interesting and elevated snack.

9. Make It Memorable

Dishes that win *Top Chef* challenges (or become signatures of any restaurant or chef, for that matter) are often described as *craveable*, and stay with us long after an episode has aired or a plate has been cleared from the table. Writing this book, I sought to capture the flavors and eating experiences that have lingered in my mind, and turn them into recipes that I (and I hope you, too!) will want to make again and again. There's often at least one inspired element, flavor, or technique that makes me want to return to a really good dish. To that end, this book aims to give you an unexpected twist in every recipe. Whether it's stirring cardamom and lemon into warm honey before drizzling it over yogurt with roasted figs (page 2); making a savory soy-lime crema for simple fish tacos (page 115); or adding a shot of bourbon to homemade marshmallows (page 202), *Bringing It Home* is all about craveable, memorable dishes. I hope that my tips will help you create your very own craveable and memorable dishes, too.

10. Maybe They Should Call It *Top Scallop*

Too many scallops have been cooked in the *Top Chef* kitchen to even begin to count. I, along with the other judges, started noticing this pattern around Season 5 and it's become a bit of a running joke with our fans ever since. In truth, there are several reasons why our cheftestants constantly turn to this much-loved mollusk. Scallops can be prepared in all sorts of ways: from raw to medium-rare or even fully cooked; in pastas and rice dishes; as the star of a main course or with other fish. Great for all seasons, they pair well with countless flavors and, perhaps most important of all, they're incredibly quick to cook. When you're up against the clock, there are few ingredients more elegant and quick to prepare than seafood in general, and scallops in particular (for a detailed scallop cooking lesson, see page 106). The takeaway is this: You don't need to make a whole roast or complicated multicourse meal to impress your family or dinner party guests. Try my Scallops & Peas with Mint Gremolata (page 105) or Rustic Fish Soup (page 77); both are sophisticated yet deceptively quick and easy to prepare.

11. Cooking Is a Team Sport

On *Top Chef*, the focus is on the individual victor but in reality the accomplishments of a single chef or cook rarely guarantee the success of a professional kitchen or restaurant as a whole. The camaraderie shared by staff in both the front and back of the house in any well-run restaurant is a vital aspect of the culture and explains why our cheftestants often support and inspire each other, creating lasting friendships along the way. Professional kitchens are structured hierarchically, with the *chef* (French for "boss") at the helm, and his or her brigade of sous chefs and cooks in their given positions, all contributing to a common goal. It's important that chefs and cooks recognize their own strengths and those of their colleagues. When *Top Chef* contestants are put into team competitions, those who understand how to maximize the various skills of their team do best. The lesson at home? Know your strengths and don't be afraid to ask for help, allowing your friends and family to contribute by doing what they enjoy. One friend loves to make cocktails? Let them! Another wants to bring the salad? Great! In my kitchen, everyone is encouraged to roll up their sleeves and jump in as they choose. My husband, Jeremy, is our family's designated salad and sauce maker, for example, and with his help every meal is prepared quickly and easily. (Lucky for me, he's also great at cleanup!). As you will soon see, Jer's sauce for grilled halibut (page 102) is a family favorite, and I am thrilled and proud to include it in this book.

12. Own It

When you're under pressure in the kitchen, it's easy to start doubting yourself, which can lead to a downward spiral of second-guessing and defeat. But even the best chefs have days when their vision isn't perfectly executed. If an imperfect outcome can't be salvaged, the best thing to remember is this: It's just food! Don't worry so much. Most of the time you're your own worst critic and far more conscious of your missteps than anyone else will be. As we say to our *Top Chef* contestants, intention is imperative, but we often won't know if a dish didn't come out exactly as you had intended unless you bring your blunder to our attention. Instead of fixating on an imperfection, do your best to accept it. Make a modification, if possible, then step back and own both your triumphs *and* your mistakes, all of which will ultimately make you a stronger cook.

When I was developing the recipes for this book, my Banana-Cardamom Upside-Down Cake with Salty Caramel (page 225) was particularly difficult to perfect. Each time I tried to turn the baked cake out of its pan, a portion of the banana topping would stick. The cake was so delicious that I couldn't help but serve it to friends nonetheless, cut into slices and patched up first so they were never the wiser. Everyone adored it. Still, I was determined to fix the issue. About a dozen cakes in, with both a new approach to the caramel and a genius tip from a food stylist friend, I finally nailed it: After cooling the cake completely, I gently warmed it in the skillet over a low flame just enough to loosen the caramel. This allowed the cake to cleanly and beautifully turn out of the skillet onto a serving plate, with the caramel lusciously oozing down the edges—just as I had imagined it in my mind when I first dreamt it up. Looking back, I am particularly proud of this recipe, not only because I love it, but also because I had the fortitude to acknowledge the imperfections along the way and keep on trying until I got it just right.

13. Know How to Make One Great Dessert

Viewers are often curious why contestants on *Top Chef* frequently fail when it comes to dessert. In many restaurants, the magic of pastry happens in its own kitchen or in a very separate area from where savory chefs work, offering little or no interaction between the two crafts. This said, you don't have to be a pastry chef to have an understanding of this territory. Being a well-rounded cook means not shying away from sweets. Even for those who don't love to bake there are many easy, crowd-pleasing desserts that don't rely on fussy techniques, fancy equipment, specific work surfaces, and the like. In other words, sweets can be joyfully simple. My Chocolate Banoffee Pie (page 206) and Classic Butterscotch Pudding (page 226) are just two of the many decadent desserts you can make from this book without even turning on the oven.

14. Reach from Your Roots

It's wonderful and worthwhile to explore the world and its many cultures through cooking, but it's important to start in a place you know well and are comfortable with. I've seen this time and again on *Top Chef* with contestants who hit their stride when they take inspiration from their roots first, rather than simply focusing on fancy techniques and modernist tricks. Of course there's a place in the kitchen for innovation, but building a foundation on what you know and who you are is the most powerful place to begin. Food memories can help guide you to your personal cooking style and provide a boost of confidence, as ease often comes from what's familiar. The dishes that linger most vividly in my mind, from both my travels and eating adventures, are more often than not those that link a cook with his or her own unique story. I've included many of my personal family recipes in this book—from my Ratatouille Galette (page 62) and Not Your Mama's Horseradish Brisket (page 140) to a very special French-Canadian Tarte au Sucre (page 209). It's these sorts of recipes that evoke strong memories for me, helped me define myself as a cook, and gave me a solid foundation from which I continue to experiment and build.

15. Just Keep Cooking

There's always a bit of extra chaos in the kitchen at the beginning of every season of *Top Chef*, as contestants settle in and familiarize themselves with both the kitchen and the game. Confidence soon builds and with each challenge, the cooking gets better and better. The same applies in the home kitchen. When you first start cooking, making a new dish (or even cooking at all) might feel awkward. The only way over this hump is to just keep cooking. Friends often come to me with the following lament and conviction: "I'm just not a good cook." Convinced they lack any natural ability, they feel frustrated and often impatient, and so turn away from the craft. I stand true to the philosophy that even if you aren't initially comfortable in the kitchen, with patience and practice, you can become a good cook. Over time, you'll develop efficiency, spontaneity, creativity, and confidence—all of which will continue to grow with every dish you make. Start by mastering a few recipes you're particularly drawn to and expand from there. I often suggest working first on soups, as they involve several building block techniques (many of which have been discussed here), and are hearty and comforting. Try starting with my Rainy Day Ribollita with Lots of Greens (page 75); Moroccan Lentil & Chickpea Soup with Chermoula (page 69); or Chilled Corn Soup with Chive Oil, Paprika, & Lime (page 78). As you keep cooking, you'll begin to see and understand patterns and rhythms; you'll become more fluent and your natural instincts will develop and emerge.

Begin the Day

YOGURT WITH ROASTED FIGS, HONEY, & PISTACHIOS 2

CHOCOLATE-GINGER SCONES 5

**BUMBLEBERRY BUCKWHEAT PANCAKES
WITH CINNAMON CREAM 6**

QUINOA CEREAL WITH STONE FRUIT JAM 9

PEANUT BUTTER, COCONUT, & BANANA OATMEAL 10

MY ULTIMATE BREAKFAST SANDWICH 11

SOFT-BOILED EGGS WITH BUTTERY HERB SOLDIERS 15

Flavored Butters 16

Citrus-Tarragon Butter • Scallion-Basil Butter •
Chili-Cilantro Butter

**VIETNAMESE OMELET WITH
SHRIMP & FRIED SHALLOTS (BANH XEO) 19**

BLOODY MARY EGGS 20

EGGS IN CRISPY POTATO SKINS WITH AVOCADO SALSA 23

THE PERFECT BAGEL BRUNCH 24

Three Cream Cheeses 25

Toasted Fennel Seed-Lemon Cream Cheese • Aleppo-Chive
Cream Cheese • Everything Cream Cheese

Beet-Cured Salmon 26

◆

YOGURT WITH ROASTED FIGS, HONEY, & PISTACHIOS

⅓ cup coarsely chopped unsalted pistachios

8 fresh figs, quartered

2 teaspoons turbinado sugar

3 tablespoons honey

1 (1-inch) strip lemon zest

⅛ teaspoon ground cardamom

Small pinch kosher salt

3 cups plain Greek yogurt (full-, low-, or nonfat)

I've long loved fresh figs, but years ago—at Spring Restaurant in Paris—I discovered the wonders of eating them *roasted* and drizzled with honey. The quick, simple cooking technique concentrates the fruit's jammy flavor and the honey complements its delicate sweetness. Amazing for breakfast, I also often serve this dish as a light, not-too-sweet dessert. Any fig variety that you like will work well here.

Heat the oven to broil with the rack about 6 inches from the heat source. Line a small baking sheet with foil.

In a small skillet, toast the pistachios over medium-low heat, occasionally shaking the pan back and forth, until the nuts are fragrant and lightly golden, 5 to 7 minutes. Transfer to a plate and let cool.

Meanwhile, arrange the figs on the baking sheet, cut-side up, and sprinkle with the sugar to evenly cover. Broil until the figs are tender and the sugar is melted and begins to caramelize, 3 to 4 minutes.

In a small microwave-safe bowl, combine the honey, zest, cardamom, and salt. Microwave at 5-second intervals until the honey is runny and just warm, 5 to 10 seconds. (If you don't have a microwave, gently warm the mixture in a small saucepan over low heat, keeping a close watch so as to not let it boil or burn.) Remove and discard the lemon zest.

Spoon the yogurt into serving bowls. Top with the figs and pistachios, then drizzle with the honey.

KITCHEN WISDOM: Fresh Figs

In the market, look for fresh figs that are tender but not mushy, with skins free from cracks or bruises. Figs keep best refrigerated for 1 to 3 days, depending on their freshness when purchased. Rinse them just before cooking or eating, no earlier, since added moisture can cause spoilage during storage.

Known for its deep-purple skin and tender pale-pink flesh, the popular Black Mission fig is named after the Spanish Franciscan missionaries who introduced the fruit to North America in the mid-1700s, when they came to Southern California to spread their faith. Along with calimyrna (aka Smyrna), a larger, green-skinned type, Mission figs are among the most widely available varieties in the United States.

CHOCOLATE-GINGER SCONES

1½ cups unbleached all-purpose flour

1½ cups whole-wheat flour

1 tablespoon baking powder

1 teaspoon ground ginger

¼ teaspoon ground cinnamon

1 teaspoon kosher salt

½ cup turbinado sugar, divided

5 ounces bittersweet chocolate (70%), coarsely chopped (about 1 cup)

4 ounces crystallized ginger, coarsely chopped (⅔ cup packed)

1⅓ cups well-shaken unsweetened full-fat coconut milk (from a 14-ounce can)

¼ cup plus 2 tablespoons room temperature coconut oil plus more for brushing

1 teaspoon pure vanilla extract

At the age of 75, after a lifetime of distinctly non-exclusionary eating, my dad surprised us all when he announced he was becoming vegan! One of the things he missed most in his new way of life was a good scone, so I set out to make him a "legal" version that would be as good as the sort made with butter and cream. In this recipe, a mixture of coconut oil and coconut milk forms a delicious crumb, and a blend of whole-wheat and all-purpose flours lends a rich nuttiness. The fact that they are vegan is really just a plus. Most importantly, these scones are packed with chocolate and ginger—a flavor duo my dad and I both love—and they are absolutely, undeniably *craveable*.

Heat the oven to 425°F with the rack in the middle. Line a baking sheet with parchment paper.

In a large bowl, whisk together the all-purpose flour, whole-wheat flour, baking powder, ground ginger, cinnamon, salt, and ¼ cup plus 2 tablespoons of the sugar. Using a wooden spoon, stir in the chocolate and crystallized ginger. Form a well in the center of the mixture. Add the coconut milk, coconut oil, and vanilla to the well, then stir together just to combine (do not overwork); the mixture will be shaggy.

Divide the dough into 2 equal pieces. On a lightly floured surface, pat each piece into a 6-inch round that is 1 inch thick. Using a sharp knife, cut each round into 6 wedges. Transfer the wedges to a baking sheet, spacing at least 1 inch apart. Brush the tops of the scones with coconut oil, then sprinkle with the remaining 2 tablespoons sugar. Bake until browned on the bottom, about 15 minutes. Serve warm or at room temperature.

BUMBLEBERRY BUCKWHEAT PANCAKES with Cinnamon Cream

Pancake Batter

1 cup buckwheat flour

1 cup unbleached all-purpose flour

⅓ cup plus 2 tablespoons sugar

1 teaspoon kosher salt

1 teaspoon baking powder

½ teaspoon baking soda

2¼ cups chilled well-shaken buttermilk (low-fat or whole; see Note)

2 large eggs, lightly beaten

2 tablespoons coconut oil, melted, plus more for griddle

2 teaspoons freshly grated lemon zest (from about 1 lemon)

1 (6-ounce) container blackberries (about 1½ cups), cut in half if large

1 (6-ounce) container raspberries (about 1¾ cups)

1 (6-ounce) container blueberries (about 1⅓ cups)

Cinnamon Cream

1 cup heavy cream

¼ cup nonfat Greek yogurt

½ teaspoon ground cinnamon

Pure maple syrup, warmed, for serving

Note: *In place of buttermilk, you can use 1½ cups whole milk mixed with 2 tablespoons fresh lemon juice or distilled white vinegar for this recipe.*

In my house, a stack of hot-off-the-griddle pancakes is not complete without a dollop of cinnamon-spiked cream and…bumbleberries! Bumbleberries, for those not familiar, are not actually a type of berry, but a combination of those you love most. I've always loved this goofy offbeat term, which is common in Canada, where I'm from and where bumbleberry pie is a summertime must. For these pancakes, I fold my bumbleberries into a hearty buckwheat batter and use some as part of the topping, too. The jumble of juicy berry flavors adds a vibrancy that can't be achieved with just one berry alone.

For the batter: In a large bowl, combine the buckwheat flour, all-purpose flour, sugar, salt, baking powder, and baking soda. Add the buttermilk, eggs, coconut oil, and lemon zest; stir together until just combined (a little lumpy is OK; do not overmix). Allow the batter to rest for 15 minutes. Gently fold in all but ⅓ cup of each type of berry.

For the cinnamon cream: Beat the cream in a medium bowl to medium peaks. Fold in the yogurt and cinnamon and continue beating just until stiff peaks form. Cover and refrigerate until ready to serve.

Heat a heavy-bottomed griddle over medium heat; brush with coconut oil. Working in batches, drop ⅓-cupfuls of the pancake batter into the griddle. Cook the pancakes until the undersides are deep golden and bubbles start to form around the edges, about 3 minutes, then flip. Reduce the heat to low and cook 1 to 2 minutes more, until the underside is golden, too. Repeat with the remaining batter. Serve the pancakes topped with a generous dollop of cream, the remaining berries, a drizzle of warm syrup, and any remaining cream on the side.

KITCHEN WISDOM: Bumbleberries

Bumbleberries are not limited to pancakes and pie! Try them in cocktails, like my Maple Berry Muddler (page 188), as a topping for ice cream sundaes, and more.

To make a true bumbleberry mixture, a minimum of three types of berries must be used. Nonberry fruits, like apple and rhubarb can also be included. Though I hear the term less often in the States than in Canada, bumbleberry pie is said to have originated in western Massachusetts.

QUINOA CEREAL

with Stone Fruit Jam

Jam

1 pound stone fruit (peaches, plums, apricots, and/or nectarines; or see Kitchen Wisdom), pitted and cut into ¾-inch cubes

⅓ cup packed light or dark brown sugar

¾ teaspoon ground cinnamon

¼ teaspoon freshly grated nutmeg

½ vanilla bean, split, bean reserved and seeds scraped; or ½ teaspoon pure vanilla extract

1 (1-inch) strip lemon zest

1 teaspoon lemon juice

¼ teaspoon kosher salt

Cereal

1½ cups quinoa, rinsed well

3 tablespoons packed light brown sugar, plus more for serving

½ vanilla bean, split, bean reserved and seeds scraped; or 1 teaspoon pure vanilla extract

½ teaspoon ground cinnamon

½ teaspoon kosher salt

3 to 4 cups plain sweetened almond milk, plus more for serving

¼ cup coarsely chopped unsalted raw almonds

3 tablespoons pepitas (raw pumpkin seeds)

2 tablespoons sesame seeds

Pure maple syrup for serving (optional)

In 2010, the *Top Chef* crew flew around the world to Singapore to shoot our Season 7 finale. Traveling that far from the U.S. for work, I couldn't help but tack on an extra adventure, so Jeremy and I made a stop in Bali on the way. We stayed on the southern tip of the island, in an area called Uluwatu, known for its sacred temple inhabited by a rambunctious band of monkeys. On our hotel breakfast menu, I was surprised to find a warm quinoa cereal with cooked fruit which, though not a traditional specialty, was deliciously bright and satisfying. I love making my own version at home, topping it with a quick homemade fruit jam and crunchy toasted nuts and seeds.

For the jam: Combine all of the ingredients (including the vanilla bean and seeds or extract) in a small saucepan. Add 3 tablespoons water and bring to a simmer over medium heat. Reduce the heat and cook, stirring occasionally, until the fruit is tender and the liquid is reduced to a medium-thick syrup, 15 to 20 minutes. Remove and discard the vanilla bean, if using, and the lemon zest.

For the cereal: Heat the oven to 350°F with the rack in the middle.

In a medium saucepan, combine the quinoa, brown sugar, vanilla bean and seeds or extract, cinnamon, salt, and 3 cups of the almond milk. Bring to a boil, then reduce the heat to low. Cover and cook at a gentle simmer, stirring occasionally, until most of the liquid is absorbed and the quinoa is tender, 18 to 20 minutes. (Some brands require longer cook time and more liquid. If your quinoa is not tender at this point, add the additional cup of almond milk and continue cooking 5 to 10 minutes longer.) Remove and discard the vanilla bean, if using, and adjust the seasoning to taste.

Meanwhile, spread the almonds, pepitas, and sesame seeds on a rimmed baking sheet. Bake until fragrant and lightly golden, 8 to 10 minutes. Transfer the nuts and seeds to a plate and let cool.

Serve the cereal with additional almond milk, with the jam and toasted nuts and seeds on top. Sprinkle with additional brown sugar or drizzle with maple syrup if you like a little added sweetness.

KITCHEN WISDOM: Rustic Fruit Jam

This recipe calls for summer stone fruit, which, of course, is not found year-round. But this rustic jam is easily adaptable to winter fruit, too, and is just as versatile and delicious. Try it with firm-ripe Anjou or Bartlett pears, or sweet or tart apples. For firmer fruit, increase the cook time to 25 to 30 minutes. With winter fruits, I leave the skins on, but you can peel them, if you like. Whichever fruit you use, you can double or even triple the recipe. The jam keeps, covered and refrigerated, for 1 to 2 weeks and is also tasty spread on toast, mixed into yogurt, or eaten with a spoon right out of the jar.

PEANUT BUTTER, COCONUT, & BANANA OATMEAL

1 teaspoon coconut oil or neutral oil, such as canola or grapeseed

3 bananas, sliced crosswise about ¼ inch thick, divided

2 cups old-fashioned oats (see Kitchen Wisdom)

½ teaspoon ground cinnamon

¼ cup chia seeds (optional)

Kosher salt

3½ to 4 cups nut, soy, or cow's milk, plus more for serving

4 tablespoons smooth peanut butter, divided

Unsweetened coconut flakes for serving

Light or dark brown sugar or coconut sugar for serving

My husband, Jeremy, is crazy for the combo of peanut butter and banana (often with coconut or chocolate added into the mix), an affinity that he passed along to our daughter, Dahlia Rae. So I came up with this oatmeal to create a hearty, quick-cooking breakfast that they both would love. I bump up the nutrients by adding chia seeds when I have them on hand. Using coconut oil to cook the bananas enhances the overall coconut flavor, but any neutral oil, like canola or grapeseed, works well, too.

In a medium saucepan, heat the oil over medium heat. Add about two-thirds of the banana slices and cook, stirring occasionally, until softened and lightly golden, about 5 minutes.

Add the oats, cinnamon, chia (if using), and ¼ teaspoon salt, then stir in 3½ cups milk and 2 tablespoons of the peanut butter to combine. Bring just to a boil, then reduce to a gentle simmer. Cook until the milk is absorbed and the oatmeal is thick and creamy, 5 to 10 minutes; add the remaining ½ cup milk if the oats are not tender when the milk is absorbed. Remove from heat.

Divide the oatmeal among four serving bowls. Dollop each with the remaining peanut butter, drizzle with a little more milk, and top with the coconut flakes, brown sugar, and reserved banana slices.

KITCHEN WISDOM: Rolled Oats

Rolled oats are sold in a few different styles that vary in thickness and cook time. Quick-cooking types require less time and less liquid, while standard old-fashioned and extra-thick varieties need a bit more liquid and a few more minutes to cook through. This recipe gives instructions for old-fashioned oats, but any type you want to use is fine. Take a look at the package instructions and follow liquid and cook time amounts accordingly.

MY ULTIMATE BREAKFAST SANDWICH

3 tablespoons unsalted butter, divided

4 large eggs

Kosher salt

Freshly ground black pepper

8 slices seeded rye bread

6 tablespoons mayonnaise

2 tablespoons spicy brown mustard

20 peppadew peppers (see Notes), drained, halved

¼ pound aged sharp cheddar, sliced

2 large kosher dill pickles, thinly sliced lengthwise (8 slices; see Notes)

4 tomato slices (each about ¼ inch thick), from 1 large ripe beefsteak tomato

Hot sauce

4 large crisp green leaf lettuce leaves

Notes: *Peppadew peppers are sold in jars, and often available at supermarket olive bars and cheese shops. Similarly, you can often find jarred, presliced pickle strips at the grocery store, sometimes labeled as* stackers.

The perfect fried egg sandwich means different things to different people. Find just the right one and you are guaranteed bliss for many mornings (or late nights!) to come. For me, a lot has to do with the layering strategy (a well-thought-out stack can help keep layers from sliding out the side of the sandwich!), as well as how the eggs are cooked (I like mine fried with edges slightly crispy, and yolk just runny enough to coat everything when you take a bite, without getting lost to the plate). Another equally important factor is the inclusion of a little acidic tang to play off the fat of the egg yolk and cheese. My answer to this is mustard and pickles. I discovered these unconventional additions when I was in college in Montreal, and often frequented a burger joint called La Paryse. My favorite dish on the menu was the egg sandwich with pickles. Now, when I wake up a little rough around the edges and need a substantial meal to start the day, this is it.

In a 10- to 12-inch nonstick skillet, heat 1 tablespoon of the butter over medium-high heat until melted and foam subsides. Crack the eggs into the skillet and cook sunny-side up for 1 minute. Reduce the heat to low and continue cooking until the whites are just set and the yolks are runny, about 3 minutes more. Season with a generous pinch each of salt and pepper, then transfer to a plate; set aside.

Arrange the bread slices on a cutting board; spread about 2 teaspoons mayonnaise on the top of each. Using the same skillet, melt 1 tablespoon of the remaining butter over medium-high heat, swirling the pan to evenly coat. Add 2 of the bread slices, mayonnaise-side down; reduce the heat to medium.

Spread the bread slices with about 1½ teaspoons of mustard each, then top each with one-fourth of the peppadews and cheese, and a generous pinch of pepper. Cook until the cheese is melted, about 3 minutes, then top each with 2 pickle slices, 1 tomato slice, and several generous dashes of hot sauce.

Top each sandwich with a remaining bread slice, mayonnaise-side up. Using a metal spatula, flip the sandwiches. Continue cooking until the underside of the bread is golden, about 3 minutes more. Transfer sandwiches to a cutting board, flipping the sandwiches onto the board so that the tomatoes are closest to the top. Lift the top bread slices and slide one egg and one lettuce leaf into each sandwich on top of the tomato, then replace the bread. Repeat with the remaining ingredients to make two more sandwiches.

Transfer each sandwich to a plate and cut in half. Serve with extra hot sauce (and lots of napkins!) on the side.

Recipe continues

SOFT-BOILED EGGS

with Buttery Herb Soldiers

4 large eggs

1 or more of the Flavored Butters (page 16)

4 slices rustic country bread, toasted, then cut crosswise into ½-inch-wide soldiers

Kosher salt

Freshly ground black pepper

Special equipment: 4 egg cups (see Kitchen Wisdom)

It's no secret that I love eggs. In my personal life and on *Top Chef*, I'm known for being a serious stickler when it comes to proper egg cookery. My obsession with this delicious, nutritious, and versatile ingredient goes back to the soft-boiled eggs my mom served in beautiful little "eggy cups" when I was growing up. I loved the sprinkle of salt on top, and the buttered rectangular toast "soldiers" she served alongside for dipping. These days, I serve the eggs in my own collection of egg cups (another obsession!), adding a fun and flavorful update: Using common pantry spices, citrus zest, or fresh herbs, I make flavored butter (also called compound butter) for the soldiers. Melted over the crisp warm bread that is then dipped into the perfectly runny eggs, this quick, easy twist makes the dish even more memorable. Have your butters prepared ahead and toast your bread while boiling the eggs, so that everything is at just the right temperature for serving.

Bring a medium saucepan of water to a boil. Using a slotted spoon, gently lower the eggs into the pot and begin timing immediately, boiling the eggs for 5 minutes. Using the slotted spoon, transfer the eggs to a colander and rinse under cold running water for 1 minute. Place the eggs upright into egg cups.

Using a paring knife, tap around then cut off the top ½ inch of each egg. Serve the eggs with flavored butters to spread on the soldiers for dipping, small spoons for digging out the whites once you've finished the yolks, and salt and pepper for seasoning.

KITCHEN WISDOM: Egg Cups

If you don't have egg cups, fill small serving bowls with uncooked rice to hold the cooked eggs upright.

FLAVORED BUTTERS

◆

These bright, savory butters add so much personality to otherwise mundane eggs and toast. Make all or just one for slathering on your soldiers. Leftover flavored butters can be tossed with hot pasta; sliced and placed over just-grilled steak or fish; or added to pan sauces.

Citrus-Tarragon Butter

- 4 tablespoons (½ stick) unsalted butter, at room temperature
- 1 tablespoon finely chopped tarragon
- 1 tablespoon finely chopped scallion (light green and white parts)
- ½ teaspoon freshly grated orange zest
- ⅛ teaspoon kosher salt
- ⅛ teaspoon freshly ground black pepper

Scallion-Basil Butter

- 4 tablespoons (½ stick) unsalted butter, at room temperature
- 2 tablespoons finely chopped basil leaves
- 1 tablespoon finely chopped scallion (light green and white parts)
- ⅛ teaspoon kosher salt
- ⅛ teaspoon freshly ground black pepper

Chili-Cilantro Butter

- 4 tablespoons (½ stick) unsalted butter, at room temperature
- 3 tablespoons finely chopped cilantro
- ¾ teaspoon chili powder
- 1 teaspoon freshly grated lime zest
- ½ teaspoon fresh lime juice
- ⅛ teaspoon kosher salt
- ⅛ teaspoon freshly ground black pepper

To make each butter, mix together the ingredients for each flavor. Spoon into small bowls and serve immediately. Or wrap in plastic wrap and refrigerate or freeze for up to 3 weeks.

VIETNAMESE OMELET

with Shrimp & Fried Shallots (Banh Xeo)

Dipping Sauce (Nuoc Cham)

2 tablespoons warm water

2 tablespoons lime juice

2 tablespoons rice vinegar

1½ teaspoons sugar

2 tablespoons fish sauce (such as nuoc nam or nam pla)

1 tablespoon reduced-sodium soy sauce

1 small Thai chili, seeded and thinly sliced; or ¼ teaspoon crushed chili flakes

1 small garlic clove, finely chopped

Fried Shallots

1 cup thinly sliced shallots (about 2 large)

½ cup canola oil

Kosher salt

Freshly ground black pepper

Omelet

4 large eggs

½ cup cold water

2 tablespoons fish sauce (such as nuoc nam or nam pla)

¾ cup unbleached all-purpose flour

½ teaspoon baking powder

1 pound large shrimp, peeled, deveined, and cut into ½-inch pieces

2 scallions, cut into ¼-inch slices

½ cup bean sprouts (optional)

⅓ cup thinly sliced basil leaves, divided

1 tablespoon canola oil

2 tablespoons torn mint leaves

Sriracha hot sauce for serving

Special equipment: 10- to 12-inch oven-safe nonstick skillet

Jeremy and I spent our honeymoon in Vietnam. It was the trip of a lifetime. After a few days in Hanoi, we flew to Hoi An, a small, centuries-old village with a vibrant history, a garment- and craft-making tradition, a fabulous market, and great food. There we discovered *banh xeo*, savory pancakes made with eggs and often rice flour that are cooked with shrimp, sprouts, and sometimes pork, then piled with fried shallots, fresh Thai basil, and mint. We ate them for breakfast and lunch, dipped in *nuoc cham*, an addictive sweet-salty concoction of fish sauce, chilies, lime juice, and garlic. The dish is remarkably easy to make at home (if you've ever made a frittata, you'll see some similarities); we make it often for ourselves and for brunch and dinner parties, too.

For the dipping sauce: In a small bowl, whisk together the warm water, lime juice, vinegar, and sugar until the sugar is dissolved. Stir in the fish sauce, soy sauce, chili, and garlic and set aside.

For the shallots: Place a mesh sieve over a bowl. Combine the shallots and canola oil in a small saucepan or skillet (not nonstick); cook over medium-low heat, stirring occasionally, until the shallots are golden brown and caramelized, 18 to 22 minutes (this happens quickly at the end). Remove from the heat. Using a slotted spoon, transfer the shallots to the prepared sieve. Let drain well, then transfer to a paper towel-lined plate; drain and blot with paper towels to absorb excess oil, then transfer to a clean, dry paper towel and season generously with salt and pepper. Set aside (shallots will continue to dry and crisp as they sit).

For the omelet: In a medium bowl, whisk together the eggs, cold water, and fish sauce. In a separate large mixing bowl, sift together the flour and baking powder. Make a well in the center of the dry ingredients then pour in the wet ingredients. Using a whisk, work from the center out to slowly incorporate the dry ingredients. This will help avoid lumps. Once incorporated, whisk vigorously to combine until the batter is smooth. Fold in the shrimp, scallions, sprouts (if using), and 3 tablespoons of the basil. Let the batter rest for at least 15 minutes (or up to 1 hour) to let the air bubbles settle and ensure even cooking.

Heat the oven to broil with the rack about 6 inches from the heat source. In the 10- to 12-inch oven-safe nonstick skillet, heat the oil over medium-high heat until shimmering. Pour in the egg mixture, spreading out the shrimp evenly. Cook until the edges bubble up and begin to dry and crisp, 5 to 7 minutes, then broil for 4 to 6 minutes, watching carefully until the omelet has puffed up and is golden around the edges, and the egg is set. Carefully slide the omelet onto a large serving platter. Sprinkle with fried shallots, mint, and the remaining basil. Cut into wedges. Serve the dipping sauce and Sriracha on the side.

BLOODY MARY EGGS

2 (28-ounce) cans whole tomatoes, drained well

2 tablespoons extra-virgin olive oil, plus more for serving

1 medium yellow onion, finely chopped

2 celery ribs, thinly sliced, plus celery leaves picked from the inner heart of the bunch for serving

1 garlic clove, finely chopped

Celery or kosher salt

¼ cup plus 2 tablespoons (3 ounces) vodka

2 teaspoons Worcestershire sauce

1 teaspoon hot sauce (such as Tabasco)

Freshly ground black pepper

3 tablespoons plus 1 teaspoon prepared or freshly grated horseradish, divided

½ cup pimento-stuffed green olives, coarsely chopped

2 teaspoons distilled white vinegar

8 large eggs

4 slices rustic country bread, toasted and drizzled with extra-virgin olive oil

Note: *Any leftover sauce can be kept, covered and refrigerated, for up to 3 days. Spoon it over toast or crackers for a snack, or thin it out with a little water and use it as a base for simmering mussels or braising fish.*

This recipe—one of my favorites to make at home—was born out of my love for two of the greatest brunch classics in existence: poached eggs and Bloody Marys. I came up with it in 2014 during a head-to-head challenge with chef Marcus Samuelsson on our short-lived TV show, *The Feed.* The idea was to create a dish that would soothe both the belly and the head the morning after a late night out. I took cues from favorites like eggs in purgatory and shakshuka, both of which feature eggs cooked in a spicy tomato sauce. The dish not only won me the challenge, but Marcus was so impressed he put a version of it on his brunch menu at Red Rooster, his Harlem restaurant. The sauce doubles easily and can be made 3 days ahead, which is great when you're hosting a crowd.

In a medium bowl, use clean hands to break up the tomatoes into small pieces. Heat the oil in a medium saucepan over medium heat. Add the onion, celery ribs, and garlic; cook, stirring occasionally, until softened, about 7 minutes. Stir in ¼ teaspoon celery salt, then add the vodka. Cook until the liquid is evaporated by half, about 8 minutes. Add the tomatoes, Worcestershire, hot sauce, a generous pinch of black pepper, and 3 tablespoons of the horseradish. Gently simmer, stirring occasionally, until the sauce is slightly thickened, 20 to 22 minutes. Stir in the olives and remaining 1 teaspoon horseradish, then remove from the heat. Adjust the seasoning and hot sauce to taste.

Meanwhile, fill a large wide saucepan halfway with water and add the vinegar. Bring to a gentle simmer over medium heat. One at a time, crack 4 eggs into a small bowl and carefully add each to the simmering water. Poach, gently spooning simmering water over the top of each egg, until the whites are set but the yolks are still slightly runny, 3 to 4 minutes. Using a slotted spoon, carefully lift the poached eggs, one at a time, from the water, and drain on paper towels. Season with celery salt and black pepper. Repeat with the remaining 4 eggs.

Divide the tomato sauce into four shallow serving bowls. Place a toast slice in the center of each bowl and top with two poached eggs. Garnish with celery leaves and a drizzle of olive oil before serving.

KITCHEN WISDOM: Horseradish

I opt for fresh horseradish whenever possible, as it delivers the purest and spiciest characteristics of the root. If the fresh stuff isn't available, the jarred prepared variety works, too. Choose a refrigerated brand over the shelf-stable options. Not only will you skip the artificial flavorings and preservatives, you'll get a brighter, more complex flavor and heat.

EGGS IN CRISPY POTATO SKINS

with Avocado Salsa

Kosher salt

4 baking potatoes

Extra-virgin olive oil for brushing and drizzling

Freshly ground black pepper

1 cup shredded sharp cheddar cheese (4 ounces), divided

8 large eggs

2 medium ripe tomatoes, coarsely chopped

2 tablespoons finely chopped yellow onion

½ garlic clove, finely chopped

2 tablespoons coarsely chopped cilantro, plus more for serving

½ avocado, cubed

1 small jalapeño, seeded and finely chopped

**KITCHEN WISDOM:
Baked Potatoes**

To prep ahead, the potatoes can be baked up to 3 days in advance. The rest of the dish then comes together in less than 30 minutes.

For over 40 years, my husband's family has rented a big house in Gloucester, Massachusetts, every summer. Upwards of 25 parents, grandparents, cousins, aunts, uncles, sisters, brothers, and a few dear friends pile in to share a beachside vacation. In effect, this sleepy New England fishing village has become an Abrams family second home and one of my favorite places on earth. One of our family rituals is breakfast, at least one morning during our stay, at Lee's—a tiny downhome Main Street diner that serves fantastic hearty food. Lee's is a third-generation family restaurant that is open fisherman's hours—5:00 a.m. to 1:00 p.m.—daily. They specialize in breakfast, including the most brilliant play on classic eggs and home fries: In lieu of cubed or shredded potatoes, Lee's packs perfectly scrambled eggs and melted cheddar cheese into crispy, salty scooped-out baked potato skins! Though there's nothing like experiencing the dish at Lee's, here is my home version, with unscrambled eggs baked directly in the skins, which serve as brilliant cooking vessels and help cut down on cleanup.

Heat oven to 450°F.

In a large bowl, dissolve 2 tablespoons salt in ½ cup lukewarm water. Roll the potatoes in the salt water to moisten, then drain and discard the water. Place the potatoes on a wire rack set into a rimmed baking sheet. Bake until tender, about 50 minutes. Remove from the oven and let stand until cool enough to handle, about 20 minutes.

Cut the potatoes in half lengthwise and scoop out the flesh (if you have a grapefruit spoon handy, put it to use here!), leaving a ¼-inch border all around, to create a bowl. Reserve the scooped-out potato flesh for another use (mashed potatoes for dinner!). Brush the potato halves all over with olive oil. Season the flesh generously with salt and pepper. Return the potatoes to the wire rack, flesh-side down, and bake until the skin begins to crisp, about 10 minutes.

Remove the potatoes from the oven and turn them flesh-side up. Sprinkle the cavities of the potato skins with about half of the cheese. Carefully crack one egg into a small bowl, then pour into one of the potato skins. Repeat with the remaining eggs and skins. Season each egg with a pinch each of salt and pepper. Bake until the egg whites are just set, 12 to 14 minutes.

Meanwhile, make the salsa: Stir together the tomatoes, onion, garlic, cilantro, avocado, jalapeño, ¼ teaspoon salt, and a generous pinch of pepper. Adjust the seasoning to taste.

Remove the skins from the oven and sprinkle with the remaining cheese, then continue baking until the cheese is melted, about 2 minutes more. Arrange the skins on serving plates. Drizzle with oil, sprinkle with cilantro and a pinch of black pepper, and spoon the salsa on top.

THE

Perfect
Bagel
Brunch

WITH BEET-CURED SALMON

SERVES 8 TO 12

Weekend brunch is a meal worth savoring and, when I have the time, I try to make it as special as possible, inviting friends and family to linger around my table. Along with eggs of all kinds, cured salmon and warm, fresh bagels are favorites in my house. Curing your own salmon is both deceptively easy and perfect for serving (and impressing!) a crowd. Beets add a touch of sweetness and a stunning pink-to-red ombré color, created as the salty-coated salmon absorbs the beets' dark purple juices during the curing process. The cream cheeses with flavorful mix-ins add another fun savory twist to the traditional feast of bagels, lox, and cream cheese. Both the salmon and the cream cheeses can easily be doubled or even tripled if you're serving a larger crowd.

Beet-Cured Salmon
(page 26)

Toasted bagels

1 or more of the Three Cream
Cheeses (opposite)

Toppings: sliced cucumber,
red onion, tomatoes, capers,
lemon wedges

Thinly slice the salmon and arrange on a large platter. Pile the toasted bagels on a plate and the toppings and cream cheeses in separate bowls. Dig in!

THREE CREAM CHEESES

Toasted Fennel Seed–Lemon Cream Cheese

2 teaspoons fennel seeds

8 ounces plain cream cheese, at room temperature

Pinch kosher salt

2 teaspoons freshly grated lemon zest

2 generous pinches freshly cracked black pepper

Aleppo-Chive Cream Cheese

8 ounces plain cream cheese, at room temperature

Pinch kosher salt

⅓ cup finely chopped fresh chives

2 teaspoons Aleppo pepper

Everything Cream Cheese

1 tablespoon sesame seeds

8 ounces plain cream cheese, at room temperature

Pinch kosher salt

1 tablespoon poppy seeds

1 teaspoon dried onion flakes

½ teaspoon garlic powder

Feel free to make one, two, or all three of these piquant cream cheeses. Each makes 8 ounces of cream cheese. A good rule of thumb when serving a crowd is 2 ounces of cream cheese per person. The cheese can be mixed up to 3 days ahead, and you can use full-fat or low-fat cream cheese. Keep them covered and refrigerated until ready to serve.

For the Toasted Fennel Seed–Lemon Cream Cheese: In a small, dry skillet, toast the fennel seeds over medium heat, occasionally shaking the pan back and forth, until the seeds are fragrant and lightly toasted, 3 to 5 minutes. Transfer to a cutting board and let cool, then coarsely crack with a mortar and pestle, or by rocking the bottom of a heavy skillet back and forth over the seeds.

In the bowl of an electric stand mixer fitted with the whisk attachment or in a mixing bowl with a standard hand mixer, whisk the cream cheese and salt on medium-high until airy and smooth, 1 to 2 minutes. Fold in all but a generous pinch each of the cracked fennel seeds, lemon zest, and pepper. Transfer to a serving bowl and sprinkle with the remaining fennel seeds, zest, and pepper.

For the Aleppo-Chive Cream Cheese: In the bowl of an electric stand mixer fitted with the whisk attachment or in a mixing bowl with a standard hand mixer, whisk the cream cheese and salt on medium-high until airy and smooth, 1 to 2 minutes. Fold in all but a generous pinch each of the chives and Aleppo pepper. Transfer to a serving bowl and sprinkle with the remaining chives and Aleppo pepper.

For the Everything Cream Cheese: In a small, dry skillet, toast the sesame seeds over medium-low heat, occasionally shaking the pan back and forth, until the seeds are lightly golden, 4 to 6 minutes. Transfer to a plate and let cool.

In the bowl of an electric stand mixer fitted with the whisk attachment or in a mixing bowl with a standard hand mixer, whisk the cream cheese and salt on medium-high until airy and smooth, 1 to 2 minutes. Fold in the sesame seeds, all but a pinch of the poppy seeds, the onion flakes, and garlic powder. Transfer to a serving bowl and sprinkle with the remaining poppy seeds.

Recipe continues

BEET-CURED SALMON

¾ pound beets (4 to 5 medium), well-scrubbed, trimmed, and quartered

2 teaspoons coriander seeds

2 teaspoons white peppercorns

⅔ cup kosher salt

⅔ cup sugar

⅔ cup finely chopped fresh dill

Finely grated zest of 1 lemon

1 (2-pound) skin-on salmon fillet

Special equipment: food-safe rubber gloves (if needed); 13 x 9-inch baking dish

In the bowl of a food processor fitted with the shredding blade, shred the beets. (If you don't have a food processor, put on the rubber gloves and use the large holes of a box grater to grate the beets.) Set aside.

In a small, dry skillet, heat the coriander seeds and white peppercorns over medium-low heat, occasionally shaking the pan back and forth, until the spices are fragrant and lightly toasted, 5 to 7 minutes. Transfer to a cutting board and let cool. Coarsely crush with a mortar and pestle, or by rocking the bottom of a heavy skillet back and forth over the seeds. Place in a bowl and stir in the salt, sugar, dill, and lemon zest to combine.

Before beginning the curing process, check for pin bones in the fish by running your index finger along the center seam of the flesh (you'll feel them if they're there). Working one by one, using tweezers or small needle-nose pliers, grasp the tip of each bone, then pull up and out at a slight angle to remove.

Rinse the salmon under cold running water and pat dry with paper towels. Place in a nonreactive baking dish, skin-side down. Rub about one-third of the salt mixture into the top and sides of the fish, then pat the remaining mixture over the top and sides, fully covering the fish. Top with the beets and their juices.

Cover the fish with plastic wrap, pressing the wrap directly onto the fish, then place a second baking dish or a heavy pan on top and weight the dish with several heavy cans. Cure in the refrigerator for 3 days.

Gently scrape off the curing mixture and discard before cutting the salmon into thin slices (see Chef Tech).

The cured salmon keeps, covered and refrigerated, for up to 1 week or frozen for up to 3 months. Cut into portions before freezing to avoid freezing again once thawed.

Slicing for success: Cured salmon is firmest when it's chilled, which makes for easy and more uniform slicing, so be sure to slice it straight from the fridge. Starting from the front end of the fish (which is also the wider end) and using a sharp, long knife, slice the flesh thinly and on an angle, applying a gentle pressure and a long back-and-forth motion. Just before the knife reaches the skin, angle the sharp end of the blade slightly upward to separate the slice from the skin. Slice only as much of the fish as you plan to serve at one time.

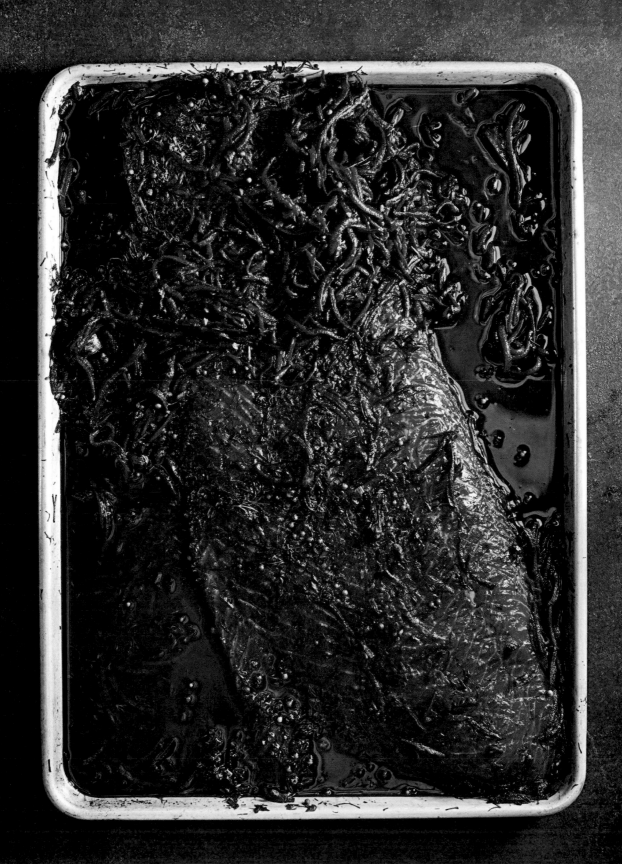

Beet-Cured Salmon,
page 26

Aleppo-Chive Cream Cheese,
page 25

Everything Cream Cheese,
page 25

Toasted Fennel Seed–Lemon Cream Cheese,
page 25

Salads & Vegetables

PEPPERY GREENS WITH TAHINI DRESSING 33

WARM FARRO BOWLS WITH ROASTED CAULIFLOWER & KALE 35

LENTIL, GRILLED RADICCHIO, & SWEET ONION SALAD 39

SHRIMP & GRAPEFRUIT SALAD WITH GINGER-CHILI DRESSING 42

SUMMER VEGETABLE SALAD WITH CHARRED LIME VINAIGRETTE 45

GRILLED CORN WITH MISO-CHILI BUTTER 49

GRILLED RADISHES WITH ANCHOVY-MINT BUTTER 53

SALT-AND-VINEGAR SMASHED POTATOES 54

ZUCCHINI THREE WAYS
Shaved Zucchini Salad with Harissa-Citrus Dressing & Mint 58
Roasted Zucchini with Coriander Vinaigrette 60
Ratatouille Galette 62

PEPPERY GREENS

with Tahini Dressing

¼ cup sunflower seeds

1 teaspoon extra-virgin olive oil

¼ teaspoon ground cumin

¼ teaspoon ground ginger

Kosher salt

2 medium carrots, peeled

3 ounces torn mustard or dandelion greens (7 loosely packed cups)

3 ounces baby arugula (6 loosely packed cups)

1 firm-ripe avocado, pitted and cubed

Tahini Dressing (page 34)

Aleppo pepper, for sprinkling (optional)

I was 18 and working in the kitchen on a kibbutz in Israel when I fell in love with tahini. Since then, the thick sesame paste has been one of my go-to staples. I use it to make my own hummus (page 167), but that's not all. Tahini is great in dips and salad dressings; sauces for noodles, meat, and fish; and even baked goods. For this salad, its rich, nutty flavor complements robust, spicy greens. Lightly toasted cumin- and ginger-dusted sunflower seeds add a bright note and satisfying crunch.

In a small skillet, stir together the sunflower seeds, oil, cumin, ginger, and ⅛ teaspoon salt until well combined. Cook over medium heat, stirring constantly, until the seeds are fragrant and lightly golden, about 4 minutes. Remove from the heat and set aside to cool.

Using a sharp vegetable peeler (I find the Y-shaped kind easiest to use), peel the carrots lengthwise into ribbons (you will have a few carrot scraps, which can be saved for another use or an instant snack). In a large bowl, combine the carrot ribbons, greens, avocado, and a generous pinch of salt. Drizzle the dressing over the salad and toss to combine. Adjust the seasoning to taste. Sprinkle with the sunflower seeds and Aleppo pepper, if desired.

KITCHEN WISDOM: Aleppo Pepper

Aleppo pepper is a wonderfully complex dried chili flake with a subtle sweetness and medium heat. It's great to cook with (try it in place of more common red pepper flakes in meat and fish dishes, and soups and stews), and as a finishing pepper over toasts, egg dishes, salads, meats, and more. The eponymous spice has long been cultivated in Aleppo, Syria (which, unfortunately, is often in the news due to the Syrian Civil War), and it is used widely in Mediterranean and Middle Eastern cuisines. If you can't find Aleppo pepper, try Turkish Marash pepper, which is smokier and spicier than Aleppo, or Antebi pepper, also from Turkey and a little more mild and fruity. Another great choice is Urfa pepper (sometimes called isot pepper), which is sweeter than Aleppo, and the smokiest of the four mentioned here.

Tahini Dressing

For Peppery Greens with Tahini Dressing (page 33)

This dressing is a family favorite. I often make a double or triple batch to use on salads of all types, serve with crudités, and drizzle over roasted vegetables. It keeps, covered and refrigerated, for up to 1 week.

¼ cup plus 2 tablespoons fresh lemon juice
  (from about 2 large lemons)

⅓ cup well-stirred tahini (see Sources, page 241)

1 small garlic clove, finely chopped

¼ teaspoon Aleppo pepper (see Kitchen Wisdom, page 33)
  or pinch red pepper flakes

¼ teaspoon kosher salt

2 teaspoons cold water

In a medium bowl, whisk together the lemon juice, tahini, garlic, Aleppo pepper, salt, and water until smooth.

WARM FARRO BOWLS

with Roasted Cauliflower & Kale

1 small head cauliflower (about ¾ pound), leaves removed and thinly sliced, florets and core cut into 1-inch pieces

7 tablespoons plus 1½ teaspoons extra-virgin olive oil, divided

Kosher salt

Freshly ground black pepper

¼ teaspoon red pepper flakes

1 small red onion, very thinly sliced

1 tablespoon red wine vinegar

1 cup farro

4 large eggs

⅓ pound shiitake or wild mushrooms, stemmed, caps quartered

1 garlic clove, finely chopped

½ cup plus 2 tablespoons mix of finely chopped tender herbs (including two or more of the following: mint, chives, tarragon, chervil, and basil), divided

1½ teaspoons freshly grated lemon zest

2 tablespoons fresh lemon juice

4 cups thinly sliced kale leaves

KITCHEN WISDOM: Prepping Ahead

All of the cooked and prepped elements in this recipe keep well, covered and refrigerated, for up to 3 days. Let the farro and cooked vegetables come to room temperature, or gently warm just before eating. Keep the boiled eggs refrigerated and unpeeled until you're ready to eat.

The best grain bowls combine hearty ingredients, great textures, and lively flavors. They also require a little extra time to prepare, due to their multiple components. Don't let this deter you, though—the effort is more than worth it! Here, freshly chopped herbs, quick-pickled onion, and a lemony dressing, plus earthy farro and roasted vegetables can all be prepared ahead (see Kitchen Wisdom), making assembly super-swift.

Bowls make great lunches for taking to work—tuck each element into its own corner of a recycled take-out container or bento lunch box and tote along the dressing in a small sealed jar.

Heat the oven to 400°F. Line a rimmed baking sheet with parchment paper.

Toss together the cauliflower florets and core pieces on the baking sheet with 2 tablespoons of the oil, ¼ teaspoon salt, and a generous pinch of pepper, then spread in a single layer. Roast, stirring once halfway through, until golden and tender, 40 to 45 minutes. Stir in the red pepper flakes and cauliflower leaves and let cool on a wire rack.

While the cauliflower is roasting, toss together the red onion, vinegar, and ⅛ teaspoon salt in a small bowl; set aside.

In a large saucepan of salted boiling water, cook the farro until tender but still firm to the bite, 18 to 20 minutes. Drain and transfer to a large bowl; set aside. Rinse out the saucepan.

Fill the saucepan with clean water and bring to a boil. Using a spoon, gently lower the eggs into the water and cook for 7 minutes. Drain, then rinse the eggs under cold running water for 1 minute; set aside.

In a large nonstick skillet, heat 2 tablespoons of the oil over medium-high heat until hot but not smoking. Add the mushrooms and cook, stirring just once or twice, until golden brown, about 8 minutes. Stir in the garlic, 2 tablespoons of the mixed herbs, and a generous pinch each of salt and pepper. Remove from the heat and set aside.

In a small bowl, whisk together the lemon zest and juice and ¼ teaspoon salt. In a slow and steady stream, whisk in 3 tablespoons of the oil; set the dressing aside.

To the farro, add ½ teaspoon salt, a generous pinch of pepper, the remaining ½ cup chopped herbs, and 1½ teaspoons oil and toss to combine.

Drain the vinegar from the onions. Peel the eggs under cold running water, then cut in half lengthwise.

Divide the farro, cauliflower, mushrooms, and kale among four large shallow serving bowls. Arrange the egg halves and pickled onions on top. Drizzle with the dressing and serve.

Warm Farro Bowls with Roasted Cauliflower & Kale, *page 35*

LENTIL, GRILLED RADICCHIO, & SWEET ONION SALAD

2 dried bay leaves

1 garlic clove, gently smashed and peeled

5 cups cold water

¾ cup small brown or green lentils (See Kitchen Wisdom), picked over and rinsed

Kosher salt

Extra-virgin olive oil for brushing

1 medium sweet onion such as Vidalia, cut into ¼-inch-thick rounds

1 large head radicchio, quartered lengthwise, keeping root end intact

Freshly ground black pepper

1 small fennel bulb, thinly sliced

½ cup coarsely chopped basil leaves, plus more for sprinkling

Lemon-Shallot Vinaigrette (page 40)

3 cups loosely packed baby or torn arugula (2 ounces)

I love the earthy-sweet flavors in this hearty lentil salad. It's a dish I turn to year-round and often for dinner parties. It looks gorgeous on a big platter and holds up well as it sits. Grilling radicchio gives the vegetable a great charred flavor, and plays off the flavors and textures of sweet grilled onion and shaved fresh fennel.

Combine the bay leaves, garlic, and water in a medium saucepan and bring to a boil. Add the lentils and ½ teaspoon salt and reduce to a simmer. Cook, uncovered, until the lentils are tender but still firm enough to hold their shape well, 18 to 22 minutes. Drain, spread on a large plate, and set aside to cool. Remove and discard the bay leaves and garlic.

While the lentils are cooking, prepare a grill or grill pan for medium-high heat. Lightly brush the grill with oil. Season both sides of the onion slices and the cut sides of the radicchio with salt and pepper. Grill the vegetables, turning once halfway through, until the onion slices are tender with a light char and the radicchio is wilted and tender at the core, 8 to 10 minutes. Transfer to a cutting board and let cool slightly, then coarsely chop the radicchio and separate the onion rings.

Combine the cooled lentils, onion, radicchio, fennel, basil, ¼ teaspoon salt, and a generous pinch of pepper in a serving bowl. Add the vinaigrette and toss the salad together, then add the arugula and gently toss just to combine. Adjust the seasoning to taste and sprinkle with additional basil.

KITCHEN WISDOM: Lentils

When shopping for lentils, seek out small brown or green types, like French green (also called du Puy) or Spanish pardina lentils, both of which have a nice firm-tender bite and hold their shape best once cooked. Black beluga lentils are also great, but are less widely available and more expensive. Regardless of variety, any lentil that's cooked too long will become mushy. Since lentil cook times may vary (as legumes age they require longer cooking times), it's best to test them several times during the cooking process, and always judge by taste rather than minutes.

Lemon-Shallot Vinaigrette

MAKES ⅓ CUP

For Lentil, Grilled Radicchio & Sweet Onion Salad (page 39)

2 tablespoons fresh lemon juice

2 tablespoons red wine vinegar

1 medium shallot, finely chopped (about 2 tablespoons)

¼ teaspoon kosher salt

2 tablespoons extra-virgin olive oil

In a medium bowl, stir together the lemon juice, vinegar, shallot, and salt. Let stand for 10 minutes, then whisk in the oil.

The vinaigrette will keep, refrigerated in a small, airtight container, for up to 1 week.

Ginger-Chili Dressing

For Shrimp & Grapefruit Salad with Ginger-Chili Dressing (page 42)

2 tablespoons fresh grapefruit juice (from the grapefruit prep
   in salad recipe)

1 tablespoon fresh lime juice

2 teaspoons light brown sugar

1 small Thai chili, seeded and thinly sliced; or ½ small jalapeño,
   seeded and finely chopped

1 teaspoon finely grated peeled fresh ginger

1 teaspoon finely chopped lemongrass (from the lemongrass prep
   in salad recipe)

1 teaspoon fish sauce (such as nuoc nam or nam pla)

¼ teaspoon kosher salt

2 tablespoons extra-virgin olive oil

In a medium bowl, whisk together the grapefruit juice, lime juice,
sugar, chili, ginger, lemongrass, fish sauce, and salt. Whisk in the oil.

The dressing will keep, refrigerated and in a small, airtight container,
for up to 1 week.

SHRIMP & GRAPEFRUIT SALAD with Ginger-Chili Dressing

1 lemongrass stalk, tough outer leaves removed

Ice water

2 (⅛-inch-thick) coins unpeeled fresh ginger

Kosher salt

1 pound large shrimp, peeled and deveined

1 large pink grapefruit

1½ cups mung bean sprouts (see Kitchen Wisdom)

1 avocado, pitted and cubed

¼ cup torn fresh basil, plus more for serving

¼ cup coarsely chopped cilantro leaves, plus more for serving

Ginger-Chili Dressing (page 41)

¼ cup dry roasted salted peanuts, roughly chopped

1 small Thai chili, seeded and thinly sliced; or ½ small jalapeño, seeded and finely chopped

Lime wedges

On our travels in Bali, Jeremy and I stayed at a little resort that offered great cooking classes. In addition to local curries and rice dishes, the chef taught us this citrusy, simple salad, which has since become a staple at home. The combination of poached shrimp, tart grapefruit, spicy chilies, and fresh mint is bright and clean. Crunchy bean sprouts add terrific texture.

Finely chop 1 teaspoon lemongrass from the thick end of the stalk and set aside for the dressing. Bruise the remaining stalk with the back of a chef's knife.

Fill a large bowl with ice water. Place the lemongrass stalk in a large saucepan and add the ginger coins, 1 teaspoon salt, and 5 cups water. Bring to a boil, then reduce to a simmer. Add the shrimp and cook until opaque and bright pink, 2 to 3 minutes. Using a slotted spoon, transfer the shrimp to the ice water. Let stand 1 to 2 minutes, then drain and pat dry. Discard the aromatics.

Using a sharp knife, cut away the skin and bitter white pith from the grapefruit. Cut in between the membranes to release the grapefruit sections into a large bowl. Cut the grapefruit segments into bite-sized pieces and place in a large mixing bowl. Squeeze and pour excess juice from the membrane into a separate bowl and reserve 2 tablespoons of the juice for the dressing (drink the rest!).

Add the shrimp, sprouts, avocado, basil, cilantro, 3 tablespoons of the dressing, and a generous pinch of salt to the grapefruit segments; gently toss to combine. Divide the salad among serving plates, then drizzle with the remaining dressing. Sprinkle with the peanuts, chili, and additional basil and cilantro and serve with lime wedges.

KITCHEN WISDOM: Mung Bean Sprouts

Mung bean sprouts are crisp and slightly sweet. Look for them in the produce section of good supermarkets or in Asian markets. When the sprouts are not available, I use sunflower sprouts or thinly sliced endive as a substitute.

SUMMER VEGETABLE SALAD

with Charred Lime Vinaigrette

2 ears corn, shucked

1 medium red, orange, or yellow bell pepper, cut into ½-inch-wide strips

Extra-virgin olive oil for brushing

1 pint cherry tomatoes, halved

½ English cucumber, peeled and cut into half moons

5 radishes, thinly sliced

Charred Lime Vinaigrette (page 46)

Kosher salt

Freshly ground black pepper

2½ ounces ricotta salata cheese, shaved (about ¾ cup)

⅓ cup coarsely chopped mixed fresh tender herbs, such as mint, basil, cilantro, tarragon, and/or chives

This salad was born out of my tendency to purchase far too many vegetables at my summer farmers' market, followed by a productive panic to make sure nothing goes to waste. I love the mix of raw and grilled flavors and textures here, as well as the fact that a wide variety of crunchy vegetables and fresh herbs work well, so you can riff almost endlessly according to what you have on hand.

Prepare a grill or grill pan for medium-high heat. Brush the corn and bell pepper with oil and grill, turning occasionally, until charred and tender, 6 to 8 minutes for the pepper and 12 to 15 minutes for the corn. Transfer the grilled vegetables to a cutting board as they are finished and let cool slightly.

Cut the corn kernels from the cobs and roughly chop the bell pepper. Arrange the grilled vegetables, tomatoes, cucumber, and radishes in a large bowl. Add the vinaigrette and a generous pinch each of salt and pepper; gently toss to combine. Sprinkle with the cheese and herbs and serve.

KITCHEN WISDOM: Grilling Limes

Grilling limes before juicing gives the dressing for this salad a delicious charred flavor, but that's not all. Warming the fruit also relaxes the flesh, which helps you squeeze every last drop of its tasty juices.

Charred Lime Vinaigrette

For Summer Vegetable Salad with Charred Lime Vinaigrette (page 45)

2 medium to large limes, cut in half crosswise

3 tablespoons extra-virgin olive oil, plus more for brushing

1 large garlic clove, peeled

½ teaspoon kosher salt

1 medium shallot, finely chopped (about 2 tablespoons)

Prepare a grill or grill pan for medium-high heat. Brush 3 of the lime halves with oil (reserve the remaining lime half for another use). Grill the halves, cut-side down, rotating occasionally, until charred, about 5 minutes. Transfer the grilled limes to a plate.

On a cutting board, thinly slice the garlic, then mound the salt on top. Using both the blade and flat side of a chef's knife, chop and scrape the mixture into a paste. Transfer to a medium bowl.

Juice the grilled limes (you should have about 3 tablespoons). Add the lime juice and shallot to the bowl with the garlic and whisk in the oil.

The vinaigrette will keep, refrigerated in a small, airtight container, for up to 1 week.

GRILLED CORN

with Miso-Chili Butter

4 ears corn, shucked

1 tablespoon extra-virgin olive oil

Miso-Chili Butter (page 50)

Finely chopped cilantro for sprinkling

Finely chopped scallion or fresh chives for sprinkling

Kosher salt (optional)

Lime wedges for serving

Though it's nearly impossible for me to resist an unadorned ear of grilled fresh corn, I also love the veg with a slather of really good butter. Mixing the butter with miso, cilantro, and spicy red pepper flakes is an easy way to up the ante and give the simple dish an exciting new twist. The butter, I should add, is also terrific melted and drizzled over grilled pork chops and steak, as well as on all sorts of fish and shellfish, so I often make a double batch. A fresh squeeze of lime juice balances the richness of the butter, and works great on any of the dishes mentioned above.

Prepare a grill or grill pan for medium-high heat. Brush the corn with the oil and grill, turning occasionally, until tender and slightly charred, 12 to 15 minutes.

Transfer the corn to a serving platter. Slather with the miso butter then sprinkle with cilantro, scallion, and a pinch of salt if desired. Serve warm with lime wedges squeezed over the top.

KITCHEN WISDOM: Miso

Miso is a traditional Japanese paste made from cooked and fermented soybeans. There are many miso varieties available, and each has its own character. The most commonly available supermarket types are white, yellow, and red. Generally, the darker the paste, the richer and more pungent it tastes. White miso is fermented for the shortest amount of time, usually with rice. It is mild, nutty, and very versatile. The yellow sort is fermented a little longer, sometimes with the addition of barley. Red miso, the darkest and saltiest of the three, also is the deepest and earthiest in flavor. For the Miso-Chili Butter that accompanies this recipe, white and yellow misos tend to work best, in terms of not overwhelming the flavor of the corn, but you can experiment with any miso that you like, especially if you want to make the butter to use in other dishes.

Miso-Chili Butter

For Grilled Corn with Miso-Chili Butter (page 49)

4 tablespoons (½ stick) unsalted butter, at room temperature

2 tablespoons finely chopped cilantro

1 tablespoon finely chopped scallion or fresh chives

1 tablespoon miso paste (yellow or red)

¼ teaspoon red pepper flakes

In a small bowl, stir together the soft butter, cilantro, scallion, miso paste, and red pepper flakes. Let stand at room temperature until ready to use.

The butter keeps, wrapped in plastic and refrigerated, for up to 3 weeks, or frozen for up to 3 months.

Anchovy-Mint Butter

For Grilled Radishes with Anchoy-Mint Butter (page 53)

4 tablespoons (½ stick) unsalted butter, at room temperature

4 flat anchovy fillets, finely chopped

1 tablespoon finely chopped fresh mint

Freshly grated zest of ½ lemon

¼ teaspoon freshly ground black pepper

Pinch kosher salt

In a small bowl, use a fork to mash together the soft butter, anchovies, mint, lemon zest, pepper, and salt. Let stand at room temperature until ready to use.

The butter keeps, wrapped in plastic and refrigerated, for up to 3 weeks, or frozen for up to 3 months.

GRILLED RADISHES

with Anchovy-Mint Butter

1 teaspoon extra-virgin olive oil, plus more for grilling

12 radishes with their greens attached, halved lengthwise

Kosher salt

Freshly ground black pepper

Anchovy-Mint Butter (page 51)

1 lemon wedge for serving

½ baguette, thinly sliced (optional)

Raw radishes, served with a smear of butter and a sprinkling of salt, are a delicious French snack, often served alongside a glass of wine at the beginning of a meal. I like to give the classic dish a twist by grilling the crisp red orbs—green tops included!—and punching up the accompanying butter with a little chopped anchovy, a splash of lemon juice, and some fresh mint. Grilling mellows the bite of the radishes and crisps up their greens. The umami flavor of the anchovy butter adds a bright, rich, and almost meaty flavor to the radishes. Serve with a few slices of fresh baguette to sop up any leftover puddles of butter (aka liquid gold!) that might be left on your plate.

Prepare a grill or grill pan for medium-high heat. Lightly oil the grill grate.

Arrange the radishes on a platter or baking sheet; drizzle with 1 teaspoon oil and season with ¼ teaspoon each salt and pepper. Grill the radishes until the greens are wilted and a little charred and the bulbs are crisp-tender, 2 to 3 minutes per side. Immediately transfer the radishes to a large bowl; add half of the anchovy butter and toss to coat, then arrange on a clean serving platter. Squeeze a few drops of lemon juice over the top and season with salt and pepper. Serve warm with the remaining anchovy butter and bread slices, if using, on the side.

KITCHEN WISDOM: Anchovies

Anchovies often get a bad rap because they're considered too fishy or strong tasting. But, used correctly—as in my Anchovy-Mint Butter—they're a delicious, easy, and inexpensive way to add a lively punch to ordinary dishes, even in small doses. Try finely chopping, then melting one or two into your next batch of pasta or pizza sauce, or blending a little bit into a simple lemon vinaigrette. They're even delicious over toasted and buttered crusty bread. An added bonus: These little fish are high in protein, iron, and omega-3 fatty acids, and they're a sustainable seafood choice—a win-win for you and the planet.

SALT-AND-VINEGAR
SMASHED POTATOES

2 pounds small red- or white-skinned new potatoes (1½ to 2 inches in diameter)

1 cup plus 2 teaspoons malt vinegar, divided, plus more for brushing

5 tablespoons kosher salt

4 cups cold water

2 cups ice

2 tablespoons unsalted butter

2 tablespoons finely chopped fresh chives, divided

Coarsely cracked black pepper

This recipe is inspired by the brilliant flavor of salt and vinegar potato chips, which are pretty much the one snack I am absolutely unable to resist. My roasted potato version makes a great side for steaks (see pages 136 to 139) and roast chicken, but it's also delicious alongside all sorts of vegetarian meals, or just eaten straight from the pan.

Combine the potatoes, 1 cup of the vinegar, and 1 tablespoon of the salt in a large saucepan. Add water to cover the potatoes by 1 inch. Bring to a boil, then cover and simmer until the potatoes are just tender, 15 to 20 minutes.

Heat the oven to 450°F. Line a rimmed baking sheet with parchment paper.

In a large bowl, whisk together the cold water and the remaining 4 tablespoons salt until the salt is dissolved. Add the ice. Using a slotted spoon, transfer the cooked potatoes to the ice water. Let stand for 30 seconds, then drain and pat dry. Allow the potatoes to cool slightly.

Meanwhile, in a small saucepan (or in the microwave), melt the butter with 1 tablespoon of the chives and ½ teaspoon coarsely cracked pepper. Remove the mixture from the heat and whisk in the remaining 2 teaspoons vinegar.

When cool enough to handle, use the heel of your hand to gently smash and flatten each potato to a ½-inch thickness. Arrange the smashed potatoes in a single layer on the prepared baking sheet.

Brush the potatoes with the butter mixture and sprinkle generously with salt. Flip and repeat on the other sides. Bake until the edges of the potatoes are crispy and golden, 35 to 40 minutes. Brush generously with more vinegar, then transfer to a serving platter. Sprinkle with the remaining 1 tablespoon chives and more salt. Serve hot.

Flash-cooling potatoes in salted ice water after boiling makes them easier to handle when smashing and adds to their crispness once baked. I use a similar dipping technique before baking regular potatoes, to enhance crispness as well (see Eggs in Crispy Potato Skins, page 23).

Using malt vinegar in place of ketchup as a condiment for French fries is common practice in Britain and Ireland (where fries are called chips), as well as in my homeland of Canada, a British colony until 1867. The vinegar is made by malting barley into beer and then into vinegar, which gives the final product its caramel color and subtle nutty flavor. Any leftover vinegar from this recipe can be used to sprinkle over fried fish, or in pickling mixtures, marinades, or chutneys.

Zucchini THREE Ways

There has always been zucchini in my mother's kitchen. When I was growing up, she cooked with the vegetable so often that it came to define—in those pre "veg-crazy" days —the thing that set a meal at our house apart from those at most of our young friends' homes. We were considered the "adventurous" eaters. To my brothers and me, this was not always a good thing as the green stuff scared off many a visiting friend: After all, who wants to eat zucchini when you could have hot dogs or grilled cheese!? But, I know now that my mom was onto something good. As an adult, I've come to adore zucchini and I use it in all sorts of ways, somehow subconsciously adopting her habit of always having the vegetable on hand. I hope my own daughter comes to appreciate it as much as I have!

Shaved Zucchini
Salad with
Harissa-Citrus
Dressing & Mint,
page 58

Ratatouille
Galette,
page 62

Roasted
Zucchini
with Coriander
Vinaigrette,
page 60

SHAVED ZUCCHINI SALAD

with Harissa-Citrus Dressing & Mint

1 pound mixed summer squashes, such as zucchini or yellow squash

Flaky sea salt (such as Maldon)

Harissa-Citrus Dressing (opposite)

½ cup crumbled feta cheese (about 3 ounces)

⅓ cup loosely packed mint leaves, torn

Zucchini doesn't need to be cooked or complicated to be delicious. Shaving the vegetable into thin ribbons is quick and easy, and makes a delicate base for fresh summer salads. Harissa, a pungent North African chili paste, adds nuanced notes of smoke and aromatic spices. Made with dried chilies, olive oil, garlic, cumin, coriander, and often caraway, a dollop of this aromatic condiment goes a long way, so make sure to taste and adjust with caution.

Trim the squash, then slice lengthwise into thin ribbons and transfer to a large bowl (save any scraps for another use). Sprinkle with a pinch of salt, then drizzle with the dressing. Gently toss to coat.

Divide the zucchini mixture among serving plates, or pile it onto a serving platter. Sprinkle with the cheese, mint, and a couple more pinches of salt and serve.

You don't need fancy equipment or chef-caliber knife skills to ensure thin zucchini ribbons for this salad. If you don't have a mandolin slicer, try a cheese plane, or a Y-shaped vegetable peeler. As you slice, press firmly from end to end in one long stroke and you'll get lovely even strips.

Harissa-Citrus Dressing

For Shaved Zucchini Salad with Harissa-Citrus Dressing & Mint (opposite)

1 Valencia or navel orange
2 teaspoons fresh lemon juice
1 tablespoon finely chopped shallot
¼ teaspoon kosher salt
½ teaspoon harissa (see Sources, page 240), plus more to taste
Freshly ground black pepper
2 tablespoons extra-virgin olive oil

Finely grate ½ teaspoon zest from the orange, then squeeze enough juice to yield 1 tablespoon (save the remaining orange for another use). In a small bowl, stir together the orange zest and juice, lemon juice, shallot, and salt. Let stand 10 to 15 minutes. Add the harissa and a generous pinch of pepper to the shallot mixture, then whisk in the oil; adjust the harissa to taste.

The dressing will keep refrigerated in a small, airtight container, for up to 1 week.

ROASTED ZUCCHINI

with Coriander Vinaigrette

1¼ pounds summer squash, one type or a mix of pattypan squash, small zucchini, and yellow squash

2 tablespoons extra-virgin olive oil

¼ teaspoon kosher salt

Freshly ground black pepper

½ teaspoon coriander seeds, crushed

¼ teaspoon red pepper flakes

Coriander Vinaigrette (opposite)

Flaky sea salt (such as Maldon) for serving

1 tablespoon coarsely chopped shelled unsalted pistachios (optional)

Fresh mint leaves, torn if large, for serving

Crushed whole coriander seeds bring light nutty and floral notes to this quick, elegant dish. If you're shopping at a farmers' market, grow zucchini in your garden, or are part of a CSA, you're likely to have all sorts of summer squash varieties in a number of shapes and colors—a mix of them would be very pretty here.

Heat the oven to 450°F with the rack in the middle. Line a rimmed baking sheet with parchment paper.

If using pattypan squash, cut them into ¾-inch wedges. If using zucchini and/or yellow squash, quarter them lengthwise, then cut the pieces in half crosswise.

On the prepared baking sheet, toss the squash with the oil, kosher salt, and a generous pinch of black pepper, then arrange in a single layer, cut-side down. Roast until tender and lightly golden, about 18 minutes. Sprinkle with the coriander and red pepper flakes and continue roasting until the edges are just golden, about 4 minutes more.

Transfer the squash to a serving platter, then lift up the parchment and slide any remaining spices and oil over the top. Drizzle with the vinaigrette and sprinkle with a pinch or two of flaky sea salt and the pistachios, if using. Sprinkle with mint leaves and serve warm or at room temperature.

Using a spice grinder to grind whole spices is easy and quick, but when you want to crush rather than grind the spices, try doing it by hand: Place the spices on a cutting board, then crush with the bottom of a heavy skillet, rocking the pan back and forth over the spices to lightly crush.

Coriander Vinaigrette

For Roasted Zucchini with Coriander Vinaigrette (opposite)

½ teaspoon coriander seeds
1 tablespoon extra-virgin olive oil
1 tablespoon red wine vinegar
½ garlic clove, finely chopped
⅛ teaspoon kosher salt
Freshly ground black pepper
¼ cup loosely packed mint leaves, torn if large

In a small, dry skillet, toast the coriander over medium-low heat, occasionally shaking the pan back and forth, until fragrant and lightly toasted, 2 to 3 minutes. Transfer to a cutting board and let cool, then crush with the bottom of a heavy pan.

In a medium bowl, whisk together the toasted coriander, oil, vinegar, garlic, salt, and a generous pinch of pepper. Just before serving, stir in the mint.

The vinaigrette will keep, refrigerated in a small, airtight container, for up to 1 week.

RATATOUILLE GALETTE

Galette Dough

¾ cup unbleached all-purpose flour, plus more for dusting

¾ cup whole-wheat flour

Kosher salt

½ cup (1 stick) cold unsalted butter, cubed

¼ cup sour cream

1 teaspoon freshly grated lemon zest

1 tablespoon lemon juice

Ice water

Ratatouille Filling

1 small zucchini, cut crosswise into ¼-inch-thick rounds

½ small eggplant, cut crosswise into ¼-inch-thick rounds

Kosher salt

1 large garlic clove, peeled

8 ounces (1 cup) whole milk ricotta cheese

2 teaspoons fresh thyme leaves

1½ teaspoons freshly grated lemon zest

Freshly ground black pepper

1 medium tomato, thinly sliced

1 cup cherry tomatoes, halved

1 tablespoon extra-virgin olive oil

½ teaspoon dried oregano

1 large egg

¼ cup freshly grated Parmigiano-Reggiano cheese

Jeremy and I were married on a beautiful late August day in the summer of 2008. Chef Daniel Boulud, one of my former bosses, agreed to cook the feast, which included seven different vegetable dishes served family-style. My favorite was his modern take on ratatouille, the traditional Provençal dish of stewed summer squash, eggplant, red peppers, tomatoes, garlic, and herbes de Provence. It was a stunning swirl of bright color and concentrated flavors, and I couldn't get enough. Inspired by Chef Boulud's dish, I came up with this vibrant, rustic tart. The delicious dough is easy to make and shape into a free-form crust, and fresh ricotta, infused with herbs and lemon zest, forms a creamy and aromatic base for the colorful array of vegetables that roast on top.

To make the dough: In the bowl of a food processor, combine the all-purpose and whole-wheat flours and ½ teaspoon salt; pulse to combine. Add the butter and pulse until the mixture is crumbly and only pea-sized chunks of butter remain. In a small bowl, stir together the sour cream and lemon zest and juice. Add the sour cream mixture to the flour and pulse until just combined. Pinch a little dough: If it sticks, it's ready. If not, add ice water, 1 teaspoon at a time, up to 3 teaspoons. Pat the dough into a 6-inch disk and wrap tightly with plastic wrap. Refrigerate for at least 1 hour or up to 1 day.

To make the filling: Arrange the zucchini and eggplant rounds in a single layer on a clean paper towel–lined work surface or baking sheets. Sprinkle with ½ teaspoon salt and let stand for at least 30 minutes.

Heat the oven to 400°F with the rack in the middle. Thinly slice the garlic, then mound ½ teaspoon salt on top. Using both the blade and flat side of a chef's knife, chop and scrape the mixture into a paste. In a small bowl, combine the garlic paste, ricotta, thyme, lemon zest, and a pinch of pepper.

Line a baking sheet with parchment paper. On a well-floured surface, roll out the chilled dough to a roughly 13-inch round (this doesn't have to be a perfect circle; the more rustic the better!), then transfer to the prepared baking sheet.

Gently wipe the zucchini and eggplant with a paper towel to remove excess moisture and salt. Leaving a 1½-inch border, spread all but 3 tablespoons of the ricotta mixture over the dough, then arrange the zucchini, eggplant, and tomato slices on top. Scatter the cherry tomatoes, drizzle with the oil, then sprinkle with the oregano and a pinch each of salt and pepper.

In a small bowl, whisk together the egg and 1 teaspoon water. Fold the edge of the dough up and over the filling (if the dough is sticking to the parchment, refrigerate for 10 minutes, then continue folding). Brush the folded dough with the egg wash.

Bake the galette for 25 minutes, then sprinkle with the Parmesan and dollop with the remaining ricotta mixture. Continue baking until the crust is golden, 20 to 25 minutes more. Serve warm or at room temperature.

KITCHEN WISDOM: Salting Eggplant

Cooks have long salted eggplant before cooking the vegetable, some say to draw out bitterness. After testing, I have come to believe the step is unnecessary with the quality of eggplants that are cultivated today. Salting does, however, draw out excess liquid, from both eggplant and other watery vegetables like zucchini, which allows them to roast instead of steaming here.

Soups & Stews

◆

MISHMOSH: FULLY LOADED MATZO BALL SOUP

Chicken and Stock

1 (4- to 5-pound) whole chicken, thighs and breasts separated

4 medium carrots, coarsely chopped

4 medium celery ribs, coarsely chopped

2 medium yellow onions, cut into wedges

1 head garlic, halved crosswise

8 sprigs fresh flat-leaf parsley

1 tablespoon black peppercorns

Matzo Balls

4 large eggs, lightly beaten

¼ cup schmaltz or clarified butter (see Chef Tech, page 68), melted

3 tablespoons club soda

2 tablespoons finely chopped fresh dill

1 cup matzo meal (see Sources, page 240)

½ teaspoon baking powder

Kosher salt

Ingredient list continues

Though my Grandma Snazzy, my mother's mother, seemed to barely eat a thing (to this day, I am convinced she subsisted on toast and coffee), she was a wonderful Jewish home cook. One of her specialties was chicken soup, which she lovingly made from scratch for Friday night dinners. Loaded with carrots and tender poached chicken, it was simple yet deeply delicious, and I looked forward to it all week long. Today I make my own Grandma Snazzy Soup, adding elements from my mother-in-law Noreen's version—which includes barley, lots of dill, and a bright squeeze of lemon—plus a few twists of my own: light-as-air matzo balls, sweet parsnips, and a sprinkling of Parmesan, which lends a savory richness. One slurp of this hearty hodgepodge instantly conjures up memories of being surrounded by family, being nurtured and loved. A comfort food powerhouse, and a true mishmosh in every sense of the word, it's sure to nourish and invigorate you.

For the chicken and stock: Combine all the chicken and stock ingredients in a large stockpot. Add 3½ quarts water and bring to a boil over high heat. Reduce to a gentle simmer and cook until the chicken breasts are cooked through, about 20 minutes.

Transfer breasts to a plate. Let cool slightly, then remove the meat from the bones and set aside. Return the bones to the stock. Continue to simmer, skimming foam from the surface occasionally, until the liquid is reduced by one-third, about 2 hours. Meanwhile, shred the breast meat and refrigerate, covered, until ready to use.

Strain the stock through a fine-mesh sieve into a large bowl; discard the solids. Pick through and shred the dark meat, then refrigerate with the breast meat. You should have about 4 cups meat and 10 cups stock. (The stock and chicken can be made ahead and refrigerated, covered, for up to 3 days, or frozen for up to 1 month.)

For the matzo balls: In a large bowl, whisk together the eggs, schmaltz, club soda, and dill. Stir in the matzo meal, baking powder, and 2 teaspoons salt. Refrigerate uncovered, at least 30 minutes or up to 2 hours.

Bring a large Dutch oven or wide, heavy pot of well-salted water to a boil. Scoop out the matzo ball mixture, one tablespoon at a time and, using wet hands, gently roll into balls. Add the matzo balls to the boiling water, then reduce to a gentle simmer. Cover and simmer until the matzo balls are plump, cooked through, and begin to sink to the bottom of the pot, 30 to 40 minutes. Remove from the heat. The matzo balls can be kept in the pot of warm water, covered, until ready to serve. While the matzo balls are simmering, prepare the soup.

Recipe continues

Soup

3 tablespoons extra-virgin olive oil

2 medium carrots, cut on the bias into ¼-inch pieces

2 medium parsnips, cut on the bias into ¼-inch pieces

2 celery ribs, cut on the bias into ¼-inch pieces

1 large leek, white and pale green parts only, thinly sliced

1 garlic clove, finely chopped

1 cup pearl barley, rinsed

Kosher salt

Freshly ground black pepper

¼ cup finely chopped fresh dill, plus more for serving

2 tablespoons fresh lemon juice

½ cup (1½ ounces) finely grated Parmigiano-Reggiano cheese (optional)

For the soup: In a 6- to 8-quart Dutch oven or wide, heavy pot with lid, heat the oil over medium heat. Add the carrots and parsnips and cook until starting to soften, about 3 minutes. Stir in the celery, leek, and garlic and cook, stirring occasionally, until all vegetables are softened, 5 to 8 minutes more. Add the barley, ¼ teaspoon salt, and a generous pinch or two of pepper. Cook, stirring frequently, until the barley begins to toast, about 1 minute. Add 8 cups of the chicken stock and bring to a boil. Reduce to a simmer, cover, and cook over low heat, stirring occasionally, until the barley is tender, about 30 minutes.

Add 2 cups shredded white and/or dark chicken meat to the soup and simmer to warm through, about 2 minutes. (Reserve the remaining chicken to use in salads, pastas, or other dishes or for Cold Soba Noodle Salad, page 90.) Stir in the dill and lemon juice. Remove from the heat and adjust the seasoning to taste.

Ladle the soup into bowls. Using a slotted spoon, transfer a few matzo balls into each bowl. Top with more dill and a sprinkle of Parmesan, if desired.

The soup can be made up to 3 days ahead. During this time, the barley will continue to absorb liquid, making the soup very thick. Add stock or water when reheating to return it to desired consistency, adjusting the seasoning to taste.

Back in Grandma Snazzy's day (and even when my mom was younger), Jewish home cooks used schmaltz (the Yiddish word for rendered chicken, duck, or goose fat) as a staple ingredient for frying latkes, making chopped liver and matzo ball soup, and spreading onto bread (move over butter!). Many Jewish cooks still say it's the key to the most flavorful matzo ball soup you can make. I use schmaltz in my matzo balls (see Sources, page 241), but sub easy-to-make clarified butter when it is not available (see Chef Tech, below).

Clarified butter is butter with both its milk proteins and water removed (which together make up about 20 percent of its contents), changing it from emulsified fat to pure butterfat. To clarify butter, simply melt it in a small saucepan over low heat until it comes to an active simmer. Cook until the foam that forms on top (these are the milk proteins) breaks up and sinks to the bottom of the pan, and the bubbling subsides. Remove the pan from the heat, then skim off any remaining foam and strain through a cheesecloth or coffee filter into a bowl. Keep clarified butter in an airtight container and refrigerated for up to 1 month.

MOROCCAN LENTIL & CHICKPEA SOUP with Chermoula

Toasted Spice Blend

2½ teaspoons coriander seeds or 2 teaspoons ground coriander

2½ teaspoons cumin seeds or 2 teaspoons ground cumin

Chermoula

¼ cup extra-virgin olive oil

2 tablespoons fresh lemon juice

¾ cup packed cilantro leaves

¼ cup packed fresh mint leaves

¼ cup chopped celery leaves from inner heart of bunch

2 tablespoons chopped fennel fronds

1 small garlic clove, peeled

⅛ teaspoon red pepper flakes

Kosher salt

Lentil & Chickpea Soup

3 tablespoons extra-virgin olive oil

1 medium onion, finely chopped

1 small bulb fennel, finely chopped (use the fennel fronds in the chermoula)

2 celery ribs, finely chopped (use the celery leaves in the chermoula)

1 garlic clove, finely chopped

¼ teaspoon red pepper flakes

Kosher salt

1½ cups (10 ounces) red lentils

1 (28-ounce) can diced tomatoes

1 (15-ounce) can chickpeas, rinsed and drained

Chopped cilantro for serving

A lively blend of citrus, cilantro, and mint, along with freshly toasted cumin and coriander, gives this hearty legume soup its enticing North African flavor. While toasting whole spices takes a little more effort than using ground, it's simple and quick to do, and the flavor payoff is huge.

For the spice blend: If using whole spices, in a small, dry skillet over medium-low heat, toast the coriander and cumin, occasionally shaking the pan back and forth, until fragrant and lightly toasted, 2 to 3 minutes. Transfer to a cutting board and let cool, then crush with the bottom of a heavy pan.

For the chermoula: In a blender, combine half of the spices, the oil, lemon juice, cilantro, mint, celery leaves, fennel fronds, garlic, pepper flakes, and ⅛ teaspoon salt. Blend until well combined. Transfer to a bowl. Refrigerate, covered, until ready to use.

For the soup: In a 6- to 8-quart Dutch oven or wide, heavy pot, heat the oil over medium heat. Add the onion, fennel, and celery and cook, stirring occasionally, until tender, 7 to 10 minutes. Add the garlic, pepper flakes, 1 teaspoon salt, and the remaining toasted spice blend. Cook 2 minutes more.

Add the lentils, tomatoes and their juices, and 7 cups water. Bring to a boil then reduce to a simmer. Cook, stirring occasionally, until the lentils are tender, 35 to 40 minutes. Add the chickpeas and cook 5 minutes more.

Remove the soup from the heat and stir in the chermoula. Serve topped with cilantro.

KITCHEN WISDOM: Waste Not

Using celery leaves and fennel fronds is a great way to get flavor from the parts of these vegetables that might otherwise go to waste.

Chermoula, a common North African condiment made with lemon juice, garlic, cilantro, and olive oil, is typically used as a sauce for grilled fish. But its pungent, bright flavors also shine when served with grilled meat, tossed with couscous or rice, stirred into yogurt (which makes a great sauce or dip), or swirled into soup, as I do here.

WINTER BORSCHT

2 tablespoons extra-virgin olive oil, plus more for drizzling

1 medium yellow onion, thinly sliced

Kosher salt

4 garlic cloves, thinly sliced

2 tablespoons tomato paste

2 dried bay leaves

1 teaspoon paprika

1 teaspoon caraway seeds

2 medium beets, scrubbed (not peeled) and trimmed, then shredded using a food processor or quartered and thinly sliced crosswise

1 small celery root, peeled and shredded using a food processor or quartered and thinly sliced crosswise

1 large carrot (not peeled), thinly sliced into rounds

1 quart low-sodium beef or vegetable broth

½ small red cabbage, cored and shredded (about 4 cups)

1 Granny Smith apple, peeled, cored, and cut into ¼-inch cubes

1 medium sweet potato (not peeled), cut into ¼-inch cubes

¼ cup apple cider vinegar

Chopped fresh dill for serving

Coarsely ground black pepper

Sour cream for serving, optional

2 cups shredded brisket (see page 140), optional

In my early 20s, I attended cooking school in New York City. Our class of 15 students was a diverse group, with nine countries and countless culinary traditions represented. One day, our teacher suggested that we each cook a dish from our heritage and—as she was also of Eastern European descent—handed me a book of recipes reflecting our common lineage. I chose to make borscht, the hearty beet soup. It was a gorgeous recipe: deep magenta in color, richly flavored with sweet, earthy beets, and brightened with a dash of apple cider vinegar at the finish. I lived on that soup for a whole week, keeping happily connected to my ancestors through its nourishing flavors. Though my version of the soup is fairly traditional, I do include a couple of unconventional moves, using sweet potato, apple, and celery root. The natural sweetness of these ingredients, along with the beets, balances the acidity and spices and eliminates the need for added sugars like honey. Caraway seeds add an earthy, warm anise note and are a key piece of what makes this recipe so complex and alluring.

In a 6- to 8-quart Dutch oven or wide, heavy saucepan with lid, heat the oil over medium-high heat. Add the onion and 1 teaspoon salt and reduce the heat to medium. Cook, stirring occasionally, until the onions begin to soften, about 5 minutes. Add the garlic and cook 2 minutes more. Stir in the tomato paste, bay leaves, paprika, and caraway seeds to coat, then stir in the beets, celery root, and carrot. Add the broth and 4 cups water, bring to a boil, then reduce to a simmer and cook for 15 minutes.

Stir in the cabbage, apple, and sweet potato, return to a simmer, and continue cooking until the cabbage, apple, and sweet potato are just tender, about 5 minutes more. Stir in the vinegar and cook just to blend the flavors, 3 minutes. Remove and discard the bay leaves. Adjust the seasoning to taste.

Serve hot, topped with dill and pepper, and adding sour cream and/or brisket if desired.

KITCHEN WISDOM: Meat vs Veg

The thing that excites me most about this soup is its flexibility. Make it meaty by using beef broth and (if you like) adding a little brisket. Go vegetarian with veg broth, or even vegan by skipping the sour cream garnish.

QUÉBÉCOIS PORK & BEAN STEW

1 pound slab bacon, cut into ½-inch cubes

3 tablespoons pure maple syrup, divided

2½ pounds boneless pork shoulder (Boston butt), well-trimmed and cut into ½-inch cubes

Kosher salt

Freshly ground black pepper

4 medium carrots, cut into ½-inch cubes

2 celery ribs, cut into ¼-inch pieces

1 large yellow onion, coarsely chopped

3 garlic cloves, finely chopped

1 pound dried cannellini beans, soaked overnight and drained

6 sprigs fresh thyme

2 dried bay leaves

2 quarts low-sodium chicken broth

1 tablespoon apple cider vinegar

1 cup heavy cream

As a Canadian, it's been thrilling for me to watch many of today's up-and-coming Québécois chefs reimagine traditional dishes using smart touches that incorporate the region's most cherished ingredients. This dish—a version of which I first had at a small modern bistro in Montreal on a bone-chilling winter night—is a perfect example. Meaty pork shoulder, slowly braised with white beans into a meltingly tender stew, is topped with crispy lardons…but that's not all! The surprise finish is a bowl of freshly whipped cream, seasoned with maple syrup and black pepper and passed at the table for guests to spoon and swirl into their bowls. This creamy, luxe touch—a gorgeous play on something you might only think to do for dessert—infuses the dish with serious Québécois goodness and takes it from simple to extraordinary.

In a 6- to 8-quart Dutch oven or wide, heavy pot with lid, cook the bacon over medium-high heat, stirring occasionally, until beginning to crisp, about 4 minutes. Add 1 tablespoon of the maple syrup and stir to coat. Cook, stirring occasionally, until the bacon is golden on all sides, about 6 minutes more. Meanwhile, season the pork well with salt and pepper.

Remove the pan from the heat. Using a slotted spoon, transfer the bacon to a plate, separating any stuck-together pieces; set aside. Pour off all but 3 tablespoons fat from the pan. Return the pan to medium-high heat. Add the pork and cook until browned on all sides, about 6 minutes total. Add the carrots, celery, onion, and garlic and cook until the vegetables are softened, about 6 minutes more.

Stir in the beans, thyme, and bay leaves, then add the broth. Bring to a simmer over high heat, reduce to a gentle simmer, and cook, stirring occasionally, until the beans are cooked through and the meat is very tender, 60 to 75 minutes. Remove and discard the bay leaves and thyme.

Transfer 1½ cups of the soup solids and ¾ cup of the liquid to the jar of a blender. Puree until smooth, then return to the stew. Stir in the vinegar, ¾ teaspoon salt, and ¼ teaspoon pepper. Adjust the seasoning to taste.

In a medium bowl, beat the cream to medium peaks. Fold in the remaining 2 tablespoons maple syrup and ¼ teaspoon black pepper, then continue beating until stiff peaks form.

Warm the stew then ladle into serving bowls. Top with a dollop of the maple cream and sprinkle with the reserved maple bacon. Pass the remaining cream at the table.

Chef Tech

Making your own vegetable and meat stocks from food scraps is a great way to keep waste and costs to a minimum and have a flavorful basic on hand for use in other dishes. Root ends, trimmings, and stems from vegetables like onions, carrots, leeks, celery, fennel, squash, and mushrooms; fresh herbs; and bones from raw or cooked chicken, as well as beef knuckle and marrow bones, can be stored in resealable freezer bags and kept frozen until ready to use. When you've collected one or more bags' worth, roast the vegetables and bones separately on parchment-lined baking sheets, until deeply golden, about 15 minutes for vegetables and 35 minutes for bones, then let cool. (This technique, known as "browning," enhances natural sugars and concentrates flavors, which results in more flavorful stocks. If you're pressed for time, however, you can skip it.) Place the bones and/or vegetables, and any fresh herb scraps, in a large pot. Cover with water by 1 to 2 inches, add a teaspoon of peppercorns and a bay leaf or two, if desired, then simmer for 1 to 3 hours, depending on how rich you want your stock to be. (Add water while cooking, as necessary, to keep the contents covered by one-half to one inch.) Strain the stock through a mesh sieve and discard the solids. Once cooled, transfer the stocks to airtight containers and label them with the contents and date. Homemade stocks keep refrigerated for up to 1 week or frozen for up to 3 months.

Snippet

In 1536, the French explorer Jacques Cartier, credited for discovering Canada, wrote about the sap from North American maple trees, describing it as "a kind of sugar" that was "as tasty and as delicate as any good wine from Orleans or Beaune." I'm a little bit biased, I know, but—even today— some of the best maple syrup known to man comes from Québec.

RAINY DAY RIBOLLITA

with Lots of Greens

¼ cup plus 3 tablespoons extra-virgin olive oil, divided, plus more for drizzling

3 celery ribs, thinly sliced

2 medium carrots, thinly sliced into rounds

1 medium onion, finely chopped

1 garlic clove, gently smashed and peeled

Kosher salt

2 tablespoons tomato paste

1 (28-ounce) can whole peeled tomatoes, preferably San Marzano

1 (3-ounce) chunk Parmigiano-Reggiano cheese with rind, rind cut off and reserved

¼ teaspoon red pepper flakes, plus more for serving

½ pound kale (about ½ bunch), stemmed, leaves coarsely chopped

¾ pound tender cooking greens, such as chard, escarole, dandelion, and/or chicory, trimmed, leaves and stems, coarsely chopped

2 (15-ounce) cans white beans, rinsed and drained

4 slices rustic whole-wheat bread, lightly toasted, then broken into small pieces

In the fall of 2003, Jeremy and I traveled through Tuscany. On the whole, the weather was gorgeously sunny and dry, save for one day in Siena when the heavens opened up unexpectedly and we found ourselves in the middle of a serious downpour without proper raingear or coverage. We ducked into a tiny *enoteca* to wait out the storm and decided to have lunch. Among an impressive array of wine offerings was a short menu that included ribollita, a traditional bean and vegetable soup fortified with leftover bread scraps. The soup was modest and soulful; I came home dreaming of it and have been making my own version ever since.

Heat 3 tablespoons of the oil in a 6- to 8-quart Dutch oven or wide, heavy pot over medium heat. Add the celery, carrots, onion, garlic, and ¼ teaspoon salt. Cook, stirring occasionally, until the vegetables begin to soften, about 5 minutes. Stir in the tomato paste, then add the canned tomatoes with their juices, the Parmesan rind, pepper flakes, and 5 cups water. Bring to a gentle simmer, breaking up the tomatoes with a wooden spoon, and cook until the vegetables are very tender, 20 to 25 minutes.

Add the kale and simmer until just tender, about 10 minutes. Add the tender greens, including the chard stems if using, and the beans. Continue cooking until the greens are tender, 8 to 10 minutes more. Remove and discard the Parmesan rind.

Remove the soup from the heat, stir in the toasted bread pieces, and let stand for 5 minutes. Add the remaining ¼ cup olive oil and stir well to break up the bread so that it blends into the soup a bit. Adjust the seasoning to taste. Serve hot, with pepper flakes and grated or shaved Parmesan on top.

KITCHEN WISDOM: Leafy Greens

I like using kale in this soup, plus a combination of other greens, but as long as you have 1¼ pounds total, any single sort or mix that you like works well.

Ribollita, *meaning "reboiled" in Italian, refers to the stages in which this classic farmhouse soup is traditionally served: as a thick bean and vegetable soup on the first day (with no bread added), with bread scraps added to extend the dish on the second day, and finally, poured into a wide heavy skillet on the third day and baked until the thick mixture is warmed through and a crispy crust has formed on top. If you're lucky enough to have any soup left over, give the day-three version a shot!*

RENA'S COCONUT CALLALOO

1 large bunch fresh spinach, trimmed and roughly chopped; or 8 ounces baby spinach

2 cups ¾-inch cubes peeled butternut squash (from a ¾ pound squash)

1 small green bell pepper, coarsely chopped

⅓ pound fresh okra, trimmed and cut crosswise into ½-inch pieces (about 1½ cups)

½ cup coarsely chopped yellow onion

3 scallions, coarsely chopped

4 garlic cloves, coarsely chopped

4 leafy sprigs fresh thyme, or ½ teaspoon dried thyme

1 Scotch bonnet, habanero, or serrano chili (optional)

1 (13.5-ounce) can unsweetened coconut milk

Kosher salt

Freshly ground black pepper

1 tablespoon fresh lime juice

1 cup jasmine or other long-grain rice, cooked according to package directions, for serving (optional)

Rena has been a guiding force for my family since Dahlia Rae was three months old. Calling her just Dahlia's nanny is a gross understatement of how much wisdom, humor, and patience she shows us daily. Among her many attributes is her cooking talent, especially when it comes to recipes from her native Trinidad. Over the years she has schooled me in the art of beans and rice, Caribbean curries, roti, macaroni pie, pepper beef, and chicken pilau. But it's her callaloo that we all love the most. The beauty of this mildly spicy stew lies not only in its creamy deliciousness, but also in the ease of its preparation: Every ingredient is simply piled into a pot, then you just turn on the heat and wait (as patiently as you can!) for the fragrant mix of coconut milk, squash, okra, and peppers to magically mingle into a rich, intoxicating stew. The finished mixture is blended into a thick, silky, bright-tasting potage that is healthy and vegan. Look for okra at farmers' markets and in the produce section of most large supermarkets. If the fresh vegetable isn't available, 1½ cups of thawed sliced frozen okra can be substituted.

In a 4- to 6-quart saucepan, combine the spinach, squash, bell pepper, okra, onion, scallions, garlic, thyme, and whole chili (if using). Add the coconut milk, then fill the empty can with water and add to the pot. Repeat with a second can of water. Season with ½ teaspoon salt and a generous pinch of pepper.

Bring the mixture to a boil over medium-high heat, then stir once or twice. Lower the heat to a simmer and cook, partially covered, until reduced by a quarter, about 1 hour.

Remove and discard the thyme sprigs and whole chili, if using. In the jar of a blender, puree in batches until smooth (or use an immersion blender directly in the pot). Return the soup to the pot and stir in the lime juice. Adjust the seasoning to taste.

Serve the callaloo on its own or over the rice.

KITCHEN WISDOM: Chilies

Though Scotch bonnet chilies are scorchers on the Scoville scale (which is used to measure the pungency of chili peppers), their heat is barely perceptible in this recipe. How is this possible? Because the chili is used whole, its spiciest parts (the inner ribs and pith) stay largely cocooned inside, while its sweet-fruity notes and only a subtle mellow heat cook into the soup. Scotch bonnets, which are widely used in Caribbean cooking, can be purchased from good supermarkets and Caribbean grocers. If you can't find them, habanero (another very spicy variety), and milder serrano and jalapeño chilies also work well in the recipe.

RUSTIC FISH SOUP

with Fennel & Orange

Fish Soup

3 tablespoons extra-virgin olive oil

1 small fennel bulb, coarsely chopped (about 1½ cups); plus 1 tablespoon finely chopped fronds for serving

1 small onion, coarsely chopped (about 1¼ cups)

2 celery ribs, coarsely chopped; plus 3 tablespoons finely chopped leaves from the inner heart of the bunch for serving

3 garlic cloves, finely chopped

½ cup dry white wine or Pernod

3 (8-ounce) bottles clam juice (3 cups)

1 (28-ounce) can whole tomatoes, tomatoes crushed by hand, juices reserved

4 fresh thyme sprigs, or ½ teaspoon dried thyme

Finely grated zest of 1 navel orange (about 1½ teaspoons)

¼ teaspoon red pepper flakes

Kosher salt

2 pounds firm white fish fillets such as halibut, cod, red snapper, or tilapia, cut into 1-inch cubes

Freshly ground black pepper

Buttery Garlic Toasts (optional)

3 tablespoons unsalted butter

1 large garlic clove, thinly sliced

1 fresh thyme sprig, or pinch dried thyme

¼ teaspoon kosher salt

½ baguette, cut on the diagonal into ⅓-inch slices

Fennel and orange zest may seem unusual in fish soup, but this natural duo—common players in many seafood dishes—makes a great match for mild, delicate fish like cod. Using store-bought clam juice in place of making your own fish stock eliminates the need for the extra cooking step while still providing a perfect broth base. This soup is a great main course for a dinner party, not only because it's easy and elegant but also since much of the work can be done in advance. Prepare it ahead, if you like, until just before the fish is added. Then all you need is a few quick minutes to finish the dish. Float the buttery garlic toasts on top, or use them to sop up the last spoonfuls of soup.

For the soup: In a 6- to 8-quart Dutch oven or wide, heavy-bottomed pot with lid, heat the oil over medium heat. Add the fennel, onion, celery, and garlic and cook, stirring occasionally, until the vegetables begin to soften, about 5 minutes. Add the wine and cook until the liquid is mostly evaporated, about 5 minutes. Stir in the clam juice, tomatoes and their juices, thyme, orange zest, pepper flakes, 1 teaspoon salt, and 1½ cups water. Bring just to a boil, then reduce to a simmer and cook, partially covered, until the soup is slightly thickened and the flavors are well blended, about 25 minutes. Remove the thyme sprigs if using.

Add the fish and several grinds of black pepper to the pot. Return to a simmer and continue cooking until the fish is opaque and cooked through, about 2 minutes more.

For the toasts, if making: As you are finishing the soup, heat the oven to broil with the rack 5 to 6 inches from the heat source. In a small saucepan, heat the butter, garlic, thyme, and salt over medium heat, stirring occasionally, until the butter is melted. Reduce to a bare simmer and cook for 1 minute to let the flavors blend. Remove from the heat. Arrange the bread on a baking sheet and brush with the butter mixture. Broil until lightly golden, 2 to 3 minutes.

Gently stir the fennel fronds and celery leaves into the soup. Ladle the soup into bowls. Serve warm, with the toasts if desired.

KITCHEN WISDOM: Pernod

If you have the French liqueur Pernod on hand, try using it in place of white wine in the soup. Its deep anise notes amp up the fennel flavor of the broth beautifully, adding dimension in a well-balanced way.

CHILLED CORN SOUP

with Chive Oil, Paprika, & Lime

6 medium ears corn, husked

1 tablespoon unsalted butter

1 large shallot, finely chopped (about ½ cup)

Kosher salt

1 medium Yukon Gold potato (about 6 ounces), peeled and cut into 1-inch cubes

¼ cup finely chopped fresh chives

¼ cup extra-virgin olive oil

½ cup plain Greek yogurt

1 teaspoon freshly grated lime zest

2 teaspoons fresh lime juice

Paprika for serving

Making this soup is one of my favorite ways to enjoy summer corn and preserve its delicate flavor. Simmering the cobs, cut into pieces to expose more of their surface area, brings a great punch of added corn flavor to the soup base; the pieces are removed before the rest of the soup is blended into a creamy puree.

Cut the kernels from the corn cobs, then cut the cobs crosswise into 3 or 4 pieces each; set aside.

In a wide heavy pot or Dutch oven, melt the butter over medium-low heat; add the shallot and cook, stirring occasionally, until softened, about 3 minutes. Add all but ¼ cup of the corn kernels along with ½ teaspoon salt and increase the heat to medium-high. Cook, stirring occasionally, until the corn is crisp-tender, about 5 minutes. (Meanwhile, wrap the remaining corn kernels in plastic wrap and refrigerate until you are ready to serve the soup.)

Add the corn cobs, potato, ½ teaspoon salt, and 4 cups water to the pot. Increase the heat to high and bring just to a boil, then reduce to a simmer and cook until the potato is tender, 18 to 20 minutes.

Meanwhile, in the jar of a blender, combine the chives, oil, and ½ teaspoon salt and puree until smooth. Strain the oil through a fine mesh sieve into a bowl. Discard the solids. Set the oil aside, covered, until ready to serve. Rinse the blender jar.

Remove the corn cobs from the soup and discard. In batches, transfer the soup to a blender and puree until smooth. (The puree will have bits of corn kernels throughout. I like to leave it rustic like this, but you can strain it through a fine-mesh sieve for a more refined texture if you like.) Adjust the seasoning to taste, then refrigerate, covered, until chilled, at least 2 hours or overnight.

Just before serving, stir together the yogurt, lime zest and juice, and ¼ teaspoon salt. Divide the soup among serving bowls. To serve, top with the yogurt, drizzle with the chive oil, and sprinkle with the reserved corn kernels and a pinch of paprika.

KITCHEN WISDOM: Fresh Corn

Corn sugars quickly begin to convert to starch as soon as the ears are picked from their stalks. To ensure the sweetest and most tender kernels, purchase corn at your local farmers' market or from a reputable grocer that turns over product quickly, and use within a day or two of purchase.

ROMESCO-STYLE GAZPACHO

2½ cups cubed baguette

⅓ cup coarsely chopped unsalted raw almonds

2½ pounds ripe tomatoes, seeded and coarsely chopped

1 large roasted red pepper (from a jar), coarsely chopped

2 tablespoons sherry vinegar

1 garlic clove, coarsely chopped

¼ teaspoon sweet smoked paprika

1 teaspoon kosher salt

Freshly ground black pepper

½ cup extra-virgin olive oil, plus more for drizzling

Gazpacho Toppings (page 81), optional

When I was in college, I spent 6 months studying in Seville, Spain, as part of my junior year abroad. The party of the year in the region is the *Feria de Abril*, or Seville Fair—a colorful citywide celebration that includes flamenco dancing, bullfights, parades on horseback, and hours of eating and drinking long into the night. It was there I first tasted true Spanish gazpacho, a rose-colored fresh tomato soup spiked with sherry vinegar and thickened with bread, which was completely different from the watery, chopped tomato and vegetable version that passed as the soup with the same name back home. The recipe here is made in the traditional Spanish style, with cubes of rustic bread and a healthy drizzle of olive oil blended in, but also incorporates a couple of twists. Borrowing flavors from the versatile Catalan sauce, romesco, I add almonds and roasted red peppers, which lend a nutty richness and a touch of smoky sweetness to the soup. Serve in glasses or small bowls with one or more of the toppings suggested on page 81.

Heat the oven to 350°F.

Place the bread cubes in a large bowl and add cold water to cover; let stand 10 minutes.

Meanwhile, spread the almonds on a baking sheet. Bake until lightly golden and fragrant, 8 to 10 minutes. Transfer to a plate and let cool.

Drain and firmly squeeze the bread to remove the excess liquid. In the bowl of a food processor or blender, puree the drained bread, toasted almonds, tomatoes, red pepper, vinegar, garlic, paprika, salt, and ¼ teaspoon pepper until smooth. With the machine running, slowly drizzle in the oil.

Chill the soup until very cold, at least 2 hours or overnight. Stir in water, 1 tablespoon at a time, to thin slightly if needed. To serve, sprinkle with toppings and black pepper, and drizzle with oil.

Gazpacho
TOPPINGS!

Part of the fun of making gazpacho is the tradition of topping it with a variety of tasty ingredients that add both texture and pops of flavor. Set up the toppings in little bowls and let diners choose what they like. Here are a few of my favorites:

Coarsely chopped hard-boiled egg

Chopped scallions

Thin strips of serrano ham, prosciutto, or speck

Finely chopped cucumber

Quartered cherry or grape tomatoes

Coarsely chopped toasted almonds

Finely chopped shallot

Finely chopped red bell pepper

Finely chopped flat-leaf parsley or chives

Noodles & Rice

SPAGHETTINI WITH BURST CHERRY TOMATOES & BASIL 85

ORECCHIETTE WITH SWISS CHARD & BURRATA 86

SPAGHETTI PIE 89

COLD SOBA NOODLE SALAD WITH SHREDDED CHICKEN 90

SINGAPORE-STYLE HOKKIEN NOODLES 93

DIRTY RICE 95

CHRISTMAS BRISKET FRIED RICE 97

SPAGHETTINI

with Burst Cherry Tomatoes & Basil

1 pound spaghettini or other long thin pasta

Kosher salt

½ cup olive oil, plus more for serving

1 small red onion, thinly sliced (about 1 cup)

2 large garlic cloves, thinly sliced

¼ teaspoon red pepper flakes

3 pints cherry tomatoes (about 2 pounds)

1½ cups loosely packed torn basil leaves

¼ cup finely chopped fresh flat-leaf parsley

¾ cup fresh whole-milk ricotta cheese (about 6 ounces)

Freshly grated Parmigiano-Reggiano cheese for serving

Coarsely ground black pepper

I feel like I'm performing something of a culinary magic trick when I make this simple pasta. As ripe cherry tomatoes cook in warm olive oil, their skins burst open, the sweet juices bubble away, mingling with the oil, and just like that—in the little time it takes to boil your pasta and chop a few herbs—you've created a silky, sumptuous sauce. Creamy fresh ricotta and a sprinkle of Parmigiano-Reggiano add a luxe touch to the pasta. And, since the cheeses are added just before serving, it's easy to leave them out if you don't eat dairy. I use spaghettini (which lies about halfway between spaghetti and angel hair in thickness), but any long thin pasta works just as well.

Cook the pasta in a large pot of well-salted boiling water until al dente.

Meanwhile, heat the oil in a 12-inch skillet or wide, heavy saucepan over medium-high heat. Add the onion, garlic, and 1 teaspoon salt. Cook, stirring frequently, until the onion begins to soften, about 5 minutes. Add the red pepper flakes, then stir in the tomatoes and continue cooking, stirring occasionally, until most of the tomatoes have burst, 6 to 8 minutes.

Reserving 1 cup of the pasta cooking liquid, drain the pasta. Add the pasta, along with the reserved pasta cooking water, to the pan with the sauce. Cook over medium heat, stirring, until the pasta is coated, about 30 seconds, then stir in the basil and parsley.

Divide the pasta among serving plates. Dollop with the ricotta and sprinkle with Parmesan and black pepper to taste. Drizzle with oil and serve immediately.

Salting pasta water is a vital first step in ensuring pasta is properly seasoned. A good rule of thumb for 1 pound of pasta is to use 4 quarts of water and 1½ to 3 tablespoons of kosher or fine sea salt (I generally settle on 2). Stir the salt into the rapidly boiling water just before adding the pasta, to ensure that it dissolves immediately (salt is corrosive and can otherwise "pit" and damage your pot). Return the water to a full boil, then add your noodles.

ORECCHIETTE

with Swiss Chard & Burrata

Kosher salt

1 pound dried orecchiette pasta

¼ cup extra-virgin olive oil

2 tablespoons unsalted butter

2 large garlic cloves, very thinly sliced

½ teaspoon red pepper flakes

1 pound (about 1 large or 2 small bunches) Swiss chard, leaves torn into 2-inch pieces, ribs and stems thinly sliced crosswise

3 tablespoons freshly grated lemon zest (from about 4 to 5 large lemons, divided)

3 tablespoons fresh lemon juice (from about 2 large lemons)

3 tablespoons freshly grated Parmigiano-Reggiano cheese

12 ounces burrata cheese

½ cup torn basil leaves

Coarsely ground black pepper

This easy, lemony pasta is dressed up with burrata cheese, which adds a show-stopping richness. The choice of pasta shape here is deliberate as *orecchiette* (Italian for "little ear") is the perfect vehicle for scooping up the creamy sauce and cheese. Similar shapes, like *fusilli*, *cavatelli*, *gemelli*, and *conchiglie* (small shells) are also good options.

In a large saucepan of well-salted boiling water, cook the pasta until al dente.

Meanwhile, in a large skillet, heat the oil and butter over medium heat until the butter is melted. Add the garlic, pepper flakes, and ¾ teaspoon salt. Cook, stirring occasionally, until the garlic is fragrant and golden, 2 to 3 minutes. Add half of the chard leaves and stems and continue cooking, stirring frequently, until the greens are wilted. Add the remaining chard leaves and stems, 2 tablespoons of the lemon zest, and the lemon juice. Cook, stirring, until all of the chard is just wilted. Remove the pan from the heat.

Reserving 1 cup of the cooking water, drain the pasta. Return the pasta to the pot. Add the chard and the reserved cooking water and cook over medium heat, stirring, for 30 seconds. Stir in the Parmesan cheese and adjust the seasoning to taste.

Spoon the pasta into bowls. Cut the burrata cheese into 1-inch chunks. Top the pasta with the burrata and sprinkle with the basil leaves and remaining 1 tablespoon zest. Season with salt and pepper to taste and serve.

KITCHEN WISDOM: Waste Not

The tender stems of Swiss chard are edible and delicious, and great to include whenever you are cooking this green. Simply cut away any dry or tough bits at the end of each stem then slice the rest.

Burrata's fresh milky flavor and decadent creaminess has made it a popular ingredient for North American chefs in recent years. The cheese has since become more widely available for home cooks, too. Made from fresh cow or buffalo milk mozzarella that's formed into a pocket, then filled with cream and shreds of buffalo milk curds (called stracciatella*), this delicate cheese is more perishable than most, so plan to eat it within a few days of purchase. Look for burrata at good supermarkets, Italian markets and, of course, cheese shops. If it's not available, use fresh mozzarella and a splash of heavy cream in its place.*

SPAGHETTI PIE

Unsalted butter for greasing the pan

2 tablespoons extra-virgin olive oil

1 medium yellow onion, finely chopped

2 garlic cloves, finely chopped

¾ pound broccoli or broccoli rabe, trimmed, stems and florets chopped into ¼-inch pieces (about 2½ cups)

1 pound hot or sweet Italian sausage, removed from casings

1 tablespoon tomato paste

1 (28-ounce) can whole peeled tomatoes, drained, tomatoes crushed by hand

Kosher salt

1 pound dried spaghetti

¾ cup whole milk

3 large eggs

2 teaspoons freshly ground black pepper

2½ cups (8 ounces) grated sharp yellow cheddar cheese

2½ cups (8 ounces) grated fontina cheese

1½ cups (3 ounces) freshly grated Parmigiano-Reggiano cheese, divided

1 tablespoon finely chopped fresh sage

Special equipment: 9½-inch springform pan

When we were 19, my best friend Camille and I traveled through New Zealand's North and South Islands. It didn't take long before we became completely obsessed with a local specialty that seemed to be offered at every roadside diner along the way: spaghetti sandwiches! These grilled cheese–pasta mash-ups are toasted delights, packed with oozy, melted cheese and tangy, tomato-sauced noodles. While we might consider them a double-carb disaster today, in our college years they were a heavenly snack. The memory of those decadent sandwiches still makes me giggle, so I came up with this spin, the mere mention of which always elicits joy. Spaghetti pie is a big affair, impressive in both stature and ingredients, and meant to serve a hungry crowd. You don't have to wait for your next party to make it, though. If you don't have enough eaters to tackle it, there's a bonus: Slices of the savory pie may make the best leftovers of all time.

Bring a large pot of water to a boil. Heat the oven to 425°F. Butter a 9½-inch springform pan. Tightly wrap the bottom of the pan with a large sheet of foil, crimping the foil against the outer edges to tightly seal.

In a large skillet, heat the oil over medium-high heat. Add the onion and garlic and cook for 1 minute. Add the broccoli and 1 tablespoon water and cook until the broccoli is crisp-tender, 2 to 3 minutes. Add the sausage and cook, breaking the meat into small bits, until cooked through, about 6 minutes. Stir in the tomato paste and cook 1 minute, then add the crushed drained tomatoes and ¼ teaspoon salt. Cook, stirring occasionally and scraping any bits from the pan, until the liquid is mostly evaporated, about 5 minutes. Remove from the heat and set aside.

Add salt to the boiling water and cook the spaghetti just until very al dente, 7 to 8 minutes (look for a white spot in the center when you bite into a strand). Drain the pasta (do not rinse) and reserve the pot.

In the pasta pot, whisk together the milk, eggs, pepper, and ¾ teaspoon salt. Stir in the cheddar, fontina, and 1 cup of the Parmesan. Add the sausage mixture and spaghetti; stir until well combined.

Transfer the pasta mixture to the prepared pan. Using a spatula, smooth the top. Set the pan on a rimmed baking sheet and bake until the edges are golden and bubbling, about 35 minutes.

Remove the pan from the oven. Turn on the broiler. Sprinkle the pie with the sage and remaining ½ cup Parmesan. Broil 4 to 5 inches from the heat until the cheese is golden, 2 to 3 minutes. Remove from the oven and run a knife around the inside of the pan. Let the pie rest about 10 minutes then release and remove the sides of the pan. Cut the pie into slices and serve warm.

COLD SOBA NOODLE SALAD

with Shredded Chicken

8 ounces soba noodles

2 cups cooked shredded chicken (about 8 ounces)

½ English cucumber, halved lengthwise and thinly sliced into half moons

1 cup frozen shelled edamame, cooked according to package instructions and cooled

½ cup coarsely chopped cilantro leaves, plus more for serving

2 scallions, thinly sliced on the bias

1 tablespoon sesame seeds, plus more for serving

½ teaspoon kosher salt

Soy-Lime Dressing (opposite)

Freshly grated lime zest and lime wedges for serving

This easy, chilled noodle dish is a go-to at my house, especially on warm summer days. Its punchy dressing is made from vibrant lime juice and a mix of fairly basic pantry ingredients, most of which you're likely to have on hand. I use a good bit of lime zest, in addition to the juice, because I love the floral tones it adds and it's a great way to make use of all parts of the fruit. Since this dish is so quick to prepare, we often turn to it for light weeknight dinners, or as a great make-ahead lunch to tote to the office or beach. I generally use cilantro, but if you have mint and basil, try them, too; a mix of two or more herbs adds brightness and complexity. The Soy-Lime Dressing can be easily doubled. Try it on green salads or spooned over warm rice.

Cook the soba noodles according to package directions. Drain, then rinse with cold water.

Combine the noodles, chicken, cucumber, edamame, cilantro, scallions, sesame seeds, and salt in a large bowl. Add the dressing and toss to combine. Adjust the seasoning to taste.

Divide the noodles among four serving bowls. Sprinkle with sesame seeds, cilantro, and lime zest and serve with lime wedges.

Soba noodles are made from buckwheat flour; buckwheat is not actually a grain or a cereal, but the seed of a flowering plant. Although buckwheat itself is naturally gluten-free, check your noodle package before purchasing if you have celiac disease or are gluten-sensitive. The noodles are often made with a mix of buckwheat and regular wheat, so gluten can be present.

Soy-Lime Dressing

MAKES ½ CUP

*For Cold Soba Noodle Salad with
Shredded Chicken (opposite)*

1 tablespoon freshly grated lime zest and ¼ cup
    fresh lime juice (from about 3 large limes)

2 tablespoons soy sauce

1 teaspoon Sriracha hot sauce

1 garlic clove, finely chopped

1 teaspoon packed brown sugar

2 tablespoons neutral oil, such as canola or
    grapeseed

1 teaspoon toasted sesame oil

In a bowl, whisk together the lime zest, juice,
soy sauce, Sriracha, garlic, and brown sugar.
Whisking constantly, add the neutral and
sesame oils in a slow and steady stream. The
dressing will keep refrigerated in a small,
airtight container, for up to 1 week.

SINGAPORE-STYLE HOKKIEN NOODLES

1 pound large shrimp in shells, preferably with heads on

⅓ pound skinless, boneless pork belly or thick-cut bacon, cut into 1-inch cubes, divided

1 (8-ounce) bottle clam juice

¼ teaspoon kosher salt

2 garlic cloves, thinly sliced

2 large eggs, lightly beaten

4 ounces dried udon noodles, cooked until al dente and rinsed under cold running water; or 10 ounces fresh thick yellow or white Asian wheat noodles

4 ounces dried vermicelli rice-stick noodles, soaked and drained per package instructions

1½ cups mung bean sprouts

4 scallions, thinly sliced, plus more for serving

2 Thai bird chilies, finely chopped; or 1 medium red or green jalapeño, seeded and finely chopped

3 tablespoons reduced-sodium soy sauce

1 tablespoon fish sauce (such as nam pla or nuoc nam)

2 teaspoons sesame oil

¼ pound cleaned squid tubes and tentacles, tubes cut crosswise into ½-inch rings

2 limes, cut into wedges

2 mandarin oranges, such as tangerines or clementines, cut into wedges

Sambal oelek or chili garlic sauce for serving

This dish is among the greatest of my personal discoveries in over 12 years of shooting *Top Chef*. I first tasted it in Singapore, on a street-food tour with my co-judge Tom Colicchio along with our guest judges, chef David Chang and former *Food & Wine* editor Dana Cowin, while we were shooting our Season 7 finale. The addictive combination of both tender and chewy noodles, sweet shrimp, and rich pork belly is perked up with citrus and chilies—and impossible to resist. While this recipe represents a traditional version of the dish, it is also very flexible. Shredded cooked chicken can be swapped in for the squid, or you can go the all-shrimp route. Once you've made a simple shrimp stock and have a few vegetables prepped, the dish comes together in minutes. The stock keeps for several days in the refrigerator and also freezes well, so you can make it ahead, if you like.

Reserving the shells and the heads (if using), peel and devein the shrimp. Set aside the shrimp.

Cook half of the pork belly in a large saucepan over medium-high heat, stirring occasionally, until the fat is rendered and the pork is golden on all sides, about 5 minutes. Add the shrimp shells and heads (if using) and cook until the shells are bright pink and beginning to crisp, 3 to 4 minutes. Add the clam juice, salt, and 1 quart water and bring to a boil. Reduce to a gentle simmer and cook until the stock is reduced to 3½ cups, 30 to 35 minutes. Strain the stock through a mesh sieve, pressing gently but firmly on the solids to extract as much flavor as possible; discard the solids. Return the stock to the saucepan and cover to keep warm.

In a 12-inch skillet or large wok, cook the remaining pork belly over medium-high heat until crispy and golden on all sides, about 5 minutes. Add the garlic and cook until fragrant and lightly golden, about 30 seconds. Add the eggs and cook, stirring with a rubber spatula, until scrambled and just set, about 30 seconds. Add the udon noodles and vermicelli and cook for 1 minute, then add half of the hot stock. Cook, stirring gently, until the liquid is mostly absorbed, 2 to 3 minutes.

Stir in the sprouts, scallions, chilies, soy sauce, fish sauce, sesame oil, and reserved shrimp. Add the remaining stock and cook, stirring frequently, for 1 minute. Add the squid and cook, stirring frequently, until the seafood is just cooked through and the noodles are well coated with sauce, 1 to 2 minutes more.

Divide the noodles among four wide, shallow serving bowls. Squeeze about half of the lime and mandarin wedges over the tops, then sprinkle with scallions. Serve with the remaining citrus wedges and the sambal oelek on the side.

Recipe continues

**KITCHEN WISDOM: Prepping Ahead—
Singapore-Style Hokkien Noodles**

Since this dish comes together quickly, have your ingredients prepped and near the stove for easy access while you cook. If you are making the shrimp stock ahead, you can refrigerate or freeze the shelled shrimp alongside.

Calamansi are small, fragrant citrus fruits, said to be a cross between mandarins and kumquats. The fruit is native to Southeast Asia, where it grows year-round and is widely used for its juice—not only to drink, but also to squeeze over meat, fish, or noodles, and to mix with a little soy sauce and use as a marinade or dipping sauce. While eating our way through Singapore's hawker stalls, I was fascinated to see that many of the food vendors keep small potted calamansi trees adjacent to their stoves, so they can pluck the fruit fresh from its branches to use on the spot (talk about fresh from the vine!). Since calamansi are not often found in North American markets, I use equal parts fresh lime and mandarin orange juices to mimic the flavor. While not exactly the same, it totally does the trick!

DIRTY RICE

1 cup long-grain rice, such as basmati or jasmine

1 tablespoon neutral oil, such as canola or grapeseed

½ pound ground chicken

¼ pound chicken livers, trimmed, rinsed, and chopped (see Kitchen Wisdom)

¼ teaspoon paprika

¼ teaspoon dried oregano

⅛ teaspoon cayenne pepper

Kosher salt

Freshly ground black pepper

1¼ cups low-sodium chicken broth, divided

3 celery ribs, halved lengthwise, thinly sliced

1 medium yellow onion, finely chopped

1 green bell pepper, finely chopped

1 medium jalapeño, seeded and finely chopped

1 large garlic clove, finely chopped

4 tablespoons finely chopped fresh flat-leaf parsley, divided

Hot sauce (optional)

Among the many things that make this Cajun rice dish so devilishly good are chicken livers, which crumble into little bits of rich flavor as they brown with ground meat and a mixture of chopped onions, peppers, and savory spices, muddying the rice and giving it its noteworthy name. While it is often served as a bed for pork chops, chicken, or shrimp, dirty rice is also used to stuff Cornish hens, chicken, and turkey. I also like it as a main course, with a green salad alongside.

Cook the rice according to package instructions.

Meanwhile, in a 10- to 12-inch skillet, heat the oil over medium-high heat. Add the ground chicken and livers and cook, breaking the meat into small bits with a wooden spoon and stirring occasionally, until lightly browned, 5 to 7 minutes.

Add the paprika, oregano, cayenne, ¼ teaspoon salt, and a generous pinch of black pepper and continue to cook, stirring occasionally, until a layer of crust begins to develop under the mixture, 2 to 3 minutes more.

Add ¼ cup broth to the pan. Using the wooden spoon, scrape up and stir the brown bits into the meat mixture; continue stirring until the broth is mostly absorbed. Stir in the celery, onion, bell pepper, jalapeño, and garlic. Cook, stirring 2 to 3 times (resist the urge to stir too much), until the mixture is browned and begins to stick to the pan, 8 to 10 minutes. Add the remaining 1 cup broth, then the rice, 2 tablespoons of the parsley, and ½ teaspoon salt. Cook, stirring frequently, until the broth is absorbed, about 5 minutes.

Adjust the seasoning to taste. Serve hot, sprinkled with the remaining 2 tablespoons parsley and drizzled with hot sauce, if desired.

KITCHEN WISDOM: Chicken Livers and More

While I believe the chicken livers are a must in this recipe (the dish just isn't "dirty" without them), the additional meat that you use is flexible. Try ground pork in place of chicken, or use sausage (chicken or pork, sweet or spicy), removed from its casing. Chicken livers can be found in some grocery store meat departments and at most butcher shops. Call ahead; you may need to order them in advance.

CHRISTMAS BRISKET
FRIED RICE

1 cup jasmine rice

3 teaspoons canola oil, divided

2 large eggs, lightly beaten

Kosher salt

5 scallions, cut crosswise into ½-inch lengths, white and green parts separated

3 tablespoons finely chopped peeled fresh ginger (from a 3-inch knob)

2 garlic cloves, finely chopped

¾ pound cooked brisket (page 140), shredded (about 3 cups)

½ cup frozen peas, thawed

¼ cup finely chopped cilantro stems, plus ¼ cup coarsely chopped cilantro leaves for serving

2 tablespoons soy sauce

¼ teaspoon freshly ground black pepper

Sriracha hot sauce for serving

1 lime, cut into wedges, for serving

Special equipment: Large wok or 12-inch skillet

Here's a tasty dish inspired by two North American Jewish traditions: making brisket for Hanukkah and going out for Chinese food on Christmas. I like to make an extra big Hanukkah brisket (regardless of how many people are actually coming over to eat), so that we have plenty of leftovers to put to delicious use in this fun twist on classic egg fried rice. You can use the brisket recipe on page 140, or purchase cooked brisket from your local BBQ joint or supermarket.

Cook the rice according to package instructions. Spread on a baking sheet and let cool until ready to use.

In a large wok or 12-inch nonstick skillet, heat 1 teaspoon of the oil over medium-high heat. Add the eggs and ¼ teaspoon salt and cook, stirring, until just set, 2 to 3 minutes. Transfer the eggs to a plate and set aside.

Add 1 teaspoon oil and the scallion whites to the skillet. Cook over medium-high heat, stirring occasionally, until fragrant and beginning to soften, 3 to 4 minutes. Stir in the ginger and garlic and cook until fragrant, about 1 minute more.

Add the remaining 1 teaspoon oil, then the brisket, and cook, stirring occasionally, until warmed through, about 3 minutes. Add the rice and cook, stirring frequently, until well incorporated and beginning to crisp, 3 to 4 minutes. Add the peas and reserved eggs. Stir well, breaking up the eggs with a wooden spoon, about 1 minute. Add the scallion greens, cilantro stems, soy sauce, and a generous pinch each of salt and pepper. Continue stirring, until the scallions are just tender, about 1 minute more. Adjust seasoning to taste.

Sprinkle with the cilantro leaves and serve warm with Sriracha and lime wedges.

Fish & Seafood

MUSSELS STEAMED WITH LEEKS, MUSTARD,
& TARRAGON 100

GRILLED HALIBUT WITH JEREMY'S GREEN SAUCE 102

SCALLOPS & PEAS WITH MINT GREMOLATA 105

SPICED-RUBBED SALMON WITH CITRUS YOGURT
& FENNEL SALAD 107

CHA CA SALAD WITH PINEAPPLE & MINT 108

SALT-BAKED BRANZINO 111

FISH TACOS WITH SOY-LIME CREMA 115

GRILLED OYSTERS FOR THREE NEW ORLEANS FRIENDS 116
Chardonnay-Herb Butter 117
Porchetta Marmalade 118
Sour Cherry Mingonette 119

JERK SHRIMP ROLLS 120

LAZY LOBSTER PIE 123

◆

MUSSELS

Steamed with Leeks, Mustard, & Tarragon

4 tablespoons (½ stick) cold unsalted butter, divided

2½ cups ¾-inch cubes rustic country bread

Kosher salt

Freshly ground black pepper

2 large leeks (about 1 pound total), white and light green parts only

4 pounds mussels

3 garlic cloves, finely chopped

2 cups dry white wine

2 teaspoons Dijon mustard

2 teaspoons finely chopped tarragon, plus more for serving

When my mother, Renée, was in grad school, she spent a year studying international politics in Belgium—a trailblazing move for a young woman in her day. While she was there, she fell in love with one of the country's greatest dishes: *moules frites* (mussels with French fries). She often cooked mussels at home and fed them to us kids at an early age. We didn't need any convincing to gobble them up. The tender mollusks were bathed in a rich, warm butter and wine sauce, generously showered with fresh herbs, and served with a basketful of soft rustic bread for sopping.

When I learned to cook for myself, mussels were among the first dishes I mastered. I still love how quick and easy they are to cook, and the many ways the dish can be varied. Here, I use leeks, Dijon mustard, and tarragon to flavor the broth, and make rustic croutons to sprinkle over the top. The croutons are a fun play on the classic bread element; their buttery crispness both softens in the warm broth and sops it up a bit as you get to the bottom of the bowl. I love the anise flavor of tarragon, but if you're not a fan, use basil or parsley instead.

Heat the oven to 375°F.

In a microwave-safe dish, melt 1 tablespoon of the butter. On a rimmed baking sheet, toss together the bread cubes, melted butter, and a pinch each of salt and pepper. Spread the cubes evenly, then bake, stirring once halfway through, until golden and crisp at edges, 13 to 15 minutes. Set aside.

Meanwhile, cut the leeks in half lengthwise, then thinly slice crosswise. Rinse well, then pat dry. Rinse the mussels well under cold water. Pick them over, pulling off any beards and discarding any mussels that are broken or gaping open.

In a 6- to 8-quart Dutch oven or wide, heavy pot with lid, melt 2 tablespoons of the butter over medium heat. Add the leeks and garlic and cook until softened, 8 to 10 minutes. Add the mussels. Stir to coat evenly, then add the wine. Increase the heat to medium-high, cover, and cook, gently shaking the pot once or twice, until the mussels open, 6 to 8 minutes. Season with a pinch each of salt and pepper and stir well to combine.

Using a slotted spoon, transfer and divide the mussels and leeks among four large, shallow bowls, discarding any mussels that did not open (it's OK if some of the leeks remain in the broth). Bring the cooking liquid to a simmer, then whisk in the remaining 1 tablespoon butter, the mustard, tarragon, ¼ teaspoon salt, and a generous pinch of pepper. Ladle the broth over the mussels. Top with the croutons and a pinch more fresh tarragon and serve.

KITCHEN WISDOM: Mussels

As with any fresh seafood, it's best to buy mussels from a reputable fish-monger, and to make your purchase no more than 2 days before you plan to cook. Mussels are often sold in mesh bags, and frequently tagged with harvest date and location info, which can be helpful for tracking freshness. If the tag is not included, you can ask your fishmonger for these details. You should also evaluate freshness with a quick look and smell test. Fresh mussels should have a subtle clean saline aroma. Shells that aren't tightly shut should quickly close when tapped; any mussels that don't close have gone bad and should be discarded. At home, keep mussels refrigerated in a bowl or other open container (they are alive and need air to breathe), covered with a damp paper towel.

GRILLED HALIBUT

with Jeremy's Green Sauce

3 tablespoons whole unsalted almonds (optional)

1½ teaspoons whole coriander seeds

1 lemon

1½ cups loosely packed basil leaves, divided

¼ cup plus 2 tablespoons extra-virgin olive oil, divided

1 large shallot, thinly sliced, divided

Coarsely cracked black pepper

4 (5- to 6-ounce) halibut fillets (about 1 inch thick)

⅓ cup mixed mild olives, pitted

¼ cup loosely packed fresh flat-leaf parsley

2 teaspoons rinsed and drained capers

1 small garlic clove, thinly sliced

Kosher salt

I am generally the designated cook in the family. But Jeremy certainly contributes, piping in with ideas and occasionally creating his own signature dishes, among them this family favorite. It was born one summer evening when I found myself thinking out loud about what to make with an excess of fresh herbs. Before I knew it, Jeremy had tossed them into the blender, added some olives, a few capers, and other light seasonings, pressed the button, and gave it all a good whirl. The emerald green sauce that emerged was an immediate hit. This recipe is endlessly variable. You can use any fish or seafood (think salmon, trout, shrimp, scallops, and more), or steak or chicken, too.

If using the almonds, heat the oven to 350°F. Spread the nuts on a rimmed baking sheet and toast in the oven until fragrant and lightly golden, 10 to 15 minutes. Let cool completely, then coarsely chop. Set aside.

While the nuts are toasting, toast the coriander in a small, dry skillet over medium-low heat, occasionally shaking the pan back and forth, until fragrant and lightly toasted, 2 to 3 minutes. Let cool, then coarsely crush with a mortar and pestle, or by rocking the bottom of a heavy skillet back and forth over the seeds.

Thinly slice half of the lemon. Squeeze enough of the remaining half to yield 1 tablespoon juice and set aside.

In a large bowl, combine the lemon slices with half of the coriander, 10 torn basil leaves, 2 tablespoons of the oil, half the shallot slices, and ¼ teaspoon pepper. Add the fish and turn to coat. Let stand at room temperature to marinate for 30 minutes.

Meanwhile, in the bowl of a food processor, combine the remaining coriander, basil, and shallot, along with the olives, parsley, capers, garlic, ¼ teaspoon salt, and reserved lemon juice. Pulse, adding the remaining ¼ cup oil in a slow and steady stream and stopping occasionally to scrape down the sides of the bowl, until well combined but still a little chunky. Transfer the sauce to a bowl.

Prepare a grill or grill pan for medium-high heat. Remove the fish from the marinade and arrange on a plate. Brush off any bits of lemon and herbs, then brush with the oil from the marinade.

Season the fish well with salt. Grill, turning once, until opaque and cooked through, 3 to 4 minutes per side. Transfer to serving plates. Spoon the sauce over the top, sprinkle with the almonds if using, and serve.

SCALLOPS & PEAS

with Mint Gremolata

Mint Gremolata

¼ cup finely chopped fresh mint

2 teaspoons freshly grated lemon zest

1 garlic clove, finely chopped

Scallops & Peas

3 tablespoons pine nuts (optional)

3 tablespoons extra-virgin olive oil, divided, plus more for serving

1 small shallot, finely chopped (about 3 tablespoons)

1 pound medium-thick asparagus, tough ends trimmed, spears cut on a diagonal into 1-inch lengths

Kosher salt

2 cups (8 ounces) fresh or thawed frozen peas

1 (5-ounce) package baby spinach (5 cups packed)

1 pound dry sea scallops, rinsed, tough muscle removed, scallops patted dry

Freshly ground black pepper

Scallops have become a go-to ingredient on *Top Chef* over the years, to the point where both judges and fans have often criticized "cheftestants" for using them as somewhat of a crutch. It's easy to understand why the tasty mollusks are so often chosen, especially in the heat of the moment: Sweet, buttery, and luxe, yet not terribly expensive, they can be prepared in a variety of delicious ways, and—most of all—are incredibly quick to cook. Though they are great any time of year, I love this fresh, springtime preparation, which balances a trio of vibrant green vegetables with a simple gremolata made with lots of fresh mint.

For the gremolata: In a bowl, stir together the mint, lemon zest, and garlic; set aside.

For the scallops and peas: If using pine nuts, place them in a small, dry skillet and cook over medium-low heat, occasionally shaking the pan back and forth, until the nuts are fragrant and lightly golden, about 3 minutes. Transfer to a plate and set aside.

In a large nonstick skillet, heat 1 tablespoon of the oil over medium heat until shimmering. Add the shallot and cook until softened, about 1 minute. Stir in the asparagus and ¼ teaspoon salt; cook stirring occasionally, until the asparagus is crisp-tender, about 3 minutes. Add the peas and cook until tender, 2 to 3 minutes more. Transfer the vegetables to a bowl.

Heat another tablespoon oil in the skillet over medium-high heat. Add the spinach and ¼ teaspoon salt; cook, stirring, just until wilted, 1 to 2 minutes. Transfer to the bowl with the vegetables.

Wipe out the skillet. Season the scallops with salt and pepper on both sides. Add the remaining 1 tablespoon oil to the pan. When the oil is hot, but not smoking, add the scallops and cook without touching until the bottoms are deep golden, 2 to 3 minutes, then turn and cook until just cooked through, 30 seconds to 1 minute more. Transfer the scallops to a plate.

Gently toss the vegetables with 1 tablespoon of the gremolata, then divide among serving plates. Top with the scallops. Sprinkle with the remaining gremolata and the pine nuts if using. Drizzle with a bit of oil and serve.

Recipe continues

Getting a perfect sear when cooking scallops takes a little practice, but is easy to do. Buying quality product is the first step (see Snippet). Before cooking, rinse your scallops under cold water, then pat dry with paper towels and remove the tough outer muscle that clings to its side if there is one. Using a nonstick skillet is helpful, especially for newbies, but is not a requirement. You will, however, want to use a skillet that's large enough to provide at least ½ inch space between each scallop, to let the moisture they release quickly evaporate. Heat whatever fat you choose (butter, oil, or a combination) to very hot but not smoking. Once the scallops are in the pan, resist the urge to fuss with them (this point cannot be overstated!); they'll easily release once they form a crust on the bottom, but not before. Turn them once and note that scallops quickly cook through; the second side requires just a quick "kiss" of heat, as the chefs say!

Snippet

In the U.S., the two most popular varieties of shelled scallops are sea scallops and bay scallops. Sea scallops average about 1½ inches in diameter and have a sweet but slightly denser muscle. They're found in deep ocean waters year round, and fished for by trawlers and by hand (in the latter case, they're called diver or day-boat scallops).

Bay scallops, generally found on the East Coast and in shallow bay waters, are smaller and sweeter than their deep-sea counterparts, measuring about ½ inch in diameter. When using bay scallops, adjust your cook time accordingly; they require just 1 to 2 minutes total in the pan.

When buying scallops, make sure to request that they are dry. Dry scallops remain dry once shucked, as opposed to wet scallops, which are dropped into water often treated with chemicals. The water helps to preserve the scallops longer, but also robs them of some of their natural flavor. Wet scallops take on some of that water, making them heavier, and therefore more expensive at checkout, too. The water also causes significantly more liquid to release into the pan during cooking, which results in the scallops steaming, rather than taking on a golden sear.

SPICED-RUBBED SALMON

with Citrus Yogurt & Fennel Salad

Citrus Yogurt

½ cup plain Greek yogurt

1 teaspoon freshly grated lemon zest

3 teaspoons fresh lemon juice, divided

Kosher salt

Freshly ground black pepper

Spice Mix and Salmon

1 tablespoon ground coriander

1 teaspoon ground cumin

½ teaspoon ground ginger

¼ teaspoon ground turmeric

⅛ teaspoon cayenne pepper

4 (5-ounce) skin-on salmon fillets (1½ to 2 inches at thickest point)

1½ teaspoons neutral oil, such as canola or grapeseed

Fennel Salad

1 medium fennel bulb, preferably with fronds, bulb cored and very thinly sliced, fronds picked to yield generous ½ cup

2 tablespoons thinly sliced fresh mint leaves

1 tablespoon extra-virgin olive oil, plus more for serving

Making your own savory blend of common pantry spices is a quick and easy way to take a basic skillet recipe from mundane to magnificent. Here I do just that with a curry-like mix that's a great complement to the rich flavor of salmon. Topped with a fresh simple salad and served with a tangy yogurt sauce, it's sophisticated enough for a dinner party and quick enough for a healthy weeknight meal.

For the citrus yogurt: In a small bowl, stir together the yogurt, zest, 1 teaspoon of the lemon juice, ⅛ teaspoon salt, and a generous pinch of black pepper. Set aside.

For the spice mix and salmon: In a second bowl, mix together the coriander, cumin, ginger, turmeric, cayenne, ¾ teaspoon salt, and a generous pinch of black pepper. Rub the spice mixture all over the salmon fillets.

Heat the neutral oil in a large nonstick skillet over medium-high heat until hot but not smoking. Cook the salmon, skin-side down, without disturbing, until the skin is crisped and golden, 3 to 4 minutes. Carefully turn the fillets and continue cooking, turning occasionally so that all four sides get a little heat, until the fish is just opaque in the center and cooked through, 2 to 3 minutes for medium-rare to medium. Remove from the heat.

For the fennel salad: In a large bowl, toss together the sliced fennel, fennel fronds, mint, olive oil, remaining 2 teaspoons lemon juice, ¼ teaspoon salt, and a generous pinch of black pepper. Adjust the seasoning to taste.

Arrange the fillets on serving plates. Dollop the yogurt alongside. Top with the salad, then drizzle with a little more olive oil.

KITCHEN WISDOM: Spice Blends

Spice blends such as the curry-like mix here can be almost endlessly modified. If you like a little more earthy warmth, for example, you can increase the cumin. For added heat, add a bit more cayenne. Additional curry spices, like ground mace, dried mustard, white pepper, and fennel seeds could be added to the mix.

Keep in mind that pantry spices decrease in flavor and intensity over time. It's good practice to occasionally replace old spices with new jars. You may want to purchase spices you don't use as often from bulk bins and in small amounts, to avoid winding up with unused excess. Try your hand at blending and have fun!

CHA CA SALAD

with Pineapple & Mint

Marinade and Fish

2 tablespoons finely chopped peeled fresh ginger (from a 2-inch knob)

Kosher salt

⅓ cup finely chopped peeled fresh pineapple

1 tablespoon ground turmeric

1½ pounds (1½- to 2-inch-thick pieces) cod or hake fillets, cut into 2-inch square pieces

Noodles and Dressing

4 ounces dried vermicelli rice-stick noodles

2 tablespoons fresh lime juice

2 tablespoons fish sauce (such as nuoc nam or nam pla)

2 teaspoons sugar

1 small Thai or serrano chili, seeded and thinly sliced; or ¼ teaspoon crushed chili flakes

½ small garlic clove, very thinly sliced

Ingredients continue, opposite

My close friends are all too familiar with this story from my honeymoon in Vietnam: Jeremy and I touched down in Hanoi after hours of travel, happily exhausted and armed with a well-researched list of must-dos and must-eats. Top of that list was a visit to Cha Ca La Vong, a celebrated, unassuming restaurant in the Old Quarter, famous for an eponymous grilled fish dish made with turmeric and lots of fresh dill, and served over tender rice noodles with salty peanuts and more fresh herbs. Over the course of our four days in the city, we made three attempts to go to the restaurant; each was met with an unanticipated "Sorry We're Closed" sign, or a lineup of diners that was longer than could be accommodated. Finally realizing my defeat, I broke into tears right there on the street. It was a moment I am not proud of, my passion and persistence had gotten the better of me, but the experience taught me a great lesson: The beauty and benefit of travel isn't always found in the checking off of everything on your list, but in the ability to engage with and adapt to the unexpected turns of your adventure. Back home, I let go of the ridiculous episode, rolled up my sleeves, and learned to make the dish myself. Here's a delicious version, served with a bright cabbage slaw.

To marinate the fish: Mound the ginger and 1 teaspoon salt on a cutting board; using both the blade and flat side of a chef's knife, chop and scrape the mixture into a paste. Place in a large bowl and add the chopped pineapple. Using the tines of a fork, mash together to crush and blend the pineapple into the paste. Stir in the turmeric to combine. Add the fish. Cover your hands with plastic bags (produce bags work well) or latex gloves and toss together the fish and paste until the fish is well-coated. Let marinate, covered, for 1 hour at room temperature, or in the fridge for 2 hours or overnight.

For the noodles: Place the noodles in a large heatproof bowl; pour 5 to 6 cups boiling water over the top and let stand for 3 minutes. Drain and run under cold water to cool completely. Drain again and return to a dry bowl, then snip with kitchen shears in a few places (snipping makes the noodles more manageable to eat).

For the dressing: In a second bowl, vigorously whisk together the lime juice, fish sauce, sugar, and 3 tablespoons water for about 30 seconds to dissolve the sugar. Stir in the chili and garlic.

Add ¼ cup of the dressing to the noodles; toss to combine. Set aside the remaining dressing.

Recipe continues, opposite

Salad

6 cups shredded napa cabbage
(from a 1-pound head)

1 cup ½-inch cubes peeled fresh
pineapple

¼ cup coarsely chopped fresh
dill plus more for serving

¼ cup coarsely chopped fresh
mint plus more for serving

¼ cup coarsely chopped
cilantro plus more for serving

¼ cup neutral oil, such as canola
or grapeseed, plus more if
needed

1 bunch (7 to 8) large scallions,
trimmed, cut crosswise into
1½-inch lengths, white parts
cut in half lengthwise

½ small garlic clove, thinly
sliced

Fresh lime wedges for serving

¼ cup coarsely chopped roasted
salted peanuts for serving

Thai or small serrano chili,
thinly sliced, for serving

Special equipment: Latex
gloves or plastic produce
bags for hands

For the salad: In a large bowl, toss together the cabbage, cubed pineapple, herbs, and 2 tablespoons of the remaining dressing. Set aside.

To cook the fish and finish the dish: Line a large plate with paper towels. In a 10- to 12-inch nonstick skillet, heat the neutral oil over high heat until hot but not smoking. Add the fish, a few pieces at a time so as not to cool the oil too quickly. Cook, turning pieces once, until opaque and cooked through, 2 to 3 minutes per side (if your fish is thinner than 1½ inches, cook it in two batches and cut cooking time accordingly).

Remove the pan from the heat. Using a slotted spoon, transfer the fish pieces and all of the bits in the pan to the prepared plate. Return the pan to medium-high heat and add 1 teaspoon more oil if needed. Add the scallions, garlic, and ¼ teaspoon salt and cook, stirring constantly, until the scallions are wilted and tender, about 3 minutes. Remove from the heat.

Divide the noodles and salad among four large, shallow bowls. Place the fish and scallions on top. Drizzle with the remaining dressing, then squeeze lime wedges over the top. Sprinkle with the peanuts, the tasty pan bits, and fresh herbs and chilies.

KITCHEN WISDOM: Turmeric

Be extra-tidy while working with turmeric: Its yellow color, which is derived from curcumin, is a powerful coloring agent, which means it's also quick to stain skin, countertops, clothing, and more.

SALT-BAKED BRANZINO

2 tablespoons whole fennel seeds

1 small fennel bulb, trimmed and thinly sliced, fronds reserved if available

6 large egg whites

6 cups kosher salt, plus more for seasoning

2 tablespoons freshly grated lemon zest

2 (1½- to 2-pound) whole branzino, cleaned, leaving head and tail intact

2 lemons, 1 thinly sliced into rounds, 1 cut into wedges for serving

1 small orange, thinly sliced into rounds

8 sprigs fresh thyme, plus more chopped leaves for serving

4 sprigs fresh dill, plus more chopped leaves for serving

Extra-virgin olive oil for serving

Spending 12 years alongside Tom Colicchio at the *Top Chef* Judges' Table has been one of the highlights of my experience working on the show. A dedicated political activist, father, fisherman, and, of course a masterful chef, Tom has shared his multifaceted wisdom with me, and I'm a better cook, mom, and person because of it. One of the many cooking techniques he regularly extolls is salt baking, which involves cooking whole fish, whole chicken, or even unpeeled root vegetables in a thick salt crust. The crust both lightly seasons whatever's inside and helps to lock in its flavor and juices. The skin of the fish, chicken, or veg acts as a barrier to the salt, leaving the interior perfectly seasoned. Since there is little added fat, it's also a healthy way to cook. Cracking open the golden salt crust to reveal what's underneath never fails to impress. If you're a first-timer at this, fear not; once you literally get the feel for what you're doing, you will see how easy it is. The technique is also very forgiving, so great results are just about always guaranteed. Thank you, Tom!

Heat the oven to 425°F. Line a heavy rimmed baking sheet or a large roasting pan with parchment paper.

In a small skillet over high heat, toast the fennel seeds until just fragrant, about 1 minute. Transfer to a plate and let cool. Meanwhile, if available, finely chop enough fennel fronds to yield ¼ cup.

In a large, clean mixing bowl, whisk the egg whites until just foamy then add the chopped fennel fronds, if using, and the fennel seeds, salt, and lemon zest. Stir together the mixture with your hands (it should have the texture of wet sand).

Rinse the fish under cold running water, then pat dry. Stuff the fish cavities evenly with the fennel, lemon, and orange slices, and the thyme and dill sprigs, reserving any extra aromatics that won't fit in the cavities.

Spread a ¼-inch-thick layer of the salt mixture on the prepared baking sheet, just large enough for the two fish to be arranged on top, with about a ½-inch space between them and a 1-inch border on all sides. Arrange any leftover aromatics on the salt layer and top with the fish. Then cover them completely and evenly with the remaining salt mixture, packing the mixture around and between the two fish (see Kitchen Wisdom, page 113).

Recipe continues

Bake the fish until an instant-read thermometer inserted into the thickest part of one fish, behind the head, registers 135°F, 25 to 28 minutes (the salt crust should be lightly golden and hard). This will take into account carry-over cooking time. Remove the pan from the oven and let rest on a wire rack for 10 minutes.

Run a knife along the side of the crust, then lift off the salt in large pieces. Brush off any excess salt. Remove and discard the aromatics from the cavities of the fish.

To fillet the fish, transfer it to a large platter or cutting board. Run the tip of a paring knife along the top fillet in three places: first, along the top of the backbone, then between the top fillet and the collarbone, and finally where the top fillet meets the tail. Insert a small metal spatula or a fish knife under the top fillet and gently push and lift it off the backbone, then transfer it to a plate. From the tail end, lift off and remove the skeleton. Gently remove the remaining bones from the bottom fillet and transfer it to a plate as well. Serve drizzled with olive oil and sprinkled with chopped thyme and dill, with lemon wedges alongside.

KITCHEN WISDOM: Salt Baking

The key to success with salt baking is to make sure that you've created a full covering of salt crust—under, over, and all around—every part of your fish, chicken, or vegetable. If you need to make extra salt mixture to form a complete shell, scale it up accordingly. If branzino is not available, snapper, sea bream, trout, sea bass, and porgy are all great substitutes. Some of these options are larger than branzino, so you may only need to purchase one fish instead of two. To feed four people, go for 3 to 4 pounds total of whole precleaned fish.

FISH TACOS

with Soy-Lime Crema

Marinade and Fish

¼ cup extra-virgin olive oil, plus more for the grill

2 tablespoons red wine vinegar

¼ cup chopped cilantro leaves, plus more torn leaves for serving

2 garlic cloves, finely chopped

2 tablespoons very thinly sliced scallions

1 pound flaky white fish fillet, such as cod, hake, or pollack

Kosher salt

Freshly ground black pepper

Soy-Lime Crema

½ cup sour cream, preferably full-fat

1¾ teaspoons reduced-sodium soy sauce

1 tablespoon fresh lime juice

½ teaspoon cold water

16 small corn tortillas

1½ cups thinly sliced cabbage (any type or color is fine)

6 small radishes, thinly sliced

¼ cup very thinly sliced scallions

Pickled jalapeños

Lime wedges

Hot sauce, preferably Mexican

My friend Sam Elkin, one of the masterminds behind the Nashville and Austin Food and Wine Festivals, is a passionate eater and cook who has a knack for discovering great food products and often shares his finds with me. He recently introduced me to Have'a Corn Chips, a brand of tortilla chips seasoned with an unlikely but totally addictive combo of soy sauce and lime. The Asian flavor, together with a corn chip, creates a delicious umami explosion and is a combination I now turn to often when I'm developing Mexican-style recipes. Here, it's the inspiration for a savory crema that sets these tasty tacos apart.

To marinate the fish: In a small baking dish, whisk together the oil, vinegar, chopped cilantro, garlic, and scallions. Add the fish, turn to coat, and let stand at room temperature for 30 minutes, turning once halfway through. Remove the fish from the marinade and gently pat off excess liquid, leaving a few bits of the marinade on (do not brush off). Season well with salt and pepper.

For the Soy-Lime Crema: While the fish is marinating, in a bowl, stir together the sour cream, soy sauce, lime juice, and water. Chill until ready to serve.

To grill the fish and tortillas: Prepare a grill or grill pan for medium-high heat. Brush the grill lightly with oil. Grill the fish, turning once halfway through, until opaque inside, 3 to 5 minutes per side. Transfer to a cutting board and let rest for 5 minutes.

Meanwhile, grill the tortillas until warmed through and charred in spots, about 1 minute per side. Wrap the tortillas in a clean dishtowel to keep warm.

To serve: Using two forks, gently flake the fish and place on a platter. Serve with the warm tortillas, soy-lime crema, cabbage, radishes, scallions, jalapeños, lime wedges, and hot sauce.

Grilled Oysters
FOR THREE NEW ORLEANS FRIENDS

SERVES A SMALL GROUP OR A CROWD

In 2011, I was lucky enough to call New Orleans home for six weeks while we shot Season 11 of *Top Chef*. Pregnant at the time with Dahlia, I had to refrain from drinking (hard to do in that town) and say no to raw oysters (even harder!). It was then I discovered *grilled* oysters, which I gleefully downed by the dozen. The combination of smoky and salty briny flavors is a match made in heaven, and the grilling takes no time at all (it also makes shucking a breeze, as the oysters pop open themselves by way of the heat from the grill). Here I've created three condiments to serve atop the brilliant bivalves, each one dedicated to a dear New Orleans chef friend who helped make my time there so special.

**As many dozen oysters as you wish to serve,
well-scrubbed**

1 or more of the three sauces:
Chardonnay-Herb Butter (page 117) ◆ *Porchetta Marmalade (page 118)*
Sour Cherry Mingonette (page 119)

Heat a grill to medium-high. Grill the oysters, cupped-side down and covered, until they start hissing and just begin to open, 2 to 5 minutes (smaller oysters will cook more quickly than larger). Transfer to a large plate (discard any that remain tightly shut) and let cool slightly.

Use an oyster knife or screwdriver to release and remove the top shells. As you work, keep the cupped sides of the oysters down and do your best to retain as much liquid as possible. Using the oyster knife or a paring knife, cut the muscles connecting the oysters to their shells.

Serve warm, with one or more of the sauces.

CHARDONNAY-HERB BUTTER

½ cup (1 stick) cold unsalted butter, divided

1 garlic clove, finely chopped

½ teaspoon freshly grated lemon zest

1 tablespoon fresh lemon juice

4 ounces (½ cup) unoaked Chardonnay

¼ cup finely chopped fresh flat-leaf parsley

2 tablespoons finely chopped fresh chives

¼ teaspoon kosher salt

Freshly ground black pepper

Emeril Lagasse is many things, most of which many of us know: He's one of the warmest, most enthusiastic, and generous chefs and food personalities around, and he's a fiercely proud champion of his adopted city of New Orleans. He is also a lover of good Chardonnay. As I drizzle this silky butter sauce over a plate of just-grilled oysters I can't help but smile, reminded of the many nights I've spent with Emeril enjoying lively conversation and a great meal. This sauce, a classic emulsion, works best when the butter is very cold. After cutting it into cubes, keep it chilled until ready to use.

In a medium skillet, melt 1 tablespoon of the butter over low heat; cube and chill the remaining butter. Add the garlic to the skillet and cook, stirring occasionally, until tender (do not brown), about 2 minutes. Stir in the lemon zest and juice, then add the wine. Increase the heat to medium, bring the mixture to a simmer, and cook until reduced to 2 tablespoons, 5 to 8 minutes.

Whisking constantly, add the remaining butter a few cubes at a time, allowing each addition to incorporate before adding the next. Remove from the heat and stir in the parsley, chives, salt, and a generous pinch of pepper. Adjust the seasoning to taste and serve warm over the grilled oysters.

PORCHETTA MARMALADE

½ pound thick-cut bacon, cut crosswise into ½-inch pieces

1 small fennel bulb with fronds, bulb halved, cored, and thinly sliced; fronds finely chopped

1 large shallot, thinly sliced (about ½ cup)

1 garlic clove, finely chopped

3 tablespoons balsamic vinegar

2 tablespoons packed dark brown sugar

2 teaspoons finely chopped fresh sage

1 teaspoon finely chopped fresh rosemary

½ teaspoon freshly grated orange zest

⅛ teaspoon red pepper flakes

Kosher salt

Chef John Besh, the charming and talented chef/owner of many of New Orleans' top restaurants, makes one of the best slow-roasted, fennel-scented, crackling-covered pork loin roasts (aka porchetta) on the planet. Inspired by a version we cooked together for a charity event at his home, I came up with this marmalade. In addition to making a crazy-delicious grilled oyster topping, it's also an unbeatable condiment for scallops or pork chops, sandwiches, eggs, and cheese plates.

In a medium saucepan, cook the bacon over medium-high heat, stirring occasionally, until golden and crisp, about 8 minutes. Pour off all but 2 tablespoons of the fat.

Reduce the heat to medium, then stir in the sliced fennel bulb, shallot, and garlic. Cook, stirring occasionally, until softened, 10 to 12 minutes. Stir in the vinegar, sugar, sage, rosemary, zest, pepper flakes, and a pinch of salt, then add ½ cup water. Bring to a boil, then reduce to a bare simmer. Cook, stirring occasionally and reducing the heat as necessary to keep the mixture barely simmering, until thickened, 50 minutes to 1 hour.

Remove the marmalade from the heat and let cool to room temperature. Transfer to a blender or food processor and pulse, scraping the sides of the blender jar or food processor as needed, until you have a coarse marmalade. Dollop the marmalade on the grilled oysters, then sprinkle with the fennel fronds.

The marmalade keeps, in an airtight container and refrigerated, for up to 1 week. Bring to room temperature or gently warm before serving.

SOUR CHERRY MIGNONETTE

3 tablespoons dried tart cherries

¼ cup plus 2 tablespoons red wine vinegar

1 teaspoon finely chopped shallot

½ teaspoon coarsely crushed black peppercorns

Pinch of ground cardamom

At my friend Alon Shaya's eponymous Middle Eastern restaurant, Shaya, he serves a classic Persian specialty that you don't see often in the U.S., let alone the Deep South: sour cherry rice. His contemporary take on the dish, infused with golden saffron, ground Persian lime, and a beguiling spice blend called *baharat*, and then topped with rehydrated dried sour cherries, was love at first bite for me, and the impetus for this tangy sauce.

Place the cherries in a small heatproof bowl and add boiling water to just cover. Let stand, covered, until plump, about 15 minutes. Reserve 2 tablespoons of the liquid, then drain the cherries. Pat the cherries dry, then coarsely chop.

In a medium bowl, combine the vinegar, shallot, black pepper, and cardamom. Add the chopped cherries and reserved liquid; stir to combine. Spoon the mignonette over the grilled oysters.

JERK SHRIMP ROLLS

2 teaspoons olive oil, plus more for grilling

1 pound large shrimp, peeled and deveined

Kosher salt

5 scallions, divided

Freshly ground black pepper

¼ teaspoon ground allspice

3 tablespoons coarsely chopped peeled fresh ginger (from a 2-inch knob)

1 large clove garlic, chopped

1 tablespoon fresh thyme leaves

1 Scotch bonnet pepper, stemmed, seeded, and chopped

2 tablespoons plus 2 teaspoons fresh lime juice

⅓ cup mayonnaise

4 hot dog buns

2 tablespoons unsalted butter, melted

Some of my most memorable meals have been at roadside jerk shacks in and around Negril, Jamaica. At each shack, chicken (and often fish, lobster, and shrimp) is rubbed with an intoxicating blend of sweet and spicy seasoning and herbs that make up *jerk*: chilies, ginger, scallions, garlic, and allspice. Each shack makes its own version of the seasoning, and—having dutifully sampled many—I can honestly say that I haven't yet met a jerk chicken or fish that I didn't wholeheartedly love. The seasoning has inspired my own riffs on jerk, including this shrimp roll. Blending the style of a classic New England lobster roll with those spicy-sweet jerk flavors, it's a wildly delicious mash-up and, since it's quick to assemble and easy to double or triple, one that's great for feeding a crowd.

Heat a grill or grill pan to high heat and brush it with oil. In a bowl, toss the shrimp with 2 teaspoons oil and ½ teaspoon salt. Grill until bright pink, opaque, and slightly charred, about 3 minutes per side. Transfer to a plate and set aside to cool, then coarsely chop.

Clean the grill and brush with more oil if required. Season four of the scallions with salt and pepper; grill until softened and charred in spots, about 2 minutes per side. Allow to cool, then trim off the root and coarsely chop.

In a food processor, combine the grilled scallions, allspice, ginger, garlic, thyme, Scotch bonnet, lime juice, and ¾ teaspoon salt. Pulse to form a coarse paste, scraping down sides a few times between pulses to evenly incorporate. Transfer to a mixing bowl and stir in the mayonnaise. Fold in the shrimp.

Split open the hot dog buns and brush the insides generously with the melted butter. Grill over high heat on the grill or grill pan until just golden, about 2 minutes. Thinly slice the remaining scallion. Divide the shrimp mixture among the buns, sprinkle with the sliced scallion, and serve.

KITCHEN WISDOM: Jerk Mayo

I always make extra jerk mayo when I make these sandwiches. A great veggie dip or sauce for leftover roast chicken, it keeps, covered and refrigerated, for up to 1 week.

Snippet

Jerk refers to a dry spice rub, a wet spice-paste marinade, and a cooking technique that involves the grilling and often smoking of chicken and other meat or fish. The term is said to have come from jerking, a Jamaican method for flavoring and cooking meat over pimento wood, and may have evolved from the Peruvian term charqui (meaning jerked or dried meat), brought to Jamaica by the Arawak peoples who were early settlers there. Charqui also eventually became "jerky" in English, referring to the dried meat snack.

LAZY LOBSTER PIE

3 tablespoons kosher salt

4 live lobsters (about 1½ pounds each)

2 cups panko (Japanese breadcrumbs)

1 cup freshly grated Parmigiano-Reggiano cheese

2 tablespoons finely chopped fresh chives, plus more for serving

2 tablespoons finely chopped fresh flat-leaf parsley

2 teaspoons freshly grated lemon zest

½ teaspoon cayenne pepper

1 cup (2 sticks) unsalted butter, melted

2 teaspoons fresh lemon juice

Lemon wedges for serving

Every summer, we spend a week or two in Gloucester, Massachusetts, where upwards of 25 of Jeremy's extended family members gather from far and wide. Along with relaxing and renewing ties, we spend a good bit of time cooking, eating, beaching, eating, reading, eating, and, what else? Well, you get the picture. Part of the fun is touring the local lobster and fried clam shacks to eat some of the best clam bellies, lobster rolls, and "chowda" imaginable. For years, one of our favorite spots, the Lobster Pool, served a crazy-good dish called Lazy Lobster Pie. It's a mix of chopped fresh lobster meat smothered in melted butter, topped with crushed Ritz crackers, baked into a casserole, then broiled to golden brown perfection. On our last visit, new owners had taken it off the menu, much to my dismay. So now I make my own, with fresh herbs, a little lemon, and a sprinkling of toasty panko breadcrumbs. You can bake it in one large casserole dish, or in individual ramekins for a more elegant look.

Fill a large, heavy stockpot about half full with water; add the salt. Bring the water to a rolling boil over high heat. Plunge the lobsters headfirst into the pot (see Kitchen Wisdom), then cover and cook until just done, 10 to 12 minutes after the water returns to a boil. Using tongs, transfer the lobsters to a colander to drain. When cool enough to handle, crack the shells and remove the meat from tails, claws, and legs; discard the shells or save them for stock. Cut the meat into ½-inch pieces; set aside.

Heat the oven to 350°F with the rack in the middle.

In a medium bowl, combine the panko, Parmesan, chives, parsley, zest, and cayenne. In a small bowl, stir together the butter and lemon juice, then stir the butter mixture into the breadcrumb mixture to combine.

Arrange the lobster meat in a 1½-quart gratin or shallow baking dish. Cover with the breadcrumb mixture. Bake until bubbling, about 15 minutes. Increase the oven temperature to broil, then broil until the topping is golden and crisp, 1 to 2 minutes. Remove from the oven and let stand 5 minutes, then sprinkle with additional chives. Serve warm with the lemon wedges on the side.

KITCHEN WISDOM: Lobster

To boil the lobsters as humanely as possible, it's best to cook them in two batches, so the water returns to a boil more quickly once they are added. If live lobsters aren't available, or you want to skip the lobster-cooking step for convenience or to save time, you can purchase 1½ pounds of cooked lobster meat to use in this recipe.

Poultry & Meat

◆

PIRI PIRI ROAST CHICKEN

2 dried ancho chilies, stemmed, seeded, and torn into pieces

1 (4- to 4½-pound) chicken

3 lemons

5 garlic cloves, coarsely chopped

⅓ cup coarsely chopped peeled fresh ginger (from a 3-inch knob)

1 medium serrano chili, seeded and coarsely chopped

1 medium shallot, coarsely chopped

2 tablespoons paprika

1 teaspoon ground coriander

2 tablespoons coarsely chopped cilantro leaves and tender stems, plus more for serving

Kosher salt

4 tablespoons extra-virgin olive oil, divided

1¾ pounds small to medium potatoes (1 to 2 inches in diameter), small ones left whole, larger cut lengthwise in half

Freshly ground black pepper

Smothered in a paste of chilies, garlic, lemon, herbs, and spices, then grilled or roasted to perfection, piri piri chicken is a deeply flavorful dish with roots in Portugal and Africa. The first time I tasted it was on a trip to my father's native South Africa in 1989. I had flown with him to visit my grandparents and other close family. One day they took me for lunch at Nando's, a wildly popular chain of fast-casual restaurants in Johannesburg that specializes in piri piri (and has since expanded to London, Australia, Singapore, Canada, and the U.S.); I was instantly hooked. Over the course of our two-week vacation, I not only requested we go back several times, but also asked my father to purchase multiple bottles of their custom hot sauces to bring home to Canada. Making the chicken at home is easy and deeply satisfying. Although my recipe calls for ancho and serrano chilies, it's only mildly spicy. If you like a palpable heat, add chili flakes or cayenne pepper to the spice blend.

Bring a small saucepan of water to a boil, add the ancho chilies, and remove from the heat. Let stand for 20 minutes. Meanwhile, spatchcock the chicken (see Chef Tech).

Grate the lemon zest from one lemon. Squeeze enough juice from the same lemon plus one of the remaining lemons to yield ¼ cup. Cut the remaining lemon into ⅛-inch slices and remove and discard the seeds; set aside the slices.

In a blender or food processor, combine the ancho chilies and 2 tablespoons of their soaking liquid, the lemon zest and juice, garlic, ginger, serrano chili, shallot, paprika, coriander, 1 tablespoon of the cilantro, and ¾ teaspoon salt. With the machine running, drizzle in 2 tablespoons of the oil to form a thin paste.

Gently push 3 tablespoons of the paste under the skin of the chicken, then rub your hands over the outside of the chicken to evenly distribute the paste underneath, pushing it to where you cannot reach with your hand. Put the chicken in a 1-gallon resealable plastic bag.

Pour the remaining paste over the chicken. Pressing out the air, seal the bag. Using clean hands, rub the outside of the bag to work the marinade into all of the nooks and crannies of the bird, then place the bag in a bowl and let the chicken marinate at room temperature at least 1 hour; or refrigerate overnight, turning the bag a couple of times midway through and allowing the chicken to come to room temperature before cooking.

Heat the oven to 425°F. Put a roasting pan or 9 x 13-inch baking dish in the oven and heat for 10 minutes. Meanwhile, in a large bowl, toss the potatoes with ½ teaspoon salt, a generous pinch of pepper, and the remaining 2 tablespoons oil. Remove the chicken from the bag, reserving the paste. Spread about half of the paste from the bag over the top of the chicken, then generously season the chicken all over with salt and pepper.

Remove the pan from the oven and immediately add the potatoes and their oil, scraping all of the oil from the bowl into the pan. Arrange the chicken on top, breast-side down, then spread the chicken with the remaining paste. Carefully return the pan to the oven (remember it's hot; wear mitts!). Roast for 15 minutes. Turn the chicken breast-side up and roast 10 minutes more. Liberally baste the potatoes and the bird with pan juices. Tuck the reserved lemon slices between the potatoes, both under and around the bird. Continue roasting until the juices run clear when the thigh is pierced with the tip of a paring knife or an instant-read thermometer inserted into the thickest part of the thigh registers 165°F, 15 to 20 minutes more.

Transfer the chicken to a cutting board; let rest for 10 minutes, then carve and serve with the potatoes, lemon slices, juicy pan drippings, and chopped cilantro.

Chef Tech

♦

To spatchcock the chicken, pull off and discard the excess fat from around the cavities, then rinse the chicken, pat dry very well with paper towels, and place on a cutting board, backbone-side up. Using kitchen shears, cut along each side of the backbone and remove it. Turn the chicken breast-side up and gently but firmly press on the breastbone to crack it and flatten the chicken. From the edge of the cavity, use your fingers to gently loosen the skin from the meat of the breasts and thighs.

Like so many countries with a history of colonization, the food of South Africa is heavily influenced by the many cultures that have played a role in shaping its people. Portugal's influence on the Cape of Good Hope is not widely considered, but dates back as early as explorers Bartolomeu Dias and Vasco da Gama during their explorations through the spice route to India in the late 15th century. The substantial Portuguese population that brought chilies to Angola and Mozambique during the 400-year Portuguese occupation most likely created piri piri chicken. The dish was then made prevalent in South Africa by the large influx of Portuguese to the country after Angola and Mozambique gained independence in the 1970s.

Piri Piri
Roast Chicken,
page 126

ZA'ATAR CHICKEN SCHNITZEL with Israeli Salad

Israeli Salad

1 red, yellow, or orange bell pepper, cut into ⅓-inch cubes

½ English cucumber, cut into ⅓-inch cubes

½ small red onion, cut into ¼-inch pieces

1 pint cherry tomatoes, quartered

¼ cup finely chopped fresh flat-leaf parsley

¼ cup coarsely chopped fresh mint

2 tablespoons extra-virgin olive oil

1 tablespoon fresh lemon juice

½ teaspoon za'atar (see Kitchen Wisdom)

1 teaspoon sumac (optional)

Kosher salt

Freshly ground black pepper

Schnitzel

½ cup unbleached all-purpose flour

Kosher salt

Freshly ground black pepper

2 large eggs

1 cup panko (Japanese breadcrumbs)

1½ tablespoons za'atar (See Kitchen Wisdom, opposite)

Freshly grated zest of ½ lemon

4 (¼-inch-thick) chicken cutlets (about 1 pound)

½ cup extra-virgin olive oil

Lemon wedges for serving

One of my favorite crispy chicken preparations, schnitzel is a perfect weeknight dish, since only a short list of mostly basic pantry ingredients is required. I always understood this simple breaded cutlet to be popular German and Austrian fare (and that Italians have a version, too). It wasn't until I went to Israel in my late teens, to travel and work on a kibbutz, that I learned it's ubiquitous there, as well—brought to the country by Eastern European immigrants. My fellow kibbutzniks made many variations of schnitzel, but the Middle Eastern rendition was the one I loved most. To re-create it today is easy, thanks to the relatively widespread availability of the Middle Eastern spice blend za'atar. Served with a crisp, bright Israeli salad, this schnitzel is equally at home on a dinner plate as it is packed into a pita with a spoonful of hummus and a drizzle of hot sauce.

To start the salad: In a large bowl, combine the bell pepper, cucumber, onion, tomatoes, parsley, and mint. Cover and refrigerate until ready to use.

For the schnitzel: Heat the oven to 200°F. Place an ovenproof platter or a baking sheet in the oven to warm.

In a wide, shallow bowl, stir together the flour, 1 teaspoon salt, and a generous pinch of pepper. Whisk together the eggs and a pinch of salt in another shallow bowl. Combine the panko, za'atar, lemon zest, and a pinch of salt in a third shallow bowl.

Using the flat side of a meat pounder or a rolling pin, gently pound each cutlet between 2 sheets of plastic wrap to an ⅛-inch thickness. Pat the cutlets dry and season both sides lightly with salt and pepper. Dredge in the seasoned flour, shaking off excess. Dip in the eggs, letting excess drip off, then gently press into the panko mixture to completely coat. Transfer the cutlets to a large plate.

Heat the ½ cup oil in a 10- to 12-inch skillet over medium-high heat until hot but not smoking. Fry the cutlets in 2 batches, turning once, until cooked through and crispy, about 3 minutes per side. Drain each batch on paper towel–lined plates, season with salt, then transfer to the platter in the oven to keep warm.

To finish the salad, add the 2 tablespoons oil, lemon juice, za'atar, sumac if using, and a generous pinch each of salt and pepper to the vegetable mixture. Toss to combine. Serve the schnitzel with the salad piled on top and lemon wedges on the side.

KITCHEN WISDOM: Za'atar

Za'atar—an earthy, citrusy, eastern Mediterranean mix of dried herbs and seeds that often includes marjoram, thyme, sumac, cumin, and toasted sesame seeds—is a spice blend that I can't seem to get enough of. A tasty seasoning for flatbread, baked chicken, or fish, I also love it swirled with good olive oil into Greek yogurt for an amazing snack or dip. And, sprinkled over fried or scrambled eggs? Absolute heaven! Lucky for me, za'atar is easy to come by in my Brooklyn neighborhood. If it's not available in your neck of the woods, you can easily find it online (see Sources, page 241).

GINGER-CHILI CHICKEN WINGS with Shishito Peppers

Nonstick cooking spray

3 pounds chicken wings, tips removed, drumettes and flats separated

1 teaspoon ground ginger

⅛ teaspoon cayenne pepper

2 teaspoons chili powder, divided

Kosher salt

Freshly ground black pepper

2 tablespoons plus 1½ teaspoons canola oil, divided

2 large limes

3 garlic cloves, finely chopped

2 tablespoons grated peeled fresh ginger (from a 2-inch knob)

3 tablespoons honey

2 tablespoons reduced-sodium soy sauce

1 pound shishito or Padrón peppers

Special equipment: commercial-grade 13 x 18-inch rimmed aluminum or stainless steel baking sheet and same-sized cooling rack.

Chicken wings may be popular sports bar snacks, but I've never needed a sporting event as an excuse to eat them. Day or night, and anytime of the year, if wings are on the menu, I'm in. At restaurants, they're most often fried, which yields the classic crispiness we all know and love. But for those who don't like to fry at home, I've got good news: Roasting wings at a high oven temperature delivers deliciously crispy results with little mess or fuss. I like to give my wings some Asian flair, flavoring them with a sweet and spicy glaze of pantry spices, fresh ginger, honey, and soy sauce, and serve them with blistered Japanese peppers called shishito. (If you can't find the peppers, or simply prefer to save room in your belly for more wings, it's perfectly fine to leave them out.)

On a heat scale of 1 to 10, with 10 being the spiciest, these wings fall in around a 5. To dial that flame up or down, simply adjust the cayenne pepper to taste.

Heat the oven to 475°F. Spray a cooling rack with cooking spray then set it into a 13 x 18-inch rimmed baking sheet. Rinse the wings under cold running water and pat dry.

In a large bowl, whisk together the ground ginger, cayenne, 1½ teaspoons of the chili powder, 2 teaspoons salt, ½ teaspoon pepper, and 1 tablespoon of the oil. Add the wings to the spice mixture and toss to coat evenly. Arrange the wings, skin-side up, on the prepared rack. Roast for 20 minutes (you're likely to get a bit of smoke, but the wings will not burn), then rotate the pan and reduce the oven temperature to 400°F. Continue roasting until the wings are cooked through and crispy, about 20 to 25 minutes more.

Meanwhile, squeeze 1 tablespoon of lime juice (from about half of one lime) into a small bowl; set aside. Cut the remaining limes into wedges; set aside.

In a small saucepan, heat 1 tablespoon oil over medium. Add the garlic and grated ginger and cook until the garlic begins to sizzle, about 30 seconds. Stir in the lime juice, honey, soy sauce, ½ teaspoon salt, and remaining ½ teaspoon chili powder. Bring to a simmer and cook for 3 to 4 minutes to slightly reduce and thicken. Set the glaze aside.

In a large bowl, toss together the peppers, ¼ teaspoon salt, and the remaining 1½ teaspoons oil. Heat a large skillet (preferably cast iron or stainless steel; not non-stick) over medium-high heat until hot but not smoking. Cook the peppers in two or three batches (avoid crowding the pan), without stirring for the first 2 minutes, then turning and tossing occasionally, until blistered and just beginning to collapse, 8 to 10 minutes total per batch. (The pan will smoke and peppers may pop a bit; this is OK.) Transfer batches as they finish to a large platter. While hot, season generously with salt, then squeeze a wedge or two of lime over the top.

Once the wings are cooked, transfer to a large mixing bowl, pour the glaze over them, and toss well to evenly coat. Pile the wings on top of the peppers on the platter. Squeeze the remaining lime wedges over the top and serve.

Shishito peppers are small and slender, and generally harvested while green in color. Commonly sold at Asian markets, they're also often found at Western grocery stores and—from summer into fall—at farmers' markets. A Galician pepper called Padrón shares similar qualities in size and taste, and makes a great substitute. The spice level of both of these varieties is, to my mind, delightfully unpredictable, ranging from mild to quite hot (until you take a bite, there's no way to know what you'll get). Part of the fun of eating them is the inherent risk—a good excuse to keep a crisp, cold beer, or other beverage of your choice, alongside!

PASTRAMI-STYLE ROAST TURKEY

SERVES 4 TO 6

Canola oil for brushing

1 large garlic clove, smashed and peeled

Kosher salt

1 tablespoon light brown sugar

1 tablespoon plus 2 teaspoons freshly ground black pepper

1 tablespoon ground coriander

1 tablespoon smoked paprika

½ teaspoon mustard powder

2 tablespoons unsalted butter

2 dried bay leaves

1 skin-on boneless turkey breast half (2 to 2½ pounds), butterflied (See Chef Tech, opposite)

Special equipment: kitchen twine

Many years ago I was introduced to pastrami-style roast turkey breast at a local Jewish deli and loved it so much that I set out to make a version at home. It is now one of our family favorites, and a recipe I often double to enjoy for dinner and then in sandwiches for several days after. The classic peppery spices are key, but a huge part of the appeal of this dish is also how simple it is to prepare. Boneless turkey breast is commonly sold at supermarkets in a variety of sizes, and you can ask to have it butterflied, or easily do this at home (see Chef Tech, opposite). The simple technique allows you to spread the spices evenly over the meat, which is then rolled and tied. This results in a perfect distribution of spices, as well as a pinwheel effect once the meat is sliced. Serve it with roasted vegetables, sweet potatoes, or a tangy slaw on the side.

Heat the oven to 450°F with the rack in the middle. Lightly brush a small roasting pan or medium oven-safe skillet with oil.

Thinly slice the garlic, then mound with 1 teaspoon salt on a cutting board; using both the blade and the flat side of a chef's knife, chop and scrape the mixture into a paste. Place in a bowl. Add the sugar, pepper, coriander, paprika, and mustard and stir to combine.

In a small saucepan, heat the butter and bay leaves over medium until the butter is melted; set aside.

Spread the butterflied turkey breast on a cutting board skin-side up. Carefully run your fingers between the skin and the flesh of the turkey from one end, being careful not to pull the skin completely off. Spread about a quarter of the spice rub under the skin, then turn the turkey skin-side down. Spread about half of the remaining rub over the meat. Roll and tie firmly with twine every 2 inches to make a compact cylinder. Spread the remaining rub all over the outside of the meat. Season generously and all over with ¾ teaspoon salt. Place seam-side down in the prepared roasting pan.

Spoon about half of the butter over the turkey, then place in the oven and reduce the temperature to 400°F. Roast, basting with the remaining butter halfway through, until an instant-read thermometer registers 165°F in the center, 40 to 45 minutes.

Transfer to a cutting board and let rest, loosely covered with foil, for 10 minutes. Slice the turkey and serve.

To butterfly a boneless turkey breast, remove and discard any netting and/or pop-up thermometer. Unroll and lay the breast flat on a cutting board, skin-side down with the long side facing you. Holding the blade of a chef's or boning knife parallel to the board and working from the narrowest end of the meat, make a horizontal cut halfway into the thickest part of the breast. Continue cutting until you are all but ¾ inch through, making sure not to cut all the way to the other side. Open the breast flat like a book. Cover with plastic wrap and use the back of a small, heavy skillet or meat mallet to pound out any thicker areas so that the meat is fairly uniform in thickness.

Pastrami is an Eastern European curing method for beef that traditionally includes a combination of coriander, paprika, mustard seed, black pepper, garlic, and brown sugar. Brought to New York from Romania in the second half of the 19th century as a method of meat preservation, it is usually applied to the cut of beef called navel, *which is cured, smoked, and steamed. Of course regional variations can be found around the world. In Canada, where I was raised, we eat what is called* smoked meat, *a similar preparation, but made with slightly different seasonings (sugar is generally omitted) and using brisket in place of navel. The larger fat cap of the brisket makes the finished product more tender when steamed.*

HANGER STEAK

with Arugula-Mint Chimichurri

2 garlic cloves, thinly sliced

1 large shallot, thinly sliced

2 tablespoons coarsely chopped fresh oregano leaves

3 sprigs fresh thyme

2 teaspoons coarsely cracked black peppercorns, plus more for seasoning

¼ cup olive oil

1 (2-pound) hanger steak, about 1 inch thick, trimmed

Kosher salt

Freshly ground black pepper

2 cups baby arugula

Arugula-Mint Chimichurri (opposite)

Giant porterhouse and Delmonico steaks are a decadent indulgence, and fun to serve when the bank account allows. But I never tire of the rich, meaty flavor and ease of the less-pricey hanger steak, especially when char-grilled and paired with a punchy herb-packed chimichurri sauce. This is one of my go-to all-season meals, one that I love to serve with roasted potatoes and whatever salad greens look best at the market that day. If hanger steak is not available, try skirt or flank instead.

In a shallow baking dish, combine the garlic, shallot, oregano, thyme, peppercorns, and oil. Add the steak and rub to coat all over. Marinate, covered, for 2 hours at room temperature, or refrigerate for at least 4 hours or overnight (if chilling, let the meat stand at room temperature for 30 minutes to 1 hour before grilling).

Heat a grill or grill pan over medium-high heat. Remove the steak from the marinade (discard the marinade) and season generously with salt and pepper. Grill, turning once, about 5 minutes per side for medium-rare. Transfer to a cutting board and let rest for 10 minutes.

Divide the arugula among four serving plates. Slice the steak and arrange on top of the arugula. Spoon 1 to 2 tablespoons of the chimichurri on top and serve the remaining sauce on the side.

KITCHEN WISDOM: Steak Cuts

Hanger, flank, and skirt steaks come from the chest and side of the steer—well-exercised areas that yield tougher cuts. But what these cuts lack in texture, they make up in spades when it comes to deep, beefy flavor. The secret to turning any one of them into a fabulous dinner, and coaxing out maximum tenderness, lies in simply understanding how to cook and slice them. While acid-based marinades are often used to help break down and tenderize these cuts, the three most important rules to adhere to are these: Limit cooking techniques to broiling and high-heat grilling. Cook to no more than medium-rare—they will otherwise turn chewy and dry. After resting the meat, cut it thinly against the grain, which means crosswise or perpendicular to the muscle structure lines that run through the meat.

Arugula-Mint Chimichurri

For the Hanger Steak with Arugula-Mint Chimichurri (opposite)

1⅓ cups coarsely chopped baby arugula

⅓ cup coarsely chopped fresh mint

1 tablespoon fresh oregano leaves

2 garlic cloves, gently smashed and peeled

½ teaspoon red pepper flakes

¼ teaspoon kosher salt

2 tablespoons red wine vinegar

⅓ cup extra-virgin olive oil

Place the arugula, mint, oregano, garlic, red pepper flakes, salt, and vinegar in the bowl of a food processor. Pulse, scraping down the bowl as necessary, until well combined. Transfer to a bowl and stir in the oil.

The chimichurri will keep, refrigerated in a small, airtight container, for up to 3 days.

Salt-and-Vinegar
Smashed
Potatoes,
page 54

Hanger Steak
with Arugula-
Mint Chimichurri,
page 136

NOT YOUR MAMA'S HORSERADISH BRISKET

1 (5½-pound) first-cut brisket

Kosher salt

Freshly ground pepper

3 tablespoons olive oil

2 medium yellow onions, thinly sliced

4 garlic cloves, finely chopped, divided

4 medium carrots, cut crosswise into 1-inch pieces

2 medium parsnips, cut into 1-inch half moons

2 celery ribs, cut crosswise into 1-inch pieces

2 cups dry red wine

3 cups low-sodium beef broth, heated to a simmer

2 dried bay leaves

4 medium Yukon Gold potatoes, peeled and cut into 1½-inch pieces

1 teaspoon Dijon mustard

½ cup drained prepared horseradish, divided

Special equipment: extra-wide (18 inches) heavy-duty aluminum foil; fat separator (if available)

My mother, and grandmother before her, passed along a few traditional Jewish recipes that remain holiday staples for me to this day—beef brisket among them. No matter how ubiquitous the dish may be, I crave it like clockwork at Rosh Hashanah (the Jewish New Year), and again for Hanukkah. Over the years, I have modified my mother's sacred recipe (much to her dismay!), coating the beef with a garlic and horseradish crust and deglazing the pan with red wine to give the dish bright balance and a rich sauce. I hope that my daughter will one day make this brisket for her own family, adapting it as she sees fit.

Heat the oven to 350°F with the rack in the middle. Season the brisket all over with 1 tablespoon salt and 2 teaspoons pepper. In a large roasting pan set over 2 burners, heat the oil until hot but not smoking. Add the brisket and cook over medium-high heat, turning, until browned all over, 5 to 7 minutes per side. Transfer the brisket to a rimmed baking sheet, fat-side up.

Pour off all but 2 tablespoons of fat from the pan. Add the onions and half of the garlic and cook over medium heat until softened, about 3 minutes. Add the carrots, parsnips, and celery and season with ¼ teaspoon each salt and pepper. Continue cooking until the vegetables are browned, about 6 minutes. Using a slotted spoon, transfer the vegetables to a plate; set aside.

Add the wine to the pan and bring to a boil over high heat. Cook, scraping up browned bits from the bottom of the pot, for 1 minute. Return the brisket to the pan, fat-side up. Add the broth and bay leaves and bring to a simmer over medium-high heat. Cover the pan tightly with the extra-wide foil, sealing the edges; transfer to the oven and braise for 2 hours.

Remove the pan from the oven, then carefully loosen and remove the foil. Scatter the reserved vegetables and the potatoes around the brisket. Reseal the pan tightly with the foil, return to the oven, and braise until the brisket is very tender, about 1 hour more. Meanwhile, in a small bowl, stir together the mustard, ¼ cup of the horseradish, and the remaining garlic.

Carefully loosen and remove the foil and spread the horseradish mixture over the top of the brisket. Return to the oven and cook, uncovered, until the top is browned, about 20 minutes.

Transfer the brisket to a carving board and loosely cover with foil to keep warm. Remove and discard the bay leaves. Using a slotted spoon, transfer the vegetables to a serving platter and loosely cover with foil to keep warm.

Pour the juices from the pan into a fat separator and let stand until the fat rises to the surface. Pour the juices into a small saucepan; discard the fat. (If you don't have a fat separator, pour the liquid into a bowl and let cool completely, then refrigerate overnight or freeze until the fat solidifies. Skim off and discard the fat.)

Gently warm the juices over low heat. Whisk in the remaining ¼ cup of horseradish, then season to taste with salt and pepper.

Thinly slice the brisket against the grain and transfer to the platter with the vegetables. Spoon a little of the warm pan juices over the brisket and pass the remaining juices at the table.

Note: *This recipe can be made ahead through to when the brisket is braised and the top is browned. Cool in the pan juices, cover, and refrigerate for up to 3 days. Refrigerate the vegetables in a separate container. Before serving, skim the fat from the surface of the pan juices. Slice the brisket while it's cold, then arrange in a roasting pan or baking dish with the vegetables and pan juices; cover the pan tightly with foil, sealing the edges. Heat in a 350°F oven until the vegetables and meat are warmed through, about 30 minutes. Transfer the vegetables and meat to a platter and season the juices with the horseradish and salt and pepper directly in the pan.*

GREEK-STYLE LAMB
MEATBALLS OVER ORZO

⅔ cup crumbled feta (3 ounces), divided

1¼ pounds ground lamb

1 large egg

⅓ cup chopped pitted kalamata olives

¼ cup plain breadcrumbs

1 tablespoon plus 1 teaspoon finely chopped fresh oregano, divided

¼ cup chopped fresh dill, divided

Kosher salt

Freshly ground black pepper

1 large lemon

2 tablespoons olive oil, divided

1 small yellow onion, coarsely chopped

2 garlic cloves, finely chopped

1 (28-ounce) can crushed tomatoes

2 dried bay leaves

½ pound (1½ cups) dried orzo pasta

I first met Andrew Carmellini in 2002, when he was chef de cuisine at Café Boulud. I was doing marketing, PR, and events for chef/owner Daniel Boulud at the time and spent hours at the café, hanging around Andrew for one reason or another (usually because his kitchen always had the best staff meal). Among the many things I loved about the Café Boulud menu was a changing section highlighting a specific world cuisine. Andrew left Café Boulud in 2005 and has since gone on to create many of New York's most successful restaurants, including Locanda Verde, where his lamb meatball sliders caused a nationwide stir when the restaurant opened in 2009. Andrew's meatballs, and his exploratory nature, inspired this recipe. The combination of olives and lemons contributes a salty brightness that complements the richness of the lamb.

In a large mixing bowl, combine half of the feta with the lamb, egg, olives, breadcrumbs, 1 tablespoon of the oregano, 2 teaspoons of the dill, 1 teaspoon salt, and ¼ teaspoon pepper. Grate the zest from half of the lemon over the top. Work the mixture together with your hands, then shape into 20 balls, each about 1½ inches in diameter. Set the meatballs on a plate.

In a 6- to 8-quart Dutch oven or wide, heavy pot with lid, heat 1 tablespoon of the oil over medium-high heat. In batches, brown the meatballs on all sides, about 6 minutes total. Transfer to a paper towel-lined plate.

Add the onion to the pan and cook, stirring occasionally, until beginning to soften, 3 to 4 minutes. Add the garlic and cook until softened and fragrant, about 2 minutes more. Stir in the tomatoes, bay leaves, remaining 1 teaspoon oregano, and 3 tablespoons water. Bring to a simmer and cook until the flavors are blended and the sauce is slightly thickened, about 15 minutes.

Remove the bay leaves from the tomato sauce and discard. Stir in half of the remaining dill and 1 teaspoon salt, then add the meatballs. Cover and gently simmer over low heat, stirring once halfway through, until the meatballs are cooked through, 12 to 15 minutes.

Meanwhile, cook the orzo in a large pot of salted boiling water until al dente; drain and transfer to a large bowl. Toss with the 1 remaining tablespoon oil and ¼ teaspoon each salt and pepper.

Divide the orzo among serving plates. Top with the meatballs and sauce. Sprinkle with the remaining feta and dill, then grate the remaining zest from the lemon over the top. Sprinkle with extra pepper, if desired.

Snippet

Feta and feta-style cheeses vary widely, depending on where they're made, what type of milk or combination of milks are used, and age. Since 2005, the cheese has had protected designation of origin (PDO) status, a protection granted by the European Union, which named Greece as the only country in Europe that could use the name feta. (It seems to be taking some time for the EU to pressure American cheesemakers and importers to follow suit; many continue to use the term feta on their packaging.) In Greece, feta must be made in designated areas and from at least 70 percent sheep's milk (up to 30 percent goat's milk can be added). The result is a smooth, deliciously salty, and milky cheese that is slightly tangy when young and becomes sharper and more complex as it ages. Many feta-style cheeses are made in France, Denmark, Bulgaria, Israel, the U.S., and beyond, and with a variety of milks, including sheep's, goat's, and cow's. These cheeses vary in texture (some creamy, some drier), tang, and saltiness. Experiment to find the ones that you like best.

LAMB CHOPS A LA PARILLA

with Roasted Grapes & Sweet Onions

2 lemons

2 garlic cloves, finely chopped

1 tablespoon fresh rosemary leaves, coarsely chopped

Kosher salt

Freshly ground black pepper

8 (1-inch-thick) lamb rib chops

4 tablespoons extra-virgin olive oil, divided

1 pound red seedless grapes on the stem

6 sprigs fresh thyme, plus more for serving

1 medium sweet onion, such as Vidalia, cut crosswise into ¼-inch rounds

2 tablespoons honey

¼ teaspoon smoked paprika

On a whirlwind trip to Spain with my in-laws for their 40th wedding anniversary, Jeremy, his parents, and I had the pleasure of visiting a few special wineries in Rioja. We arrived at our first stop, Bodegas Muga—founded by the Martinez family in 1932 and now run by its third generation—around noon. After a tour of the vineyards and winery, we were invited for lunch. Walking from the outdoor courtyard into the family dining room, I noticed a chef feeding the flames of a wood-burning grill (a *parilla*) with grapevine clippings, which the Martinezes use to add subtle smoky notes to whatever is grilled. I still dream about that meal. In addition to sharing wine that dated back to the year of my in-laws' wedding, we enjoyed the most tender, flavorful lamb chops that any of us had ever tasted. In honor of that lunch, I created this recipe, rubbing juicy lamb rib chops with garlic, lemon zest, and other aromatics before grilling, and then serving them alongside bunches of thyme-scented roasted red grapes.

Grate 1 teaspoon zest from one lemon. Squeeze enough juice from the same lemon to yield 1½ tablespoons. Cut the remaining lemon in half crosswise; remove and discard the seeds; set aside.

In a small bowl, mix together the lemon zest, garlic, rosemary, 1½ teaspoons salt, and ¼ teaspoon black pepper. Place the lamb chops in a shallow baking dish. Rub the mixture into both sides of the eyes (the meaty part) of each chop. Using the same bowl, whisk together 2 tablespoons of the oil and the lemon juice, then pour the mixture over the chops, turning to coat. Cover and let stand at room temperature for 30 minutes.

Heat the oven to 400°F. Line a rimmed baking sheet with parchment paper. Gently rinse and pat dry the grapes (try to keep them on the stem as much as possible), then arrange on the prepared baking sheet. Brush with 1 tablespoon of the oil, then thread the thyme sprigs between the clusters of fruit. Season with a generous pinch each of salt and pepper. Roast until the grapes are tender and blistered, 25 to 28 minutes.

Meanwhile, prepare a grill for medium-high heat. Scrape the marinade from the lamb chops and season with salt and pepper. Grill to desired doneness, about 4 minutes per side for medium-rare. Meanwhile, brush the onion slices with the remaining 1 tablespoon oil and season with salt and pepper. Grill until charred and tender, about 3 minutes per side. Season the lemon halves with a pinch each of salt and pepper. Grill, flesh-side down, until grill marks appear, about 3 minutes.

In a small bowl, stir together the honey, smoked paprika, ⅛ teaspoon salt, and 1 teaspoon water. Transfer the lamb chops, roasted grapes, onions, and lemon halves to a large platter. Drizzle with the honey mixture and squeeze grilled lemon over everything.

CHANG'S STICKY BABY BACK RIBS

¼ cup soy sauce

3 tablespoons finely chopped peeled fresh ginger (from a 3-inch knob)

3 garlic cloves, coarsely chopped

2 teaspoons toasted sesame oil

½ cup hoisin sauce

3 tablespoons light or dark brown sugar

2 tablespoons dry sherry

1½ teaspoons Chinese five-spice powder

4 pounds baby back pork ribs (2 to 4 racks)

¼ cup honey

½ teaspoon chili flakes

2 scallions, thinly sliced on the bias, for serving

Chinese mustard for serving (optional)

Special equipment: extra-wide (18 inches) heavy-duty aluminum foil

KITCHEN WISDOM: Slicing Ribs

The meat of these tender ribs falls off the bone when just made; it's a messy, yet delectable affair. If you want to make them ahead, allow them to cool to room temperature, then cover tightly with foil and refrigerate for up to 3 days. Slice the ribs when cold, then, just before serving, warm them under the broiler and glaze. In addition to the convenience that making a meal ahead can offer, you'll also end up with more cleanly cut ribs, though either way you "slice" them, they are equally delish!

As I've mentioned, my Grandma Snazzy was a fabulous cook who loved to entertain. She was also a philanthropist and spent a good deal of time organizing events and fundraisers, which she often held in her home near the top of Mount Royal in Montreal. Between cooking for her family and hosting guests, she needed a hand at the stove, and for many years employed a talented Chinese chef named Chang. Chef Chang's skill, along with his love for the cooking of his homeland, instilled in my mom and her two brothers a deep appreciation for Chinese cuisine long before it was popular in Canada. Mom's penchant often led us, years later, to Toronto's vast Chinatown to feast on her favorite foods. Our family outings included samplings of dishes like *char siu bao* (which my family adopted as one of their many nicknames for me—along with Snippet—a term of endearment if you will; I learned in my twenties that it means "steamed pork bun"!), Peking duck with tender Chinese greens, and sticky sweet pork ribs. I, in turn, have Chef Chang to thank for teaching me to love and respect the complex and delicious food of China as much as I do. Chef Chang, wherever you may be, this recipe's for you.

Heat the oven to 300°F with the rack in the upper third. Line a 13 x 18-inch rimmed baking sheet with 1 (18-inch-wide) sheet of heavy-duty foil, leaving a 2 to 3-inch overhang on all sides.

In a blender, puree the soy sauce, ginger, garlic, and sesame oil until smooth. Transfer the mixture to a bowl and whisk in the hoisin, sugar, sherry, and five-spice powder.

Place the ribs on the prepared baking sheet. Set aside ½ cup of the hoisin mixture for the glaze. Brush the rest of the mixture over both sides of the ribs, then turn the ribs meaty-side down. Cover the pan tightly with foil. Bake until the ribs are very tender but not falling apart, about 3 hours.

Carefully remove the top piece of foil from the ribs. Let stand 15 minutes.

Before serving, combine the reserved sauce with the honey and chili flakes in a small saucepan. Bring to a simmer over medium-low heat, then reduce to low and cook, whisking to combine, until thickened, about 5 minutes. Line a second rimmed baking sheet with a clean sheet of foil. Transfer the ribs, meaty-side up, to the clean baking sheet (discard the fat and foil from first baking sheet).

Increase the oven temperature to broil with the rack 5 to 6 inches from the heat. Brush the ribs with the glaze, then broil until bubbling, 3 to 5 minutes. Top with the scallions and serve with Chinese mustard, if desired.

WEEKNIGHT SAUSAGE & SAUERKRAUT

1 pound small or medium red- or yellow-skinned new potatoes

⅓ pound slab bacon, cut into ½-inch batons

1 pound cooked smoked kielbasa, cut into 3-inch lengths crosswise, then cut in half lengthwise

1 medium yellow onion, thinly sliced (about 2 cups)

1 Granny Smith apple, cored and cut into ¼-inch cubes

2 teaspoons caraway seeds

1 dried bay leaf

Freshly ground black pepper

1 cup dry white wine

1 (32-ounce) jar sauerkraut, drained

6 ounces ¼-inch-thick good-quality deli ham, cut into 2-inch squares

Pumpernickel or European-style sunflower seed bread for serving

Assorted mustards for serving

During her year as a student in Europe, my mom discovered and later introduced us children to *choucroute garni*. From Alsace, the region in northeastern France that borders Germany and Switzerland, this is a hearty mix of pickled cabbage, sausage, ham, and potatoes that is cooked with white wine, onions, bay leaves, and garlic (and sometimes apples, cloves, and/or caraway seeds, too) and served with a dollop of mustard. I never attempted to make it at home until 2010, when, on the set of *Top Chef: Just Desserts*, acclaimed chef Hubert Keller—a regular *Top Chef* judge, *Top Chef Masters* finalist, and Alsace native—and I got into a long discussion about his love for the foods of his homeland. I wasn't surprised to hear that choucroute garni topped his list. I returned home inspired, and vowed to cook the dish for myself. Making the classic version is a bit of a project, with ingredients like pig's knuckles and rendered duck or goose fat, and several hours of braising involved. So I created a simplified take that captures its deep smoky flavors, but can be prepared easily on a weeknight with accessible, basic ingredients. When there's a chill in the air, it's as warming and comforting as it is delicious.

In a large, wide pot, cover the potatoes with salted cold water by 2 inches. Bring to a boil and cook until tender, 10 to 15 minutes. Drain, then transfer to a plate; let cool, then quarter.

Meanwhile, in a 6- to 8-quart Dutch oven or wide, heavy pot with lid, heat the bacon over medium heat, stirring occasionally, until the fat is rendered and the bacon is crisped on all sides, 7 to 9 minutes. Using a slotted spoon, transfer the bacon to a small bowl. Discard all but 1 tablespoon of the bacon fat from the pot.

Increase the heat to medium-high. Add the kielbasa pieces to the bacon fat, cut-side down, and cook until golden, about 3 minutes. Turn over and pile the sausages to one side of the pan. Add the onion, apple, caraway seeds, bay leaf, and a generous pinch of pepper. Cook, stirring occasionally, until the onion is softened, 5 to 7 minutes.

Add the wine; stir together the onion mixture and sausages, scraping up any brown bits from the bottom of the pot, then stir in the sauerkraut and bacon pieces. Reduce the heat to medium; cover and cook, stirring occasionally, until the flavors blend, about 10 minutes. Stir in the ham, cover, and cook for 1 minute more.

Remove and discard the bay leaf. Adjust the pepper to taste. Serve warm, with potatoes, bread, and mustards.

MY KINDA BURGER

Special Sauce

½ cup mayonnaise

1 tablespoon finely chopped shallot

2 teaspoons ketchup

1 tablespoon pickle juice (from the bread and butter pickle jar below)

½ teaspoon smoked paprika

¼ teaspoon garlic powder

¼ teaspoon hot sauce

Burgers

1⅔ pounds mixed ground meat as follows: ⅔ pound ground beef chuck, ½ pound ground brisket, and ½ pound boneless ground short rib; or 1⅔ pounds ground beef chuck (20% fat)

2 tablespoons Dijon mustard

2 large egg yolks

1 tablespoon plus 1 teaspoon rinsed and drained capers, coarsely chopped

2 tablespoons finely chopped shallot

¾ teaspoon Worcestershire sauce

½ teaspoon kosher salt

¼ teaspoon freshly ground black pepper

For Assembly

4 extra-large brioche, sesame seed, or potato buns, split

Ketchup

4 green leaf or romaine lettuce leaves, thick stems removed

1 large ripe tomato, sliced

Bread and butter pickle slices

¼ pound mild blue cheese (such as Maytag), crumbled (about ⅓ cup)

Real burger obsessives love to argue the merits of the classic American sandwich: thick or thin patty; mustard or ketchup; cheese or no cheese; brioche, potato, or sesame seed bun. And, of course, the blend of meat that grounds it (pun intended!). Generally, I'm a burger egalitarian, embracing all styles in full appreciation of this perfectly crafted food. When it comes down to making my own burgers at home, though—try as I might to vary my method—I always come back to this recipe. When I have time for a trip to my local butcher, I go for a blend of chuck, brisket, and short rib. I gently mix together the meat with mustard, capers, and Worcestershire sauce, shape into thick, generous patties (fair warning: large buns are a must here!) and grill them to juicy perfection. And then there's my special sauce, which I would never keep secret: Who am I to deny my friends and readers the unbridled pleasure of its deliciousness? One taste of this messy love of a burger, fully assembled with all the fixings, and I'm betting that it'll be your kinda burger, too.

For the special sauce: In a bowl, stir together all of the ingredients. Cover and chill until ready to use. (The sauce can be prepared up to 1 day ahead. Keep covered and chilled until ready to use.)

For the burgers: In a large bowl, use clean hands to gently stir together all of the ingredients. Divide the mixture into 4 equal portions. Gently shape one portion into a ball, then use your hands to gently flatten and shape the ball into a 4-inch-diameter, ¾-inch-thick patty. Transfer to a large plate. Repeat with the remaining portions.

Prepare a grill or grill pan for high heat. Grill the burgers, turning once, about 4 minutes per side for medium/medium-rare.

Meanwhile, grill or lightly toast the buns. Transfer the burgers to the 4 bottom buns. Dress each burger with ketchup, lettuce, tomato, pickles, blue cheese, and special sauce. Top with the top buns. Serve with any leftover special sauce on the side, and a stack of paper napkins!

My Kinda Burger, *page 149*

Party Time!
SNACKS & NIBBLES

CRUNCHY FRUIT & VEG WITH
CHILI & SUMAC 154

CRISPY CHICKPEAS WITH PISTACHIO DUKKAH 157

TWO QUICK PICKLES
Pickled Dilly Beans & Fennel 159
Spicy Pickled Pineapple 160

CORNMEAL-CRUSTED PICKLE CHIPS WITH
SMOKY MUSTARD MAYO 161

CHILI CHEESE TOAST 162

RENÉE'S CHOPPED LIVER 163

LATKE REUBENS 165

MY THREE FAVORITE DIPS
Hummus with Harissa Oil, Toasted Fennel Seeds, & Mint 167
Red Pepper, Pomegranate, & Walnut Dip 168
Creamy Herbed Goat Cheese with Za'atar 169

CRUNCHY FRUIT & VEG

with Chili & Sumac

1 English cucumber, cut into
½- by 3-inch sticks

4 large radishes, trimmed and
cut into eighths

1 large mango, peeled and cut
into ½- by 3-inch sticks

1 medium jicama, peeled and
cut into ½- by 3-inch sticks

1 large or 2 small limes

½ teaspoon flaky sea salt (such
as Maldon)

½ teaspoon chili powder

½ teaspoon sumac

2 teaspoons finely chopped
cilantro

Though I spent over a week in San Miguel de Allende, Mexico, to shoot *Top Chef*'s Season 12 finale in September 2014, I only had to be on set for three days, to work on elimination challenges (Padma and Tom handle Quickfires and kitchen walk-throughs). This left me plenty of time to explore the colonial city's winding streets and enchanting gardens, eat my weight in tacos, and drink lots and lots of good tequila. I spent hours poking around craft and furniture markets and scouting food market stalls, where vendors of everything from butchered meats, grilled corn, fresh chickpeas and avocados to spices and herbs of all kinds, congregated to sell their wares. My favorite street snack was *fruta con chile y limón:* fresh mango, cucumber, and jicama slices doused with just-squeezed lime juice and sprinkled with chili powder and salt. Neatly packed into a plastic bag for enjoying on the go, it quickly became my daily treat. At home now, whenever life calls for a plate of fruit or crudités, I put together one of these. Both the fruits and vegetables you choose and the blend of spices can be varied quite a bit: try sliced bananas, fresh coconut, celery, or bell peppers, as well as Aleppo or black pepper, and fresh mint or tarragon.

Arrange the fruit and vegetables on a large platter.

Grate all of the lime zest from the lime and cut the lime in half crosswise.

In a small bowl, combine the lime zest, salt, chili powder, sumac, and cilantro.

Squeeze the juice from the lime halves over the fruit and vegetables, then sprinkle generously with the salt mixture. Serve immediately.

CRISPY CHICKPEAS

with Pistachio Dukkah

3 tablespoons shelled unsalted pistachios

2 (15-ounce) cans chickpeas, rinsed and drained

2 tablespoons extra-virgin olive oil

Kosher salt

Freshly ground black pepper

2 teaspoons sesame seeds

1 teaspoon coriander seeds

½ teaspoon cumin seeds

½ teaspoon fennel seeds

½ teaspoon freshly grated lemon zest

Crispy chickpeas, simply tossed with salt or dressed up in more refined ways, make a great party or anytime snack. Here I make them with homemade *dukkah*, a savory Egyptian blend of nuts and spices. I've been a fan of dukkah since I first tasted it during a weeklong trip to Egypt when I was 18, at the end of a summer spent working on an Israeli kibbutz. While it often contains hazelnuts or pistachios, plus sesame seeds, coriander, cumin, and salt, rules are loose when it comes to nut types and lots of other seeds can be swapped in or added. The addictive blend is often stirred into olive oil for dipping torn pieces of warm bread, but is also sprinkled over anything from yogurt to scrambled eggs, roasted veggies to salads. (If you want to double or triple the dukkah here, you can do all that, too!) The chickpeas are great alongside cheese, charcuterie, and olives, served with cocktails or wine.

Heat the oven to 400°F with the rack in the middle.

Spread the nuts on a rimmed baking sheet; toast in the oven until fragrant and lightly golden, 4 to 5 minutes. Let cool completely.

Meanwhile, on a second rimmed baking sheet, pat the chickpeas between two layers of paper towels, repeating as necessary until they are very dry. Discard any loose skins.

Toss the chickpeas with the oil, ¾ teaspoon salt, and a generous pinch of pepper, then spread in a single layer. Roast, stirring every 10 minutes, until golden and crispy, 50 to 55 minutes (chickpeas may pop; this is OK).

Meanwhile, in a medium, dry skillet, over medium-low heat, toast the sesame seeds, stirring frequently, for 5 minutes. Add the coriander, cumin, and fennel seeds and toast, stirring frequently, until the mixture is fragrant and the sesame seeds are golden, about 3 minutes more. Transfer to a plate and let cool completely.

In the bowl of a food processor, combine the cooled nuts, seed mixture, ¼ teaspoon salt, and generous pinch pepper. Pulse the mixture just until coarsely chopped (do not let it become a paste). This is your dukkah.

When the chickpeas are ready, immediately toss with the dukkah, lemon zest, and ⅛ teaspoon salt. Serve warm or at room temperature.

These chickpeas are best eaten fresh from the oven, but can be kept, covered and at room temperature, for up to 3 days.

TWO
Quick Pickles

Every summer when I was growing up, I looked forward to making pickles with my dad, using the bushels of Kirby cucumbers he brought home from the market. His recipe for full sour dills is known by our family and friends as the very best around (I included it in my first book, *Talking with My Mouth Full*). Dad's pickles take a month to prepare and ferment; I make them in the summer, when time allows. But being such a pickle lover I also make a variety of quick pickles all year long. This easy and almost immediate (in pickling terms) way to infuse fruits and vegetables with savory, spicy, vinegary flavors can be done with basic kitchen tools and simple pantry spices, and takes less than one day. The two recipes here show both the flexibility and ease of this fun technique.

PICKLED DILLY BEANS & FENNEL

Kosher salt

1 pound green beans, trimmed

1 small fennel bulb, preferably with fronds

1 tablespoon coriander seeds

2½ cups distilled white vinegar

1 tablespoon plus 2 teaspoons sugar

2 garlic cloves, gently smashed and peeled

2 teaspoons black peppercorns

2 dried bay leaves

1 small bunch fresh dill

While these crisp, bright beauties are great on their own, they're also the perfect companions to cheese and charcuterie.

In a large pot of salted boiling water, cook the beans for 2 minutes, then drain and run under cold water to cool.

Pick the fronds from the fennel; set aside. Remove the stems and discard, or save for another use. Thinly slice the bulb lengthwise. Divide the beans and fennel slices among two 1-quart heatproof jars with lids.

In a medium, dry saucepan over medium heat, toast the coriander, occasionally shaking the pan back and forth, until the seeds are fragrant and lightly toasted, 3 to 4 minutes. Remove the pan from the heat and add the vinegar, sugar, garlic, peppercorns, bay leaves, 1 tablespoon kosher salt, and 2 cups water. Bring the mixture just to a boil over medium-high heat, then reduce to a simmer and cook, stirring occasionally, for 2 minutes.

Transfer the brine and spices to a liquid measuring cup, then pour into the jars, covering the vegetables completely and filling the jars up to ½ inch from the rim. Discard any leftover brine. Let cool to room temperature. Add the dill and the fennel fronds if using, tucking the sprigs under the brine and into the pickles a bit. Cover the jars with the lids. Refrigerate at least 24 hours before serving.

The pickles keep, covered and refrigerated, for up to 10 days.

KITCHEN WISDOM: Cutting Fruit and Veg

The safest way to cut round fruits and vegetables like fennel, is to first cut the ingredient in half, then turn it flat-side down before further cutting. This keeps it stationary while you work.

SPICY PICKLED PINEAPPLE

1 large pineapple, peeled and cut into ½-inch-thick wedges (about 6 cups; see Note)

½ teaspoon red pepper flakes

2 tablespoons coriander seeds

2 cups distilled white vinegar

1 cup sugar

1½ teaspoons kosher salt

1 garlic clove, gently smashed and peeled

20 leafy cilantro sprigs

Note: To make pineapple wedges, cut the peeled pineapple crosswise into ½-inch-thick slices. Cut each slice into 8 to 10 wedges. The core is edible, tasty, and nutritious; it will soften during the pickling process.

These bright spicy pickles are delicious straight out of the jar. I also love them tossed into salads or wraps, and served alongside fried chicken.

Divide the pineapple and pepper flakes among two 1-quart heatproof jars or containers with lids.

In a medium, dry saucepan over medium heat, toast the coriander, occasionally shaking the pan back and forth, until the seeds are fragrant and lightly toasted, 3 to 4 minutes. Remove the pan from the heat. Add the vinegar, sugar, salt, garlic, and 1⅔ cups water. Bring the mixture just to a boil over medium-high heat, then reduce to a simmer and cook, stirring occasionally, for 2 minutes.

Transfer the brine and spices to a liquid measuring cup, then pour into the jars, covering the pineapple mixture completely and filling the jars up to ½ inch from the rim. Discard any leftover brine. Let stand at room temperature until cool, then add the cilantro, tucking the sprigs under the brine and into the pickles a bit. Cover with the lids. Refrigerate at least 24 hours before serving.

The pickles keep, covered and refrigerated, for up to 10 days.

CORNMEAL-CRUSTED PICKLE CHIPS with Smoky Mustard Mayo

Smoky Mustard Mayo

½ cup mayonnaise

2 teaspoons fresh lemon juice

2 teaspoons grainy Dijon mustard

¼ teaspoon smoked paprika

⅛ teaspoon cayenne pepper

Fried Pickles

½ cup fine cornmeal

½ cup rice flour

Kosher salt

¾ cup cold water

1 large egg white

1 quart neutral oil, such as canola or grapeseed (for frying)

8 medium dill pickles, cut crosswise on the bias into ¼-inch-thick slices

Special equipment: A candy/fry thermometer

The only thing that makes a great pickle even greater is a dip in the deep fryer. I was reminded of this fact in Charleston, South Carolina, on a day off from shooting Season 14 of *Top Chef*. Jeremy, Dahlia, and I hopped in the car and headed northeast on Bypass 17 to See Wee, a family-owned restaurant with checkered tablecloths and a nearly exhaustive menu of fried fish and all the fixins'. While we waited for our she-crab soup, shrimp and grits, and hush puppies, the owner plunked down a plate of crispy pickles, fresh from the fryer. The plate was clean before I could get the question out of my mouth: "Why don't we make these at home?" Back in New York, after a bit of trial and error, I discovered that a combination of fine cornmeal and rice flour, mixed with a little salt, water, and a lightly beaten egg white makes the perfect crunchy coating. My smoky mustard mayo is an excellent foil for the tangy pickle and adds just a hint of heat.

For the mustard mayo: In a medium bowl, mix together all the ingredients. Cover and chill until ready to use.

For the pickles: In a large bowl, whisk together the cornmeal, rice flour, and a pinch of salt. Using a rubber spatula, stir in the water until well combined. In a separate large bowl, beat the egg white to stiff peaks, then gently fold into the cornmeal mixture to form a loose batter.

In a large heavy skillet, heat ½ inch oil to 375°F.

Working in batches, dip the pickle slices, one at a time, into the batter, coating completely and letting the excess batter drip off (stir the batter between batches if it starts to separate). Fry the coated pickles, turning once or twice, until golden, about 2 minutes total (adjust the heat as necessary to keep the oil around 375°F as you fry). Using a slotted spoon or tongs, transfer the fried pickles to a paper towel-lined plate to drain. Season with salt. Pile the fried pickles onto a platter and serve with the mustard mayo for dipping.

CHILI CHEESE TOAST

4 slices whole-wheat sandwich bread

1 tablespoon unsalted butter, melted

1½ cups (4½ ounces) grated Monterey Jack or sharp cheddar cheese

4 teaspoons finely chopped seeded jalapeño, Fresno, or serrano chili

1 tablespoon finely chopped peeled fresh ginger

Kosher salt

Freshly ground black pepper

In the early years of *Top Chef,* we judges took forever to come to unanimous decisions as to which contestants should stay and which should go. Conversations often dragged into the wee hours of the morning. These days, though things move along more quickly, we still engage in long, lively debates that inevitably require fueling. While craft services provides plenty of basic nibbles, sometimes we need something more substantial. During Season 7, in Washington, D.C., Padma introduced me to her favorite late-night snack: sharp cheese and pickled or fresh chilies melted over toast. I had to know more! She explained that, as a child in India, she often ate this popular open-faced sandwich. Recently, at a fashionable Indian restaurant in London, I was tickled to see it on the menu and inspired to make a version of my own. My addition of fresh ginger lends both floral and peppery notes.

Heat the oven to 425°F.

Place the bread slices on a baking sheet and brush the tops with the butter. Bake until just golden and starting to crisp, 5 to 6 minutes.

Meanwhile, in a bowl, toss together the cheese, chili, ginger, and a generous pinch each of salt and pepper.

Remove the baking sheet from the oven; increase the heat to broil with the oven rack 5 to 6 inches from the heat source. Sprinkle the cheese mixture evenly over the toasted bread slices, then broil until the cheese is bubbling and lightly golden, 2 to 3 minutes. Cut the toasts on the diagonal and serve warm.

RENÉE'S CHOPPED LIVER

1 large egg

½ pound shallots

1 tablespoon unsalted butter

Kosher salt

Freshly ground black pepper

2 tablespoons schmaltz (see Sources, page 241) or 1 tablespoon canola oil plus 1 tablespoon butter

2 garlic cloves, finely chopped

1 pound chicken livers, trimmed and rinsed (see Kitchen Wisdom, page 95)

½ cup unbleached all-purpose flour

¼ cup sherry, port, brandy, or dry red wine

1 tablespoon Dijon mustard

1 tablespoon coarsely chopped fresh parsley

⅓ cup thinly sliced cornichon pickles for serving

Crusty bread, water crackers, or matzo for serving

I can't remember a time in my childhood when a Kelly-green ceramic serving dish, filled with my mom's chopped liver, didn't occupy a regular spot in our fridge. My brothers and I simply accepted it as a constant in our lives, even if we rarely ate from it. Although it would be years before I developed a taste for the iconic Jewish dish, I was always comforted by the sweet, rich aromas that emanated from the kitchen when my mom prepared it, carefully cleaning the fresh livers before sautéing them with onions and a little Madeira or sherry. Years later, as a line cook in New York, I was excited to see the dish on casual bistro menus, sometimes blended with a little butter or cream (or both) and dressed up as a mousse (more of a French preparation than a typical Jewish one, though equally enticing). When I called my mom for her recipe, she rattled it off from the top of her head without a moment's hesitation. I add a little mustard and extra fresh herbs, but otherwise leave it as is. With such perfection, there's little reason to fuss.

Place the egg in a small pot of cold water and bring to a boil over medium-high heat. Allow the egg to boil for 1 minute, then cover the pot, remove from the heat, and let stand for 8 minutes. Drain, then submerge the egg in a bowl of ice water and let stand 1 minute. Peel and coarsely chop; set aside.

Finely chop enough of the shallots to yield ⅓ cup; set aside. Thinly slice the remaining shallots. In a medium skillet, melt the butter over medium heat. Add the sliced shallots; reduce the heat to medium-low and cook, stirring occasionally, until very tender, golden, and caramelized, 45 to 50 minutes. Remove from the heat and season with ⅛ teaspoon each of salt and pepper. Set aside.

While the shallots are caramelizing, in a large skillet, heat the schmaltz over medium heat until melted. Add the chopped shallots and cook for 1 minute, then add the garlic and cook until softened, about 2 minutes more. Meanwhile, dredge the livers in the flour, shaking off any excess, then season generously with salt. Add the livers to the pan and cook, turning once or twice, until just cooked through and barely pink in the center, 6 to 8 minutes. Reserving the skillet, transfer the livers to a food processor and let stand until slightly cooled.

Meanwhile, add the sherry to the skillet and simmer over medium heat, scraping up any brown bits, until reduced to about 1 tablespoon, 1 to 2 minutes. Transfer to the food processor, scraping to get all the bits from the pan. Add the hard-boiled egg, mustard, parsley, and ¼ teaspoon pepper. Pulse until the mixture is mostly smooth, but still textured. Season to taste with salt and pepper then transfer to a bowl. Cover the surface of the liver with plastic wrap and refrigerate until chilled, at least 1 hour or up to 1 day.

Just before serving, season the chopped liver again. Serve with the caramelized shallots, sliced cornichons, and crusty bread or crackers alongside.

LATKE REUBENS

Slaw

2 tablespoons apple cider vinegar

1 tablespoon spicy brown mustard

1½ teaspoons light or dark brown sugar

¼ teaspoon kosher salt

Freshly ground black pepper

2 tablespoons canola oil

1½ cups shredded green cabbage (about a quarter of a small head)

1 Granny Smith apple, cut into matchsticks

¾ cup thinly sliced red onion (about half small onion)

2 celery ribs, thinly sliced

2 tablespoons chopped fresh dill

Dressing

¾ cup sour cream

¼ cup ketchup

1 tablespoon prepared white horseradish

1 teaspoon hot sauce

Latkes

3½ pounds baking potatoes, peeled and quartered lengthwise

1 large yellow onion, peeled and cut into 8 wedges

½ cup unbleached all-purpose flour

2 large eggs, lightly beaten

2 tablespoons chopped fresh dill

¼ teaspoon baking powder

Kosher salt

Canola oil for frying

To Assemble

½ pound thinly sliced pastrami, slices cut in half crosswise

Chopped fresh dill

I came up with this little nosh for a holiday episode of *The Feed*, my show with chef Marcus Samuelsson and comedian Max Silvestri, in 2014. Combining my family's cherished latke recipe with the fillings of a classic Reuben sandwich, I created the ultimate Hanukkah deli delight. A perfect way to celebrate the Festival of Lights, it's also a killer Super Bowl party snack or fun accompaniment to cocktails any time of year.

For the slaw: In a large bowl, stir together the vinegar, mustard, sugar, salt, and a generous pinch of pepper. Slowly whisk in the oil until well combined.

Add the cabbage, apple, onion, celery, and dill to the dressing; toss thoroughly to combine. Adjust the seasoning to taste. Let the slaw stand at room temperature for 30 minutes before serving.

For the dressing: In a medium bowl, stir together all of the ingredients. Adjust the hot sauce to taste. The dressing can be refrigerated in an airtight container for up to 2 weeks.

For the latkes: Set a large strainer over a bowl. In a food processor fitted with the shredding disk, shred the potatoes and onion in batches. Add each batch to the strainer and let stand for 5 minutes, then squeeze dry. Pour off the liquid and rinse the bowl, then add the shredded potato mixture. Stir in the flour, eggs, dill, baking powder, and 1½ teaspoons salt. Scrape the mixture back into the strainer and set it over the bowl again; let stand for another 5 minutes.

In a large skillet, heat ¼ inch of canola oil over medium-high heat until shimmering. Working in batches, spoon a scant ¼ cup of the potato mixture into the hot oil for each latke, pressing slightly to flatten. Fry over moderate heat, turning once, until the latkes are golden and crisp on both sides, about 7 minutes. Drain the latkes on a paper towel–lined baking sheet. Season well with salt.

To assemble: Spread about 1 teaspoon of the dressing on each latke. Top with a folded slice of pastrami and a heaping tablespoon of the slaw. Garnish with dill and serve.

KITCHEN WISDOM: Grating Potatoes

There's much debate regarding best practices when it comes to making potato latkes. Honoring age-old tradition, many recipes call for box-grated potatoes. In my experience, using the shredding disk of a food processor results in longer, thinner strands that make for lighter, crispier pancakes.

MY Three Favorite Dips

Every party needs a good dip. Or three! Here are a few I make often, both for entertaining and casual snacking at home. I like to set them out with assorted crackers and crudités; they're also great as spreads on sandwiches and toast. As with most homemade dips, these are best within a day or two of blending, but will likely disappear much sooner. If making ahead, keep covered and refrigerated, leaving time to let the dips come to room temperature before serving—the flavors are boldest and brightest that way.

HUMMUS

with Harissa Oil, Toasted Fennel Seeds, & Mint

½ teaspoon fennel seeds

1 (15.5-ounce) can chickpeas, rinsed and drained

3 tablespoons well-stirred tahini

2 tablespoons fresh lemon juice

1 small garlic clove, thinly sliced

¾ teaspoon kosher salt

¼ cup ice water

1 tablespoon extra-virgin olive oil

1 teaspoon harissa (see Sources, page 240)

½ teaspoon freshly grated lemon zest

2 teaspoons thinly sliced fresh mint

Hummus, the popular Middle Eastern puree made from chickpeas and tahini, is one of the easiest dishes to prepare at home. With just a few pantry basics it can be whipped up in minutes, no cooking required. Of course decent supermarket versions abound, but nothing compares to the deep flavor and silky texture you can get when you make it yourself. Often, it's the ingredients that are drizzled or sprinkled on top that give the classic dip unique character. Here I use a spicy oil, made from a simple store-bought harissa paste, plus toasted fennel seeds and lots of fresh mint.

In a small, dry skillet, warm the fennel seeds over medium heat, accasionally shaking the pan back and forth, until fragrant and lightly golden, 1 to 2 minutes. Let cool slightly, then coarsely crush with a mortar and pestle, or by rocking the bottom of a heavy skillet back and forth over the seeds. Set aside.

In the bowl of a food processor, combine the chickpeas, tahini, lemon juice, garlic, and salt. Puree until combined. With the machine running, drizzle in the ice water. Continue to puree until you have a very smooth and creamy hummus, about 3 minutes.

In a small bowl, whisk together the oil, harissa, and lemon zest. Spread the hummus onto a serving plate. Use the back of a large spoon to swirl and create a little dip in the middle. Drizzle with the harissa oil, sprinkle with the mint and toasted fennel seeds, and serve.

KITCHEN WISDOM: Creamy Hummus

Chef Michael Solomonov, my trusted friend and Israeli food guru, claims the key to the best homemade hummus is using dried chickpeas, soaked and boiled until very tender and starting to fall apart, then draining and pureeing them for longer than may seem necessary. Heed his advice. The long whipping time makes the final product extremely airy, and hence delectably creamy and light. I call for canned chickpeas here to save time, but of course using the dried version is great, if you prefer.

RED PEPPER, POMEGRANATE, & WALNUT DIP

2 cups small torn pieces rustic whole-wheat bread (from about 1½ slices; see Note)

½ cup walnuts, coarsely chopped

1 (12-ounce) jar roasted red bell peppers, drained

2 tablespoons pomegranate molasses (see Sources, page 241)

1 tablespoon plus 1 teaspoon tomato paste

1 tablespoon fresh lemon juice

¾ teaspoon kosher salt

½ teaspoon ground cumin

⅛ teaspoon red pepper flakes

¼ cup extra-virgin olive oil, plus more for serving

Pomegranate seeds for serving (optional)

Torn fresh basil or mint for serving (optional)

Note: You can use ¾ cup coarse plain breadcrumbs, like panko (Japanese breadcrumbs), in place of the toasted bread. If you are using crumbs, they do not need to be toasted. Gluten-free bread or breadcrumbs can also be used.

I first visited the Middle Eastern spice stores, butchers, and bakeries that line Atlantic Avenue in Brooklyn when I worked for Jeffrey Steingarten at *Vogue* magazine. He had sent me to the revered emporium Sahadi's, on a hunt for rare dried chilies. I returned to the office triumphant: chilies in hand but also loaded with extra treasures, including olives in every shape, size, and color; silky dips; and savory stuffed pastries. One of the most exciting discoveries I made that day was *muhammara*, a sweet and tangy Syrian dip of walnuts, red peppers, breadcrumbs, and pomegranate molasses, that I've since taken to making at home. If you have a mortar and pestle, try it in place of the food processor. In either case, just be sure not to overblend the mixture; the rustic texture is part of its charm.

Heat the oven to 350°F. Spread the bread pieces on a rimmed baking sheet and toast in the oven for 2 minutes. Add the walnuts and continue toasting until the bread is dry and lightly golden and the nuts are fragrant and lightly toasted, about 7 minutes more. Transfer the bread and nuts to a plate and let cool completely.

Set aside about 1 tablespoon of the toasted nuts. In the bowl of a food processor, combine the remaining nuts and toasted bread with the red peppers, pomegranate molasses, tomato paste, lemon juice, salt, cumin, and pepper flakes; puree until well combined. With the machine running, add the oil in a slow and steady stream until you have a coarse mix.

Transfer the spread to a serving bowl. To serve, drizzle with additional oil and sprinkle with the reserved nuts, the pomegranate seeds, and basil or mint if using.

CREAMY HERBED GOAT CHEESE

with Za'atar

4 ounces mild soft goat cheese, at room temperature

¼ cup finely chopped mixed fresh tender herbs, such as basil, chives, tarragon, mint, dill, and parsley

¼ teaspoon kosher salt

⅛ teaspoon cayenne pepper

⅛ teaspoon za'atar, plus more for serving

⅓ cup heavy cream, well-chilled

¼ teaspoon fresh lemon juice

Extra-virgin olive oil for serving

¼ teaspoon toasted sesame seeds for serving (optional)

This dip takes inspiration from a couple of classic spreads I especially love. The first is tzatziki, the Greek cucumber-yogurt dip that's generally heavy on the garlic and dill, and sometimes includes vinegar or lemon juice. The second is Boursin, a packaged creamy Gournay cheese blended with garlic and fine herbs. I like using tart soft goat cheese as a base, then add whatever tender herbs I have in the fridge, plus a little cayenne, za'atar, and lemon juice. A touch of whipped cream lightens up the mixture, and a sprinkle of sesame seeds gives it texture and depth as a final touch.

In a medium bowl, mix together the cheese, herbs, salt, cayenne, and za'atar.

In a second medium bowl, beat the cream to soft peaks. Fold the whipped cream into the cheese mixture, then fold in the lemon juice.

Spread the mixture on a serving plate, drizzle with olive oil and sprinkle with za'atar and sesame seeds, if using.

Red Pepper, Pomegranate, & Walnut Dip, *page 168*

Creamy Herbed Goat Cheese with Za'atar, *page 169*

**Hummus with
Harissa Oil,
Toasted Fennel
Seeds, & Mint,**
page 167

Drinks

THREE HOMEMADE SODAS
Toasted Coconut–Lime Soda 176
Cherry-Vanilla Soda • Apple-Ginger Soda 177

WATERMELON LIME AGUA FRESCA 179

GOLDEN MILK–MANGO LASSI 180

SALAD IN A GLASS 181

CARDAMOM-WALNUT DATE SHAKE 184

◆

THREE

Homemade Sodas

When my brother Alan turned 13, he was given a soda maker as a gift. I was seven at the time and—between the bubbles and the canisters and the syrupy packets that came in all sorts of cola and fruit flavors—I was completely enthralled by its magic. Alan and I would pull things like mango nectar and maple syrup from the fridge and stir them together with the drink mixes to create our own custom flavors. These days, my homemade sodas are much more grown-up, and far healthier, too! I start by making pure, all-natural syrups, then a quick stir into chilled soda water is all that's needed to complete them. The syrups keep well, covered and refrigerated for up to 2 weeks, and they can be doubled or tripled, if you want to prepare them for a crowd. They are fantastic mixed into cocktails and add a little extra dimension to fruit juices as well.

From left to right: **Cherry-Vanilla Soda,**
page 177; **Apple-Ginger Soda,** *page 177;*
Toasted Coconut–Lime Soda, *page 176*

TOASTED COCONUT–LIME SODA

Syrup
1 cup unsweetened coconut chips
½ cup sugar
⅛ teaspoon kosher salt

Soda
Fresh lime juice
Ice cubes
Chilled club soda or seltzer
Lime wedges, for serving

The combination of tropical coconut and zesty lime is unlike any flavor I've been able to find in a bottle or can, and makes this bubbly beverage one of my favorites. Very fresh coconut chips may leave a touch of oily residue in the syrup after the solids are strained, but they also lend the best flavor.

For the syrup: In a medium saucepan, over medium-low heat, toast the coconut, stirring frequently, until golden, 5 to 7 minutes. Add 2 cups water, stir in the sugar and salt, and increase the heat to high. Bring the mixture to a boil, stirring occasionally to dissolve the sugar. Boil until the mixture is syrupy and reduced to ½ cup, about 12 to 14 minutes. Remove from the heat and let cool completely, 15 to 20 minutes. Strain the syrup through a fine-mesh sieve into a bowl, pressing gently but firmly on the solids to extract as much syrup as possible; discard the solids. Makes about ½ cup. The syrup can be used immediately or kept covered and refrigerated for up to 2 weeks.

To make one drink: In an 8-ounce glass, stir together 1 tablespoon of the syrup and ½ teaspoon lime juice. Top with ice and ½ cup chilled club soda or seltzer. Stir once to combine. Garnish with a lime wedge and serve.

CHERRY-VANILLA SODA

Syrup

2½ cups frozen pitted dark cherries, finely chopped (about 10 ounces)

¼ cup plus 2 tablespoons sugar

½ teaspoon coarsely ground black pepper

⅛ teaspoon kosher salt

½ teaspoon pure vanilla extract

Soda

Ice cubes

Chilled club soda or seltzer

Whole thawed frozen pitted dark cherries for serving

Black pepper and vanilla give this fruity soda a bit of complexity and a grown-up touch, without being too upscale for the kids.

For the syrup: Stir together the chopped cherries, sugar, pepper, salt, and ¾ cup water in a small saucepan. Bring to an active simmer over medium heat and cook until thick and syrupy, about 15 minutes. Strain the syrup through a fine-mesh sieve into a bowl, pressing gently but firmly on the solids and scraping the bottom of the sieve to extract as much syrup as possible; discard the solids. Stir in the vanilla and let cool completely, 15 to 20 minutes. Makes about ⅔ cup. The syrup can be used immediately or kept covered and refrigerated for up to 2 weeks.

To make one drink: Fill an 8-ounce glass with ice. Add 2 tablespoons syrup and top with ½ cup chilled club soda or seltzer. Stir once to combine. Garnish with 1 or 2 whole cherries and serve.

APPLE-GINGER SODA

Syrup

2 cups apple cider

¼ cup coarsely chopped peeled fresh ginger (from 2½-inch knob)

2 tablespoons sugar

Pinch kosher salt

Soda

Ice cubes

Chilled club soda or seltzer

Apple slices for serving

Tart with a hint of spice, this cider soda is a refreshing fall and winter pick-me-up.

For the syrup: Whisk together all of the syrup ingredients in a small saucepan, then bring to an active simmer over medium-high heat. Simmer until the mixture is reduced to ⅔ cup, 25 to 30 minutes. Remove from the heat and let cool completely, 15 to 20 minutes. Strain through a fine-mesh sieve into a bowl, pressing gently but firmly on the solids to extract as much syrup as possible; discard the solids. Makes ⅔ cup. The syrup can be used immediately or kept covered and refrigerated for up to 2 weeks.

To make one drink: Fill an 8-ounce glass with ice. Add 2 tablespoons syrup and top with ½ cup chilled club soda or seltzer. Stir once to combine. Garnish with an apple slice and serve.

WATERMELON LIME AGUA FRESCA

5 cups coarsely chopped seeded peeled watermelon (from a 3½-pound watermelon)

½ English cucumber, peeled and cut into ½-inch cubes (about 1 cup), plus sliced rounds for serving

¼ cup plus 1 tablespoon fresh lime juice

1 tablespoon sugar

1½ teaspoons packed coarsely chopped fresh tarragon leaves, plus sprigs for serving

Pinch cayenne pepper (optional)

1 cup cold water

Ice cubes

Lime wedges for serving

KITCHEN WISDOM: Adding Booze

Turn this virgin drink into a killer cocktail with a splash of tequila, vodka, or gin.

This thirst-quenching blend of watermelon, cucumber, and lime is quick to prepare and a great drink to make in a big batch for a summer party. The unexpected addition of tarragon lends a subtle anise note that makes the whole concoction sing.

In a blender, puree the watermelon, cucumber, lime juice, sugar, tarragon leaves, and cayenne pepper, if using, until very smooth. Strain the mixture through a fine-mesh sieve into a large pitcher; discard the solids. Add the water and stir well. Serve over ice with cucumber slices, lime wedges, and tarragon sprigs.

Agua fresca keeps, covered and refrigerated, for up to 1 day. Stir well before serving.

Aguas frescas, *Spanish for "fresh waters," are refreshing, non-alcoholic drinks made from fresh fruit, flowers, grains, or seeds and simply blended with sugar and water. Common in Latin America and the Caribbean, in recent years they've gained a significant North American fan base, too.*

GOLDEN MILK–MANGO LASSI

2 tablespoons unsweetened
coconut flakes

1½ cups plain low-fat yogurt
(see Note)

1 ripe red mango, peeled and
diced (about 1½ cups); or
1½ cups frozen cubed mango

½ cup well-shaken unsweetened
coconut milk

2 tablespoons finely chopped
peeled fresh ginger (from a
1½-inch knob)

½ teaspoon ground turmeric

⅜ teaspoon kosher salt

¼ teaspoon freshly ground
black pepper

⅛ teaspoon ground cinnamon

4 to 6 ice cubes (about ¾ cup)

1 tablespoon chopped unsalted
shelled pistachios

Note: *I love the way that low-fat
yogurt lightens up this rich drink,
but any sort of plain yogurt
works well. If you're using a
thicker Greek-style yogurt, add
a splash of chilled water or extra
coconut milk to achieve the
desired drinkable consistency.*

Tinkering in the kitchen one day with two of my favorite classic Indian drinks, I came up with this striking, refreshing hybrid. It combines lassi, a cooling yogurt beverage, with golden milk, a gently spiced and brightly colored tea that has developed something of a cult following in Western wellness circles in recent years, due to its inclusion of the super-spice turmeric, which is said to offer myriad health benefits. While I can't promise this drink will cure what ails you, I can tell you this: The lightly sweet tropical flavors of mango and coconut, accented with spices and gingery notes, are delicious and invigorating.

In a small, dry skillet over medium-low heat, toast the coconut flakes, occasionally shaking the pan back and forth, until the coconut is lightly fragrant and golden, about 5 minutes. Remove from the heat and let cool.

In a blender, puree the yogurt with the mango, coconut milk, ginger, turmeric, salt, pepper, cinnamon, and ice until well blended and frothy. Divide the lassi among four glasses. Serve cold, topped with the cooled toasted coconut flakes and chopped pistachios.

SALAD IN A GLASS

1 small avocado, halved and pitted

Up to 1 cup ice water, divided

2 cups cubed peeled fresh pineapple

1 unpeeled English cucumber, cut into 2-inch pieces

¼ cup packed fresh mint leaves

2 tablespoons fresh lime juice

2 tablespoons finely chopped peeled fresh ginger (from a 1½-inch knob)

Kosher salt

4 cups loosely packed roughly chopped kale (3 to 4 large leaves, stemmed)

This emerald energizer is packed with kale—but it's not overly vegetal, like some green juices are. Pineapple, ginger, and cucumber lend bright peppery melon notes with just a hint of sweetness, while avocado adds body. You don't need a juicer or any other fancy equipment to make it; a basic blender does the job perfectly.

Scoop the flesh from the avocado into a blender. Add ¼ cup of the ice water, the pineapple, cucumber, mint, lime juice, ginger, and ¼ teaspoon salt. Puree to combine. Add the kale and ½ cup more ice water and puree until smooth. Add more ice water, up to ¼ cup, to thin to desired consistency. Adjust the seasoning to taste.

Serve the juice immediately or keep chilled in the refrigerator for 1 hour, which cools and concentrates the flavors, making it even more refreshing. The juice keeps, covered and refrigerated, for up to 3 days.

Salad in a Glass, *page 181*

CARDAMOM-WALNUT DATE SHAKE

½ cup pitted dates, coarsely chopped

2 tablespoons walnut pieces

Scant ⅛ teaspoon ground cardamom

⅛ teaspoon kosher salt

Pinch ground cinnamon, plus more for serving

¼ cup cold water, plus more if needed

1 cup vanilla ice cream

¼ cup whole milk

4 to 6 ice cubes (about ¾ cup)

In the early aughts, I worked for *Vogue* magazine's esteemed food critic, Jeffrey Steingarten, as his editorial assistant. Among the countless great food lessons I learned over the course of our two years together was a deep respect for date shakes. One day, upon returning from a trip to Southern California's Coachella Valley—a desert region where more than 90 percent of the world's dates are grown—Jeffrey declared he was in love with the drink, and would make it the subject of his next article. We set about mastering a date shake recipe, fiddling with the ratio of vanilla ice cream to sticky sweet fruit, until we landed on the perfect balance. Years later, on my first of what would be many trips to the valley, I finally had a chance to taste the shake at the source, and was reminded how decadent and special it is. When I make date shakes at home, I toss in walnuts and a touch of spice for added dimension. Not sure Jeffrey would approve, but I can attest that it makes these fabled shakes even more enchanting.

Place the dates, walnuts, cardamom, salt, cinnamon, and water in a blender; blend, adding cold water by the tablespoon if needed (up to 2 tablespoons total), to form a coarse paste. Add the ice cream, milk, and ice; blend until smooth. Divide between two glasses and serve with an additional pinch of cinnamon on top if desired.

Drink Drinks

MAPLE BERRY MUDDLER 188

THE GAIL 189

CHARRED GRAPEFRUIT MEZCALITA 190

JERKALADA 192

THE NILOU 193

PICKLE JUICE MARTINI 197

KING OF THE JUNGLE 198

BITTERSWEET HOT CHOCOLATE WITH
BOURBON MARSHMALLOWS 201

◆

MAPLE BERRY MUDDLER

1 cup mixed fresh berries (raspberries, blueberries, blackberries), plus extra for serving

1½ ounces (3 tablespoons) pure maple syrup

2 ounces (¼ cup) fresh lemon juice

4 ounces (½ cup) bourbon

Ice cubes

2 pinches freshly grated lemon zest for serving

Special equipment: cocktail shaker

In addition to the fact that he's one of my favorite chefs, Hugh Acheson—a fellow *Top Chef* judge and the brains and brawn behind many exceptional restaurants, including 5 and 10 in Athens, Georgia—and I have something in common: We're both Canadian. Although he hails from Ottawa and I'm from Toronto, we share a love for our home country and one of its most delectable commodities, maple syrup. At the Food & Wine Classic in Aspen a few years ago, Hugh and I did a cooking demo that highlighted the ingredient. He made duck breasts with a maple gastrique, and pork belly with a maple–apple cider vinegar glaze. I baked a maple-berry tarte tatin and, in Hugh's honor, created this cocktail, which has since become one of my favorites. It's strong and just sweet enough—a little bit of Canada muddled with the American South. Just like Hugh!

In the cocktail shaker, muddle the berries with the maple syrup and lemon juice. Add the bourbon, then fill the shaker with ice cubes and shake vigorously until the outside of the shaker is very cold, about 30 seconds. Fill two rocks glasses with ice. Strain the cocktail into the glasses, top with a few whole berries and lemon zest, and serve.

KITCHEN WISDOM: Maple Syrup

Maple syrup is graded by color and flavor, ranging from light to dark and mildest to most robust. The lightest iteration of the syrup comes from the earliest tapping of the trees, and the grades move forth with the season. Recently revised, the grading system, which used to include three grades (A, B, and C), now encompasses four levels of solely grade A, each with a wordy description that marks their differences. When it's available, I go for "Grade A: Dark Color and Robust Flavor" (formerly known as grade B). Rich and deep, it works well for baking and cocktails as well as for serving with pancakes, waffles, and more.

THE GAIL

8 whole cucamelons, or 8 (¼-inch-thick) English cucumber slices, divided

4 ounces (½ cup) gin, preferably London dry

1½ ounces (3 tablespoons) fresh lemon juice

1½ ounces (3 tablespoons) simple syrup (see Chef Tech, page 190)

8 fresh mint leaves, plus 2 sprigs for serving

4 ice cubes

4 cups crushed ice

Special equipment: cocktail shaker

Introduced to cucamelons by a farmer friend from Ohio a few summers ago, I instantly fell in love with the fruit. How could you not? The adorable, grape-sized cucumbers look like tiny watermelons from the outside, but deliver the same satisfying crunch and refreshing light grassy notes of a common cucumber, along with a subtle tang. One evening, at a dinner at New York's Eleven Madison Park, I shared my new passion with the gifted bar director, Leo Robitschek. Moments later he arrived at our table with a custom cucamelon cocktail, which he sweetly named *The Gail!* I guzzled it down, then asked for another, and for the recipe so I could make it at home. Though cucamelons can be found at farmers' markets and specialty grocery stores in late summer, they're not yet widely available. When I can't find them, I substitute seedless cucumber, which works just as well.

In the cocktail shaker, muddle 6 of the cucamelons (or 6 of the cucumber slices). Add the gin, lemon juice, and simple syrup. Clap the mint leaves between your hands a few times to release their oils, then drop them in the shaker. Add 4 whole ice cubes, then cover and shake gently, to chill and aerate the drink without overly bruising the mint leaves, until the outside of the shaker is very cold, about 30 seconds.

Fill two 12-ounce double rocks glasses with crushed ice, then strain the drink into them. Top with more crushed ice to form a mound, then garnish with the remaining whole cucamelons (or cucumber slices) and mint sprigs.

KITCHEN WISDOM: Essential Herb Oils

I follow Leo's lead here, clapping whole mint leaves between the palms of my hands (instead of tearing or chopping them) before gently shaking the drink. The technique, though it may seem a little dramatic, is actually a very effective way to release the essential oils and perfume from the herb without bruising it. It also helps keep the cocktail free of tiny herb specks, which might otherwise wind up stuck in your teeth.

If you don't have a fancy ice maker that offers crushed ice, place whole ice cubes in a resealable plastic bag, then pound them with the bottom of a heavy pan or a meat tenderizer until crushed.

CHARRED GRAPEFRUIT MEZCALITA

1 large pink grapefruit, quartered

Olive oil for brushing

1 tablespoon fine smoked sea salt

2 tablespoons cilantro leaves, plus sprigs for serving

3 ounces (6 tablespoons) mezcal (see Kitchen Wisdom)

1½ ounces (3 tablespoons) triple sec

2 teaspoons simple syrup (see Chef Tech)

Ice cubes

Special equipment: cocktail shaker

KITCHEN WISDOM: Smoky Flavors

Use tequila instead of mezcal, and/or regular sea salt instead of smoked, if you prefer a less smoky cocktail or can't get your hands on one or both ingredients. The drink, though less complex, is delicious made any of these ways.

This refreshing cocktail has a three-point smoke game, which comes primarily from swapping out tequila for its complex, smoky cousin, mezcal. A smoked-salt rim plays up the theme, as does grilling pink grapefruit wedges, which maximizes their sweet-tart flavor and juice-ability, and adds a touch more char to the mix.

Heat a grill or grill pan to medium-high heat. Brush the cut sides of the grapefruit with olive oil, then grill until well charred, 2 to 3 minutes per side. Transfer to a plate and let cool.

Juice all but one of the charred grapefruit wedges through a mesh strainer into a bowl; discard the seeds.

Spread the smoked salt on a small plate. Rub the rim of two rocks glasses with the remaining grapefruit wedge, then swirl through the salt to coat.

In the cocktail shaker, muddle the cilantro and 1 tablespoon of the grapefruit juice, then add the remaining juice, the mezcal, triple sec, and simple syrup. Fill the shaker with ice cubes and shake vigorously until the outside of the shaker is very cold, about 30 seconds. Fill the prepared glasses with ice cubes, then strain the mezcalita into them. Garnish with cilantro sprigs and serve.

Simple syrup is sugar and water boiled together for use in sweetened cold drinks and cocktails. Making your own takes just a few minutes: simply heat an equal amount of granulated sugar and water in a small saucepan over low heat (I usually make 1 cup sugar to 1 cup water, which yields about 1½ cups simple syrup), stirring occasionally, until the sugar is fully dissolved. Remove the pan from the heat and allow the syrup to cool completely before use. Simple syrup keeps in an airtight container and refrigerated for about 1 month.

Many things differentiate the two popular Mexican spirits mezcal and tequila. Here are a few basics: Though both are derived from the agave plant, tequila is made from blue agave (agave tequilana weber), while mezcal can be made from over two dozen varieties of the plant. Additionally, while the agave heart (the piña) is most often cooked in large industrial ovens to make tequila, it's generally roasted in wood-fired underground pits for mezcal, which gives the spirit its distinct smoky aroma and flavor. Tequila is made in Jalisco and mezcal comes largely from the region of Oaxaca.

JERKALADA

3 limes

2 teaspoons kosher salt

½ teaspoon chili powder

2 generous pinches allspice

Ice cubes

1 teaspoon Pickapeppa Sauce (see Kitchen Wisdom; Worcestershire sauce can be used if this is unavailable)

½ teaspoon hot sauce (as fiery as you can stand it, preferably habanero), plus more for serving

2 bottles chilled Red Stripe beer

I created this savory beer beverage while sipping an ice-cold Red Stripe at a beachside jerk shack in Jamaica with my dear friend, Peter Jon Lindberg. Peter, one of the most prolific and poetic travel writers in America, spends much of his year traversing the globe with his wife Nilou. Their end-of-year respite in Jamaica has become an annual tradition; on several occasions, Jeremy, Dahlia, and I have been lucky enough to tag along. By adding a dash of Pickapeppa Sauce to our beer that day, along with a few shakes of fiery habanero sauce and a generous squeeze of fresh lime juice, Peter and I came up with this Jamaican version of a Mexican Michelada. We call ours a *Jerkalada*, and we've been drinking it religiously ever since.

Juice up to 2½ of the limes to get 2 tablespoons juice and set aside. Cut three wedges from the remaining lime. Rub the rim of two 16-ounce glasses with one of the lime wedges. In a small bowl, stir together the salt, chili powder, and allspice, then spread the mixture onto a small plate. Swirl the rim of each glass through the salt mixture to coat. Fill the glasses with ice and set aside.

In a small bowl, stir together the lime juice, Pickapeppa Sauce, and hot sauce. Divide the mixture between the prepared glasses. Top off with the beer and garnish with lime wedges. Serve the remaining beer and extra hot sauce alongside so guests can season and top up their drinks to their liking.

KITCHEN WISDOM: Pickapeppa Sauce

Pickapeppa Sauce, one of Jamaica's most popular condiments, has a sweet mellow heat. In addition to being a key component in this drink, it's also fantastic for flavoring meat loaf, adding to marinades, serving alongside steaks, pork chops, roast chicken, grilled fish, and much more!

THE NILOU

2 cups ice cubes, plus more for
serving

2½ cups 1-inch cubes papaya
(about 1 medium)

4 ounces (½ cup) light rum

1½ ounces (3 tablespoons) fresh
lime juice

1 ounce (2 tablespoons) honey

2 lime wedges

I have vivid memories of childhood trips to my father's native South Africa and the abundant and impressive variety of tropical fruit we feasted on there. Along with fresh guava, passion fruit, and mangos of all kinds, there was *paw paw*, or papaya, as we North Americans know it. While my family and friends devoured papaya's sweet, coral flesh, I always steered clear. Like cilantro, this fruit is polarizing—you either love it or are utterly turned off by its aroma and taste. I was of the no-go mindset for most of my life, until my friend, Nilou Motamed, *Food & Wine* magazine's former editor in chief, insisted I try this cocktail. The drink—a simple blend of papaya, a little honey, and a splash of rum and lime juice—completely transformed the flavor of the fruit from unappealing to floral and delicious and, as Nilou surmised, immediately won me over. Now I enjoy it often, and with an added bonus: It's great without the booze, as a break-fast or anytime smoothie.

Fill two highball glasses with ice. Combine the papaya, ice cubes, rum, lime juice, and honey in the jar of a blender. Blend on high until smooth, then pour into the highball glasses. Garnish with the lime wedges and serve.

From left to right: Jerkalada,
page 192; The Nilou, *page 193*

PICKLE JUICE MARTINI

1 large or 2 small sprigs fresh
  dill

3 tablespoons kosher dill pickle
  juice, divided

Ice cubes

5 ounces (½ cup plus
  2 tablespoons) vodka

1 teaspoon dry vermouth

4 pickle slices for serving

Special equipment: cocktail
  shaker or small pitcher

Jeremy's grandfather, Papa, was my hero. The patriarch of the Abrams family, he was strong and stoic, and ever the flirt with the ladies. He loved to eat and drink, and together we spent countless hours *noshing* (Yiddish for snacking) on Montreal smoked meat and bagels, and *kibitzing* (chatting, gossiping) about life. More than anything, the man loved a dill pickle, and family legend goes that it was a daily shot of pickle juice that kept him alive and robust until the ripe old age of 96. A nod to the classic dirty martini, I designed this variation in Papa's honor, and I'd like to think that he'd approve!

Muddle the dill with 1 teaspoon of the pickle juice in a cocktail shaker or small pitcher. Fill with ice, then add the vodka, vermouth, and remaining pickle juice. Stir until well chilled. Strain into two martini glasses, garnish with the pickle slices, and serve.

KING OF THE JUNGLE

2 ripe bananas, peeled and cut crosswise into ¼-inch-thick slices, plus more for serving

12 ounces (1½ cups) light rum

3 ounces (6 tablespoons) fresh lime juice

4 teaspoons simple syrup (see Chef Tech, page 190)

Ice cubes

Special equipment: cocktail shaker

Our friends Seth Gold and Brandon Creed are important men in our lives. Longtime friends of both Jeremy and me, they are also responsible for first introducing us. A few years ago, Seth launched the premium rum company, SelvaRey (Spanish for King of the Jungle). Since then, at our annual reunion in Palm Springs, California, he takes charge as our resident mixologist, whipping up rum-infused creations in a steady stream throughout the weekend. This is my favorite to date. By soaking bananas in rum for many hours, the spirit takes on a tropical flavor with no artificial sweetness. All that is needed is a little lime juice and a touch of simple syrup to create a delicious and well-rounded cocktail.

In a glass jar or pitcher, combine the banana slices and rum. Allow to soak at room temperature for at least 8 hours or overnight. Strain out the banana pieces and reserve.

In a cocktail shaker, muddle 4 pieces of the rum-soaked banana. Add half the lime juice, half the simple syrup, and 6 ounces (¾ cup) of the banana-infused rum. Fill with ice. Shake until the outside of the shaker is very cold, about 30 seconds.

Fill two rocks glasses with ice. Strain the drink into the glasses. Garnish each with a fresh banana slice. Repeat with the remaining ingredients and serve.

BITTERSWEET HOT CHOCOLATE

with Bourbon Marshmallows

3 cups whole milk

5½ ounces bittersweet chocolate (70%), finely chopped (1 cup)

Bourbon Marshmallows for serving (page 202)

My father is a chocoholic, and to a large extent I share his addiction. He tries to keep his intake to one or two small pieces of dark chocolate per day, but maintains that a cup of hot cocoa is not part of that limitation, and drinks one religiously, no matter the weather. Although I don't partake as often as he does, I do love a hot chocolate after a day in the snow, and even more so when topped with a homemade bourbon marshmallow! This drink is made with bittersweet chocolate, which makes it nice and rich, yet not too sweet.

In a large saucepan, warm the milk over low heat until it just begins to simmer. Whisk in the chocolate until smooth and velvety. Divide evenly among four to six mugs. Add a marshmallow to each and serve.

Recipe continues

Bourbon Marshmallows

For Bittersweet Hot Chocolate (page 201)

¼ cup confectioners' sugar

¼ cup cornstarch

Nonstick cooking spray

3 (¼-ounce) envelopes unflavored gelatin

½ cup bourbon, divided

¼ cup ice water

1 cup granulated sugar

1 cup light corn syrup

¼ teaspoon kosher salt

1½ teaspoons pure vanilla extract

Special equipment: candy thermometer

Making homemade marshmallows may sound intimidating, but it's actually very easy and fun. To make the marshmallows for kids, swap in water for the booze when you soften the gelatin, then simply leave out the second addition of alcohol in the last step.

In a small bowl, whisk together the confectioners' sugar and cornstarch. Lightly coat the bottom and sides of a 9 x 9-inch baking pan with nonstick spray. Add a few tablespoons of the cornstarch mixture to the pan, then shake to evenly coat the bottom and sides. Return any excess mixture to the bowl.

Combine the gelatin, ¼ cup of the bourbon, and the ice water in the bowl of a stand mixer fitted with the whisk attachment; stir once to make sure all of the gelatin is in contact with the liquid. Let soften while you make the sugar syrup.

In a small saucepan, combine the granulated sugar, corn syrup, salt, and ½ cup water. Clip a candy thermometer to the side of the pan so its base is submerged in the sugar mixture but not touching the bottom of the pan. Cook over medium-high heat, without stirring, until the thermometer registers 240°F, about 10 minutes. Remove the pan from the heat, then carefully pour the sugar mixture over the gelatin mixture.

Beat the mixture at medium speed, gradually increasing to high. Continue beating until the marshmallow is slightly cooled, very thick, and forms a thick ribbon when the whisk is lifted, 12 to 14 minutes.

Beat in the vanilla and remaining ¼ cup bourbon until evenly distributed, about 1 minute more. Scrape the marshmallow into the prepared pan and use dampened hands to spread it smoothly and evenly. Dust the top with 2 tablespoons of the cornstarch mixture and let stand, uncovered at room temperature, until set, at least 4 hours or overnight. (Reserve the remaining cornstarch mixture.)

Turn out the marshmallow onto a cutting board. Using a lightly oiled knife or pizza wheel, cut into 1-inch squares. Dust all sides of each cut marshmallow with the reserved cornstarch mixture.

The marshmallows will keep for 1 week, layered between sheets of wax paper or parchment in an airtight container at cool room temperature.

Use lightly oiled cookie cutters to cut the marshmallows into stars, hearts, animals, or other fun shapes, if you like.

Sweets

CHOCOLATE BANOFFEE PIE 206

TOASTED-HAZELNUT TARTE AU SUCRE 209

BLUEBERRY LEMONADE BARS 211

BLACK-LICORICE CHOCOLATE BUNDT CAKE 212

MAPLE-PEAR PUDDING CAKE (*POUDING CHÔMEUR*) 215

GRILLED PINEAPPLE WITH LIME ZEST & MOLASSES 216

BROWN BUTTER–OATMEAL COOKIE
& PEACH ICE CREAM SANDWICHES 219

COCONUT CREAM PUFFS 221

BANANA-CARDAMOM UPSIDE-DOWN CAKE WITH SALTY CARAMEL 225

CLASSIC BUTTERSCOTCH PUDDING 226

ROASTED STRAWBERRY–BUTTERMILK ICE POPS 228

CLEMENTINE-GINGER GRANITA 231

CAMPFIRE SUNDAES 232

CHOCOLATE HONEYCOMB CRUNCH 235

CHOCOLATE-DIPPED, DULCE DE LECHE–FILLED
SANDWICH COOKIES WITH SEA SALT 237

◆

CHOCOLATE BANOFFEE PIE

Dulce de Leche

1 (14-ounce) can sweetened condensed milk (see Kitchen Wisdom)

Chocolate Banoffee Pie

9 ounces chocolate wafer cookies, broken into pieces

1 tablespoon granulated sugar

Kosher salt

10 tablespoons (1¼ sticks) unsalted butter, melted

⅓ cup roasted salted peanuts, coarsely chopped

3 large bananas, peeled and cut crosswise into ¼-inch slices

1 pint heavy cream

1 ounce bittersweet chocolate

I made this riff on the classic British pie for my friend Melanie Dunea, the award-winning photographer and creator of the *My Last Supper* project—a spirited celebration of world-famous chefs and their fantasy final meals. Of all the sweets imaginable, I chose it as my "last dessert." I first fell in love with the pie by name alone, but then—after just one bite of the caramel, banana, and whipped cream filling and the sweet cookie-crumb crust—my mind was blown. I use dark chocolate wafers for my crust, and add a garnish of chocolate curls along with crushed roasted peanuts for a hit of crunch and salt. Luckily, I don't have to wait until my last supper to eat this pie, and I hope that you won't either. It's a crowd-pleasing, show-stopping slam-dunk anytime.

For the dulce de leche: Remove any labels from the can of sweetened condensed milk and place on the bottom of a large stockpot. Fill the pot with water, covering the can by 4 to 6 inches, then bring the water just to a boil over high heat. Reduce the heat to low, cover the pot, and continue boiling, frequently checking the water level, for 3 hours. (The can should be covered by at least 1 inch of water throughout the cooking process or it could explode.) Remove the can from the water and allow it to cool at room temperature before opening. If making ahead, dulce de leche can be kept refrigerated, unopened or in an airtight container, for up to 1 week.

For the pie: In a food processor, pulse the cookies until fine, then transfer to a large bowl. Stir in the sugar and a generous pinch of salt. Add the melted butter and stir until well combined. Press the mixture over the bottom and up the sides of a 9-inch pie plate. Refrigerate until firm, about 30 minutes.

Spread the dulce de leche in a thick layer over the bottom of the crust. Reserve 1 tablespoon of the peanuts and sprinkle the remainder evenly over the dulce de leche. Arrange the banana slices in overlapping circles in 2 layers over the dulce de leche and peanuts.

In a large mixing bowl, whip the cream until it just holds stiff peaks. Spoon the whipped cream over the bananas, covering the pie and forming a mound. With a vegetable peeler, shave the chocolate over the top, then sprinkle with the reserved 1 tablespoon chopped peanuts. Refrigerate until chilled, at least 15 minutes or up to 1 hour, before serving.

KITCHEN WISDOM: Dulce de Leche

Part of the fun of making this pie is making your own dulce de leche, by slowly simmering a can of sweetened condensed milk until the milk sugars caramelize into a thick, golden sauce. If you don't want to take the time to make your own, look for a 14- to 16-ounce jar of dulce de leche in the baking aisle of your grocery store. The rest of the pie comes together quickly, and no baking is required.

TOASTED-HAZELNUT
TARTE AU SUCRE

Hazelnut Crust

½ cup hazelnuts

1¼ cups unbleached all-purpose flour

½ teaspoon kosher salt

6 tablespoons (¾ stick) cold unsalted butter, cut into small cubes

Up to 4 tablespoons ice water

Filling

1 cup maple sugar (see Sources, page 240)

¾ cup packed light brown sugar

1 large egg

2 tablespoons unbleached all-purpose flour

2 tablespoons unsalted butter, melted

⅓ cup chilled heavy cream, plus ½ cup for serving

Special equipment: 9-inch tart pan with removable bottom

Growing up in Toronto, we traveled often to Montreal to visit my grandparents and my mom's extended family. If it was early spring, our trip included a stop at one of the many traditional *cabanes à sucre* (sugar shacks)—small cabins where sap tapped from sugar maple trees is boiled into some of the finest amber syrup in the world. There we indulged in treats like maple sugar and *tire d'érable*—a taffy-pop hybrid made by drizzling thickly boiled maple sap over icy-cold fresh snow, then turning it around a popsicle stick. All of that, while irresistible, could not steal the thunder from the pièce de résistance: rich, sticky *tarte au sucre* (sugar pie). We'd share a slice on site and often buy a whole tart to bring home. These days, I'm not always lucky enough to hit sugaring season when I visit Montreal, so instead I make the dessert at home. Easy and fun, it's also a great make-ahead for dinner parties—the chilled cream, dramatically poured tableside as the final touch, is especially impressive!

For the crust: Heat the oven to 350°F. Spread the hazelnuts on a rimmed baking sheet and toast in the oven until lightly browned and the skins start to blister, 10 to 12 minutes. Rub the hot toasted hazelnuts in a clean kitchen towel to remove skins (it's OK if not all the skins come off), then let cool completely. Transfer the cooled nuts to the bowl of a food processor and pulse until the nuts resemble a coarse meal.

In a large bowl, whisk together the hazelnuts, flour, and salt. Using your fingertips, blend in the butter until incorporated, leaving some roughly pea-sized lumps. Working with 1 tablespoon at a time, stir in 2 to 4 tablespoons ice water, just until the dough holds together.

Place the dough in the center of the 9-inch tart pan with a removable bottom. Using your fingers and a flat-bottomed measuring cup, spread and push the dough to evenly cover the bottom and sides of the pan. Prick the dough all over with the tines of a fork. Freeze until firm, at least 30 minutes or overnight wrapped tightly in plastic.

For the filling: In a medium bowl, stir together the maple sugar, brown sugar, egg, flour, butter, and ⅓ cup cream until well combined.

To assemble: Increase the oven temperature to 375°F with the rack in the middle. Remove the tart shell from the freezer and bake until the dough is just starting to brown, about 20 minutes. Pour the filling into the hot crust and continue baking until the crust is golden and the edges of the filling are just set (the center will be fairly jiggly), 35 to 38 minutes more. Cool the tart in the pan on a rack for 1 hour (the filling will continue to set as it cools), then remove the sides of the pan.

Recipe continues

At the table, just before serving, pour the remaining ½ cup chilled cream over the top of the tart, then cut into wedges.

The tart, without the cream poured over the top, can be kept, covered and refrigerated, for up to 1 day. Bring it to room temperature, then pour on the cream just before serving.

When it comes to making butter-based tart and pie crusts, I go the old-fashioned route, mixing by hand to get the most tender and flaky result. Using your hands (as opposed to a food processor or mixer) to incorporate cold butter into flour, makes it easier to see and feel the dough, and makes overmixing less likely. This helps ensure that lumps of butter (generally pea-sized) remain intact as you roll out your dough or press it into your pan. While the tart or pie is baking, those butter lumps melt and form steam pockets that create separated, "flaky" dough layers. Keeping everything very cold is key here, too. After cutting your butter into small cubes, refrigerate or briefly freeze it until ready to use. Mixing the dough in a stainless steel bowl (which can also be chilled for 10 minutes or so with your flour in it), and running your hands under cold water for a minute or two (dry them thoroughly before mixing), also helps keep everything cold.

BLUEBERRY LEMONADE BARS

Crust

1 cup (2 sticks) unsalted butter, cut into cubes, at room temperature

½ cup granulated sugar

2 cups unbleached all-purpose flour

¼ teaspoon kosher salt

Lemon Curd

5 large eggs

1 cup granulated sugar

½ cup unbleached all-purpose flour

1 tablespoon freshly grated lemon zest

1 cup fresh lemon juice (from about 6 small lemons)

3 cups blueberries, stemmed, rinsed, and patted dry

Confectioners' sugar for serving

When I was at culinary school, one of my favorite instructors, chef Frank Garofolo, taught me how to make a gorgeous classic French lemon tart. Glossy, bright, and piled high with fresh blueberries, it quickly became one of my favorite desserts and my go-to for special occasions. These days I tend to have less formal affairs to bring sweets to (hello, life with a three-year-old!), but I still love the tangy-sweet combo of lemon curd and blueberries. In this recipe, the blueberries bake right into the curd over a simple press-in shortbread crust, making compact, easy-to-eat bars. At once laid-back and elegant, they're ideal for a kid's birthday party, grown-up picnic, or midsummer night's dessert. The bars freeze surprisingly well, making them a great make-ahead dish. If good, fresh blueberries are not available, frozen berries, thawed and drained, can be substituted.

Heat the oven to 350°F. Line a 9 x 13 x 2-inch baking dish with parchment paper, leaving an overhang.

For the crust: In the bowl of an electric mixer fitted with the paddle attachment, beat the soft butter and granulated sugar on high until light and fluffy, about 3 minutes. In a medium bowl, whisk together the flour and salt. With the mixer on low, slowly add the flour mixture. Increase the speed to high and beat until the dough holds together, about 1 minute more.

Turn out the dough into the prepared pan and press it into an even layer using your fingertips. Bake until the edges are just beginning to brown, 18 to 22 minutes.

For the curd: Meanwhile, in a clean large bowl, whisk together the eggs and granulated sugar, then whisk in the flour followed by the lemon zest and juice. Allow the mixture to stand until foam appears on top, 2 to 3 minutes, then skim off and discard the foam.

Remove the pan from the oven. Pour the lemon curd evenly over the hot crust, then sprinkle the blueberries evenly over the top. Return the pan to the oven and continue baking until the filling is just set in the center (still a touch jiggly), 20 to 25 minutes. Let cool completely in the pan on a wire rack, then refrigerate until chilled, about 30 minutes or up to 1 day. Cut into 24 bars and dust with confectioners' sugar.

The bars keep, covered and refrigerated, for up to 3 days, or frozen for up to 3 months. I recommend freezing before cutting if you are making ahead, but you can also freeze bars individually. Wrap them with parchment paper and then in heavy-duty foil to avoid freezer burn. Let thaw at room temperature, then dust with confectioners' sugar just before serving.

BLACK-LICORICE
CHOCOLATE BUNDT CAKE

Unsalted butter, at room temperature, for greasing pan

1 cup unsweetened cocoa powder, plus more for dusting

3 large eggs

¼ cup canola oil

1 tablespoon plus 1½ teaspoons licorice root powder (see Sources, page 240)

1½ cups hot water

2¼ cups sugar

2¼ cups unbleached all-purpose flour

2 teaspoons baking soda

1½ teaspoons baking powder

¼ teaspoon salt

¾ cup sour cream

6 ounces bittersweet chocolate (70%), coarsely chopped (1¼ cups)

3 ounces Australian soft black licorice chews, coarsely chopped (½ cup packed)

Special equipment: 12-cup Bundt pan

My father, Ivor, is from a small town in the center of South Africa and, although his family's background is English and Eastern European, he was raised with strong Dutch influences. One Dutch passion he passed down to me is his love of black licorice, specifically the salty, chewy sort—not the soft, sweet kind. Whenever we visited family in South Africa, my dad would bring home bags of what we knew as *dubbel zout* (double salt)—coins of salted black licorice about the size of a quarter. I devoured them every chance I got, relishing the savory, saline exterior before it gave way to the barely sweet, chewy center. Dad's other sweet vice, which I also inherited, is chocolate. Not white. Not milk. Simply pure and dark. So, it was in honor of him, and our shared love of these two confections, that I concocted this deep, dark chocolaty cake, which gets a touch of sophisticated salt flavor, plus notes of molasses and anise, from what might seem to be an unlikely partner: black licorice. Paired together, the two confections make for a brilliant duo that is both delicious and not-too-sweet.

Heat the oven to 350°F with the rack in the middle. Brush the soft butter generously all over the inside of the 12-cup Bundt pan, then dust lightly with cocoa powder, shaking off any excess.

In a large mixing bowl, whisk together the eggs, oil, licorice root powder, and hot water. Add the sugar and whisk well to combine. Sift together the cocoa, flour, baking soda, baking powder, and salt in a bowl.

In three additions, add the dry ingredients to the wet ingredients, stirring between each addition until incorporated before adding the next. Fold in the sour cream, chocolate, and licorice chews.

Pour the batter into the prepared pan and bake until a wooden pick inserted into the center comes out clean, 50 to 60 minutes. Transfer to a wire rack and let the cake cool in the pan for 10 minutes. Invert the cake onto the rack; remove the pan and let cool completely. Dust with cocoa powder just before serving. Cake can be stored at room temperature, wrapped tightly in plastic, for up to 3 days.

KITCHEN WISDOM: Black Licorice

Australian black licorice, which is perfect here, is available in most grocery stores. *Dubbel zout* is less commonly available and generally too stiff to bake with. But if you're interested in stocking it for snacking purposes, it can be ordered online, as can the licorice root powder that you'll need for the cake (see Sources, page 240).

MAPLE-PEAR PUDDING CAKE

SERVES 6

(Pouding Chômeur)

7 tablespoons unsalted butter, at room temperature, divided

1 firm-ripe Bosc or other good baking pear, cored and thinly sliced

4 tablespoons packed dark brown sugar, divided

⅜ teaspoon ground cinnamon, divided

Kosher salt

1 cup pure maple syrup

¾ cup heavy cream

2 teaspoons fresh lemon juice

1 cup unbleached all-purpose flour

1¼ teaspoons baking powder

1 large egg

½ teaspoon pure vanilla extract

Vanilla ice cream, crème fraîche, or sour cream for serving

Special equipment: 2-quart gratin or 8-inch square baking dish (2 inches deep)

Every time I eat *pouding chômeur* when I'm back in Montreal, I am mystified that it hasn't yet taken the rest of North America by storm. This classic French-Canadian pudding cake is a simple, wintery delight, made in a somewhat funny fashion: Dollops of thick cake batter are dropped into a pan and then covered with a healthy pour of maple syrup, which soaks into the batter as it bakes to form a delicious, gooey cake. I like to make it with cinnamon-sugared pears, which add both dimension and texture.

Heat the oven to 350°F with the rack in the upper third.

In a medium skillet, melt 1 tablespoon of the butter over medium heat. Add the pear slices, 1 tablespoon of the brown sugar, ⅛ teaspoon of the cinnamon, and a pinch of salt. Cook, stirring occasionally, until the pear begins to soften, about 8 minutes. Remove from the heat and let cool.

Meanwhile, in a small saucepan, bring the maple syrup, cream, a pinch of salt, and ¼ cup water just to a boil, then remove from the heat. Stir in the lemon juice.

In a medium bowl, whisk together the flour, baking powder, the remaining ¼ teaspoon cinnamon, and ¼ teaspoon salt. In the bowl of a stand mixer fitted with the paddle attachment, beat together the remaining 6 tablespoons butter and 3 tablespoons brown sugar until light and fluffy, about 1 minute. Add the egg and vanilla and beat until just combined. Using a rubber spatula, fold in the flour mixture (the batter will be very thick).

Pour about ⅓ cup of the syrup mixture into the deep 2-quart gratin or 8-inch square baking dish. Dollop the batter on top in about five ¼-cupfuls, spacing the mounds evenly over the syrup. Arrange the sliced pears on top of the mounds and drizzle with any juices from the skillet, then pour the remaining syrup mixture over the top.

Set the baking dish on a rimmed baking sheet and bake until the cake is just golden but still syrupy, 30 to 35 minutes. Serve warm, spooned into bowls with vanilla ice cream, crème fraîche, or sour cream on top, if desired.

Literally "unemployment pudding" or "poor man's pudding," pouding chômeur was created in Québec City during the Great Depression, but is now served all over the province as a beloved regional treat, especially during sugaring season when local maple syrup is available in abundance.

GRILLED PINEAPPLE

with Lime Zest & Molasses

Coconut oil or any neutral oil,
   such as canola or grapeseed,
   for grilling

1 ripe medium pineapple,
   peeled, cut crosswise into
   ½-inch-thick rounds

2 tablespoons plus 1 teaspoon
   dark brown sugar

Kosher salt

Coarsely ground black pepper

1 teaspoon molasses

1 lime

The fact that my in-laws, Herbie and Noreen, share my unbridled enthusiasm for gastronomic adventure makes them excellent company in general, and superb travel companions. On a trip through northern Spain with them several years ago to celebrate their anniversary, we all agreed that one of the most memorable dishes we shared was an extraordinary and stunningly simple dessert, served at chef Albert Adrià's (since closed) Barcelona tapas bar, Inopia: sliced fresh pineapple, sprinkled with lime zest and drizzled with molasses. I make my own variation at home, grilling the pineapple, which gives the fruit a smoky note and concentrates its sweet juices. Using coconut oil adds a subtle buttery, toasted note. If you don't have it on hand, any neutral oil is just as good.

Prepare an outdoor grill or grill pan for medium-high heat. Lightly oil the grill grates.

Rub the pineapple slices on both sides with the sugar, then season with salt and pepper. Arrange on a baking sheet.

Grill the pineapple slices until grill marks appear and the pineapple is warmed through, about 4 minutes per side. Transfer the slices to a platter. Drizzle with the molasses, grate the zest from the lime over the top, and serve warm.

BROWN BUTTER-OATMEAL COOKIE & PEACH ICE CREAM SANDWICHES

Brown Butter-Oatmeal Cookies

1½ cups old-fashioned whole oats

10 tablespoons (1¼ sticks) unsalted butter, at room temperature, divided

1 cup unbleached all-purpose flour

½ teaspoon baking powder

1 teaspoon ground cinnamon

1 teaspoon kosher salt

¾ cup packed dark brown sugar

1 large egg

1 teaspoon pure vanilla extract

1 cup coarsely chopped pitted dates

¾ cup walnut halves, coarsely chopped (optional)

Peach Ice Cream

2 ripe peaches, pitted and cut into ¼-inch cubes (1½ cups)

1 teaspoon granulated sugar

1 quart premium vanilla ice cream

¼ teaspoon ground cinnamon

Alex Lee, one of the most accomplished and talented chefs I know, spent ten years at the helm of Daniel Boulud's flagship restaurant, Daniel. For a few years during his tenure, I managed the restaurant group's events and public relations. One summer day, after taping a cooking demo in Connecticut for a local TV station, Alex suggested we play hooky, and—instead of returning directly to the restaurant—find our way to a nearby creamery, known for its exceptional peach ice cream. That beguiling taste of fresh peaches and cream (so worth the detour!) was the inspiration for these ice cream sandwiches.

Browning the butter before folding it into the cookie batter contributes a rich, nutty flavor. Once you try it you may never go back to conventional cookie-making again. I opt for finely chopped dates in the cookies, because I prefer their lightly caramel flavor. But raisins can be substituted, if you prefer.

For the cookies: Heat the oven to 350°F with the racks in upper and lower thirds.

On a rimmed baking sheet, spread the oats in a single layer. Bake on the lower rack, stirring once halfway through, until fragrant and lightly toasted, about 12 minutes. Transfer the pan to a wire rack; let the oats cool completely.

Meanwhile, place 5 tablespoons of the butter in a 1- to 2-quart saucepan. Cook over low heat, swirling the pan occasionally, until the butter has a nutty aroma, is a rich brown color, and the bottom of the pan is speckled with browned bits of the milk solids, 12 to 14 minutes. Transfer the brown butter to a small bowl and let cool for 20 minutes.

In a medium bowl, whisk together the cooled toasted oats, flour, baking powder, cinnamon, and salt. In the bowl of a stand mixer fitted with the paddle attachment, or in a large bowl with a hand mixer, beat the remaining 5 tablespoons soft butter and the brown sugar on medium-high until very smooth, about 2 minutes. Add the brown butter and continue beating on medium-high until light and fluffy, 3 to 5 minutes. Mix in the egg and beat thoroughly, scraping down the sides of the bowl if necessary, until incorporated. Beat in the vanilla. With the mixer on low, or by hand, mix in the dry ingredients until just combined. Fold in the dates, and walnuts if using.

Line two baking sheets with parchment paper. Form the dough into 24 balls (each about 2 tablespoons). Arrange the balls on the baking sheets, spacing at least 2 inches apart. Press each ball into an even 2-inch round.

Recipe continues

Bake 10 minutes for soft and chewy cookies. Remove from the oven and let cool for 1 to 2 minutes on the baking sheets. Using a spatula, transfer the cookies to a wire rack to cool completely.

For the ice cream: Heat the oven to 400°F. Line a baking sheet with parchment paper.

In a small bowl, toss together the peaches and granulated sugar; let stand at room temperature for 5 minutes. Spread the mixture in a single layer on the prepared baking sheet and roast until the fruit is tender and lightly golden at the edges, 12 to 15 minutes. Remove from the oven and allow to cool completely.

Meanwhile, let the ice cream stand at room temperature until softened, 8 to 10 minutes, then transfer to a large freezer-proof bowl. Mix in the roasted peaches and cinnamon. Freeze until firm, at least 2 hours or up to 3 days.

To assemble the sandwiches: Place 12 of the cookies flat-side up on a clean work surface. Working quickly, place ⅓ cup ice cream on each. Sandwich with remaining 12 cookies, flat sides together, and gently press to adhere. Serve immediately, or wrap individually in plastic wrap and then in foil, and freeze for up to 3 days.

COCONUT CREAM PUFFS

½ cup (1 stick) unsalted butter

½ teaspoon kosher salt

1 cup unbleached all-purpose flour

4 large eggs

2 cups (6 ounces) sweetened coconut flakes

2⅓ cups well-chilled heavy cream

½ teaspoon pure vanilla extract

1½ cups plus 2 teaspoons confectioners' sugar, divided

2 tablespoons plus 1 teaspoon whole milk

Special equipment: pastry bag fitted with ¼-inch tip

My friend Katherine Yang is the best baker I know. She worked for chefs Daniel Boulud and Thomas Keller before opening her own baking company in New York, called Gigi Blue, where she makes all sorts of decadent treats with extreme attention to detail and unsurpassed technical aptitude. Among my favorites of her desserts is her coconut cake, which is layered with coconut custard and covered with meringue frosting and toasted coconut flakes. It's the most sophisticated comfort food in the world. As an ode to Katherine and her wonderful cake, I created these coconut cream puffs. Light and airy, they're easy to make for a crowd, and—with their deep toasted coconut flavor—they are, most importantly, totally indulgent.

Heat the oven to 400°F with racks in the upper and lower thirds. Line three baking sheets with parchment paper.

Combine the butter, salt, and 1 cup water in a medium saucepan and bring to a rolling boil over medium-high heat. Remove the pan from the heat and add the flour. Using a wooden spoon, stir continuously until the mixture is smooth and glossy, about 1 minute. Return the pan to the heat and cook over low heat, stirring constantly, until the dough forms a ball, pulls away from the sides of the pan, and a skin forms on the bottom of the pan, about 2 minutes. Remove from the heat and allow the dough to rest for 1 minute. Stir in the eggs, one at a time, until the eggs are well incorporated and the dough is smooth.

Dip two soup spoons in water, then shake off excess. Scoop a walnut-size piece of dough with one spoon. Use the other spoon to push the dough onto one of the prepared baking sheets. Repeat with the rest of the dough to create 24 mounds total, spacing them 1 inch apart on two of the baking sheets. Bake, rotating and changing racks halfway through, until the puffs are golden brown and sound hollow when lightly tapped, 28 to 30 minutes. Transfer the pans to wire racks and let the puffs cool completely (leave the oven on).

Meanwhile, spread the coconut flakes on the third lined baking sheet. Toast in the oven, stirring once halfway through, until lightly golden, about 8 minutes. Let cool. Transfer half of the coconut flakes to a small bowl; set aside. Transfer the remaining coconut flakes to a food processor or spice grinder and pulse until finely ground.

When the puffs have cooled, combine the cream, vanilla, and 2 teaspoons of the confectioners' sugar in a medium bowl. Beat to stiff peaks, then gently fold in the finely ground coconut. Transfer the coconut cream mixture to the piping bag with a ¼-inch tip.

Recipe continues

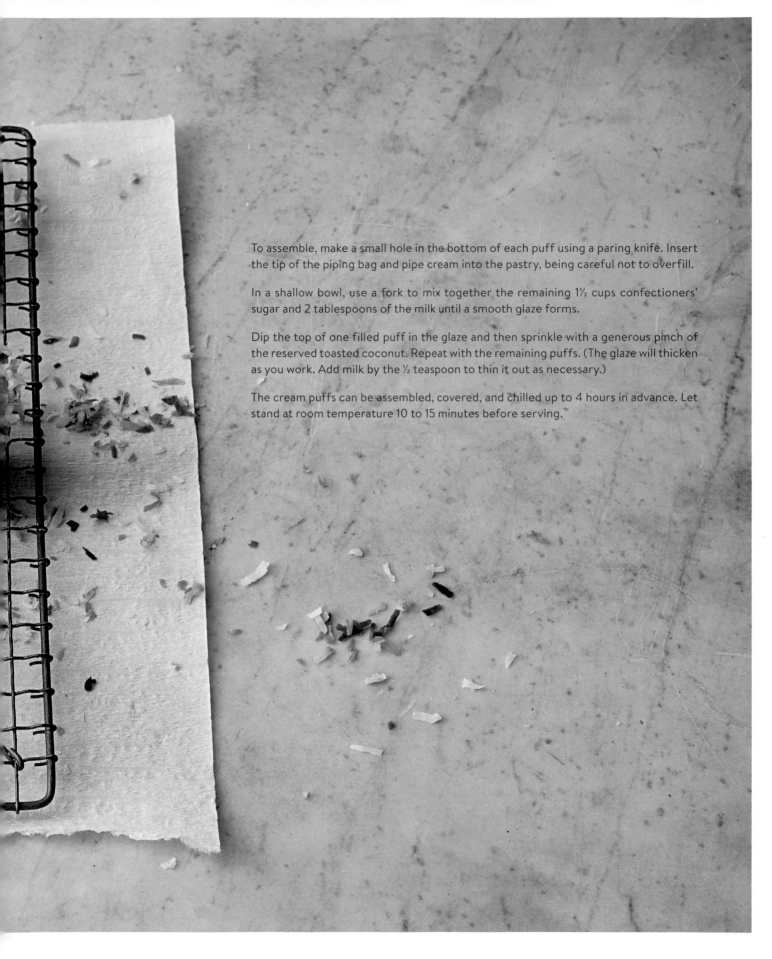

To assemble, make a small hole in the bottom of each puff using a paring knife. Insert the tip of the piping bag and pipe cream into the pastry, being careful not to overfill.

In a shallow bowl, use a fork to mix together the remaining 1½ cups confectioners' sugar and 2 tablespoons of the milk until a smooth glaze forms.

Dip the top of one filled puff in the glaze and then sprinkle with a generous pinch of the reserved toasted coconut. Repeat with the remaining puffs. (The glaze will thicken as you work. Add milk by the ½ teaspoon to thin it out as necessary.)

The cream puffs can be assembled, covered, and chilled up to 4 hours in advance. Let stand at room temperature 10 to 15 minutes before serving.

BANANA-CARDAMOM UPSIDE-DOWN CAKE

with Salty Caramel

Banana Topping

4 tablespoons (½ stick) unsalted butter

¾ cup packed dark brown sugar

¾ teaspoon kosher salt

2 firm-ripe bananas, peeled

Cake Batter

½ cup granulated sugar

½ cup packed brown sugar

6 tablespoons (¾ stick) unsalted butter, cubed, at room temperature

2 large eggs

2 bananas, peeled and mashed

¾ cup sour cream (preferably full-fat)

1 teaspoon pure vanilla extract

1¾ cups unbleached all-purpose flour

1¼ teaspoons ground cardamom

¾ teaspoon baking soda

¾ teaspoon baking powder

½ teaspoon kosher salt

Special equipment: 10-inch cast iron skillet

Banana bread was always a staple in my mom's kitchen when I was growing up. Over the years, I have riffed on her recipe in dozens of ways: adding chocolate chips, nuts, or spices; swinging from quick bread to cake; icing or dusting it with confectioners' sugar. Then, about a year ago, I decided to play with the idea of a banana *upside-down* cake, topped with banana slices and salted caramel, which both soaks into the cake and drips all around it when the pan is inverted. That little idea turned out to be a *total* keeper. Here it is.

Heat the oven to 350°F with the rack in the middle.

For the bananas: Melt the butter in a well-seasoned 10-inch cast iron skillet. Stir in the brown sugar and salt and cook over medium heat, stirring, until evenly combined, 1 to 2 minutes. Remove from the heat.

Cut the bananas in half crosswise, then the halves lengthwise in thirds. Arrange the slices, cut-side down, on top of the caramel.

For the batter: In the bowl of an electric mixer fitted with the paddle attachment, combine the granulated sugar, brown sugar, and soft butter. Beat on high until light and fluffy, 3 to 5 minutes. Reduce the speed to medium and beat in the eggs, one at a time, then the mashed bananas, sour cream, and vanilla until combined, scraping down the sides of the bowl between additions as needed.

In a medium bowl, whisk together the flour, cardamom, baking soda, baking powder, and salt. Slowly mix the dry ingredients into the banana mixture until evenly distributed. Pour the batter into the skillet over the bananas. Smooth the top evenly.

Place the skillet on a rimmed baking sheet. Bake until lightly browned and a cake tester inserted into the middle of the cake comes out clean, 40 to 45 minutes. Remove from the oven and let cool completely. To invert the cake from the pan, run a butter knife around the edge of the cake, then place the skillet over very low heat to just warm the bottom, about 2 minutes. Remove the pan from the heat, then carefully invert the cake onto a large plate.

CLASSIC BUTTERSCOTCH PUDDING

1¾ cups whole milk

½ cup heavy cream

6 tablespoons (¾ stick) unsalted butter, cut into cubes

1 cup packed dark brown sugar

2 tablespoons cornstarch

½ teaspoon kosher salt

2 large eggs

1 teaspoon pure vanilla extract

1 tablespoon Scotch whiskey (optional)

Whipped cream, shaved dark chocolate, and/or turbinado sugar for serving (optional)

As a kid, butterscotch pudding was my number one choice when it came to desserts. I love that it has recently made a comeback, and that so many restaurants are offering it on their dessert menus, often embellished with creative and sophisticated flourishes. My version keeps it homey and deeply buttery, yet each bite delivers the subtle lingering finish of real Scotch. A grown-up incarnation of my childhood favorite.

In a medium saucepan, bring the milk and cream just to simmer over medium heat. Remove from the heat.

Meanwhile, in a large saucepan, melt the butter over medium-high heat, then whisk in the brown sugar. Continue cooking, whisking constantly, until the mixture is smooth and just begins to bubble, about 2 minutes (do not overcook, or the mixture will burn). Remove from the heat.

Whisking constantly, gradually add the warm milk mixture to the butter mixture until it is fully combined.

In a medium bowl, whisk together the cornstarch and salt, then add the eggs and ¼ cup of the milk mixture and whisk to combine. Whisk in an additional ¼ cup of the milk mixture, then add the egg mixture back to the milk mixture in the pan, whisking constantly until very smooth.

While continuing to whisk, cook over medium heat until the pudding is bubbling and becomes very thick, about 2 minutes. Remove from the heat, then whisk in the vanilla, and whiskey if using.

Pass the pudding through a fine-mesh sieve into a bowl. Spoon into four serving glasses or custard cups, cover the surface with plastic wrap, and chill until cold, at least 4 hours or overnight.

Serve the pudding topped with whipped cream, shaved chocolate, and/or a sprinkling of turbinado sugar, if desired.

Snippet

There is some debate about the scotch in butterscotch. I always assumed the name of the pudding and candy referred to the inclusion of butter and Scotch whiskey as ingredients, or maybe the origin of the confection in Scotland. But research suggests otherwise. The first account of butterscotch candy was in Yorkshire, England, in 1817. It contained butter, but not a drop of Scotch. The name "butterscotch" may have come from the fact that the butter is "scorched," or burned to make pudding, and/or that the original candy is often "scored," or cut, before it hardens. I still attest that using a little Scotch adds a complex flavor you can't get any other way, and makes the dessert undeniably unique.

ROASTED STRAWBERRY–BUTTERMILK ICE POPS

1 medium to large ear corn, kernels cut from cob and reserved, cob cut crosswise into 4 to 5 pieces

Kosher salt

1 pound strawberries, hulled

3 tablespoons sugar

¾ cup buttermilk, well shaken

⅓ cup sour cream

½ cup honey

½ teaspoon pure vanilla extract

1¼ cups puffed corn cereal, such as Corn Pops or Gorilla Munch, crushed

½ cup plus 2 tablespoons freeze-dried strawberries, crushed

Special equipment: 8 (4-ounce) or 10 (3-ounce) ice pop molds

Everyone has memories of running to the ice cream truck to get a bar or cone. As a kid, the treat that drew me in was the strawberry shortcake bar: Bright pink, creamy, and sweet, I loved its deliciously textured crumb topping. Since it's now a favorite of my daughter's too, I created a fun homemade version. I roast strawberries to concentrate their juices, then blend the fruit with buttermilk and sweet corn kernels to make a just-tart pink berry base. A mixture of crushed dried strawberries and corn cereal forms the colorful coating that lends extra flavor and a crunchy bite. Whip up a batch and watch what happens. (Hint: Both kids and adults will come running!)

Heat the oven to 425°F.

In a medium saucepan, combine ¾ cup water, the corn kernels, corn cob pieces, and ⅛ teaspoon salt. Bring to a boil over medium heat. Remove from heat, cover, and let stand to cool and allow flavors to blend.

Meanwhile, toss together the hulled strawberries and sugar in a 13 x 9 x 2-inch baking dish. Roast, stirring once halfway through, until juices are bubbling, 15 to 20 minutes. Remove from oven and let cool.

Strain the corn stock into a bowl, pressing gently but firmly on solids to extract as much liquid as possible. Discard corn cobs. Reserve corn kernels in a small bowl.

In a blender, puree the strawberries and their juices with the corn stock, buttermilk, sour cream, honey, vanilla, and a pinch of salt. Gently fold in reserved corn kernels. Pour the mixture into eight 4-ounce or ten 3-ounce ice pop molds, dividing evenly. Insert ice pop sticks and freeze until firm, at least 4 hours or up to 4 days. (If using wooden sticks, freeze the mixture first for 45 minutes before inserting sticks halfway into pops. Then freeze again until pops are frozen.)

Just before serving, stir together the cereal and freeze-dried strawberries, then spread onto a flat plate. Carefully run the ice pop molds under warm water to thaw just slightly and release from their molds. Gently but firmly press each into the cereal mixture on both sides. Serve immediately.

CLEMENTINE-GINGER GRANITA

¼ cup sugar

½ cup peeled thinly sliced ginger (from a 3-inch knob), plus ½ teaspoon finely grated ginger

Kosher salt

2 tablespoons freshly grated clementine or tangerine zest (from 3 clementines or 1 tangerine)

2 cups fresh clementine or tangerine juice (from 15 clementines or 10 tangerines)

2 tablespoons fresh lemon juice

2 teaspoons finely chopped fresh basil

½ cup (4 ounces) sweetened condensed milk for serving

Shooting *Top Chef*'s Season 11 in New Orleans was a pivotal experience for me. The music, food, people, and culture of that city are forever in my heart. We shot from late May through July, and it was *hot*. I was pregnant with Dahlia and often queasy. Luckily my friend, chef Sue Zemanick, one of the city's brightest talents, introduced me to Hansen's Sno-Bliz, a NOLA institution famous for its snoballs: scoops of fluffy shaved ice doused in an array of unique homemade syrups. Resistance was futile. After tasting my way through most of Hansen's menu, I landed on my favorite: satsuma and ginger, drizzled with condensed milk. There's no way to exactly replicate it at home, since satsumas are regionally grown and Hansen's ice-shaving device, responsible for their snoballs' magical lightness, is a patented machine. Still, I have mastered a close second in the form of this granita, and on the hottest of summer days it totally hits the spot.

In a saucepan, combine the sugar, sliced ginger, a pinch of salt, and 1 cup water. Bring just to a boil, stirring to dissolve the sugar, then reduce to a simmer and cook for 5 minutes. Remove the pan from the heat, cover, and let steep for 10 minutes. Uncover and allow the mixture to cool to room temperature.

Strain the ginger syrup into a clean mixing bowl, pressing gently but firmly to extract as much liquid as possible; discard the solids. To the syrup, add the clementine or tangerine zest and juice, lemon juice, basil, and grated ginger.

Pour the mixture into an 8 x 8-inch metal baking pan, or similar wide shallow freezer-proof pan, and freeze for 2 hours. Stir and mash the frozen crystals with a fork, then freeze again, stirring and mashing every 30 minutes until the mixture is completely frozen, and the crystals are evenly broken up, fluffy, and flaky, 3 to 3½ hours total. To serve, scoop the granita into small bowls or cups and drizzle with condensed milk.

The granita keeps, covered and frozen, for up to 1 week. Just before serving, let stand at room temperature until slightly melted, about 10 minutes, then gently fluff with a fork before scooping into bowls and drizzling with the condensed milk.

Ever wonder what the difference is between mandarins, tangerines, clementines, and satsumas? Here's the scoop: Mandarins are a category of small, slightly flat oranges, and tangerines, clementines, and satsumas are all a part of that category. Tangerines are the largest, with slightly tough skin and a distinct tartness. Clementines are the sweetest and smallest mandarins; usually seedless, they have become the most common in American grocery stores. Satsumas, originally from Japan, are grown in abundance in the American South, but are less commonly available outside of the region; they are also very juicy and sweet, and have the loosest skin, making them the easiest to peel.

CAMPFIRE SUNDAES

Toasted Marshmallow Ice Cream

Nonstick cooking spray

5 ounces marshmallows (about 25 standard-sized marshmallows)

2½ cups (20 ounces) premium vanilla ice cream

Pound Cake Croutons and Toasted Hazelnuts

4 ounces pound cake, cut into 1-inch cubes (about 3½ cups)

1 tablespoon unsalted butter, melted

⅓ cup hazelnuts

Chocolate Shell

4 ounces bittersweet chocolate (70%), coarsely chopped (¾ cup)

¼ cup coconut oil, melted

½ teaspoon smoked sea salt, plus more for serving

To Assemble

12 standard-sized marshmallows

2 cups (16 ounces) premium vanilla, chocolate, or coffee ice cream

1 cup heavy cream, whipped to medium peaks

Special equipment: 3 metal or bamboo skewers (if bamboo, soak in water for 1 hour, then pat dry with paper towels before using)

Many years ago, my parents, my brother Alan, and I spent a long weekend just outside of Toronto in Prince Edward County, known for its national park, emerging wines, and great food. One night we stumbled upon an ice cream shop where I ordered a scoop of "campfire" ice cream; the flavor was amazing—a creamy, cold version of a perfectly charred toasted marshmallow that had just been lifted from the flames. Nostalgic for many childhood summer nights spent around the fire, I started playing with the flavor at home, cracking the code on a fantastic version of the ice cream, and adding a home-made chocolate shell, plus cubes of toasted pound cake and toasted nuts. The smoked sea salt here is well worth the purchase; it gives the dessert a stunning final touch and a little bit of grown-up campfire flair.

For the marshmallow ice cream: Heat the oven to broil with the rack 4 to 5 inches from the heat source. Line a baking sheet with foil and lightly coat with nonstick cooking spray. Arrange the marshmallows in a single layer on the prepared baking sheet. Broil until the tops are charred, checking frequently, 3 to 4 minutes. Let cool completely.

Combine the broiled marshmallows and half of the ice cream in the jar of a blender. Pulse until almost smooth, 1 to 2 minutes. Add the remaining ice cream and pulse until incorporated, 1 to 2 minutes more. Transfer the mixture to a container and freeze until firm, at least 8 hours or overnight.

To toast the croutons and hazelnuts: Heat the oven to 375°F. Line a rimmed baking sheet with parchment paper.

In a large bowl, gently toss the pound cake with the melted butter to coat. Spread the cake cubes over half of the prepared baking sheet and the nuts on the other half. Bake until the croutons are lightly golden and the hazelnuts are fragrant and blistered, 10 to 12 minutes. Rub the hot toasted hazelnuts in a clean kitchen towel to remove skins (it's OK if not all the skins come off), then let both the croutons and nuts cool completely. Coarsely chop the cooled nuts.

For the chocolate shell: Combine the chocolate, coconut oil, and salt in a medium microwave-safe bowl. Microwave in 15-second intervals, stirring well in between, until the mixture is melted and smooth, 1 to 1½ minutes. Let cool to room temperature.

To assemble the sundaes: Thread the marshmallows onto skewers, leaving about ¼ inch between each. Toast 2 to 3 inches above a stovetop flame, turning occasionally, until golden and slightly charred on all sides, 2 to 3 minutes. (If you do not have a gas stove, broil the marshmallows following the method used for the ice cream.)

Place a scoop each of the toasted marshmallow and vanilla, chocolate, or coffee ice cream in each of four bowls. Spoon the chocolate shell over the tops. Let stand until the shell hardens (it will turn from glossy to matte), about 30 seconds, then top with the toasted marshmallows and croutons. Dollop with the whipped cream, then sprinkle the top with the toasted nuts and a little more smoked salt.

CHOCOLATE HONEYCOMB CRUNCH

¾ cup unsweetened coconut chips (or flakes if easier to find)

Nonstick cooking spray

1½ cups salted mini pretzels, each broken into 3 or 4 pieces

½ cup roasted unsalted peanuts, coarsely chopped

1½ teaspoons baking soda

½ teaspoon kosher salt

1⅓ cups sugar

½ cup light corn syrup

12 ounces bittersweet chocolate (70%), coarsely chopped (about 2½ cups)

Special equipment: candy thermometer

Note: *For easy cleaning after making the honeycomb, fill the pot halfway with water. Bring the water to a boil, then pour it out. Clean the pot with a scouring pad and dish soap, repeating with the boiling water once or twice as necessary.*

KITCHEN WISDOM: Prepping Ahead

Once the sugar mixture begins to brown slightly the recipe moves very quickly. Have everything at the stove and ready to go. A heat-proof rubber spatula, if you have one, is helpful to control the honeycomb as you pour it out onto a baking sheet to cool.

On a visit to New York from Toronto a few years ago, my friend Mia brought me a bag of homemade chocolate-covered candy. I had no idea what was in it but I devoured it with gusto. It was insanely addictive, sweet, and a little chewy with serious crunch. In a way, it reminded me of my favorite Canadian (via Britain) chocolate bar from childhood, called Crunchie, made from chocolate-dipped honeycomb candy (aka sponge toffee): Basically, it is caramelized sugar mixed with baking soda to create a foamy, crackly candy—which doesn't actually contain any honey at all. When I asked her for the recipe she told me it was salty, buttery crackers and hard toffee pieces mixed with condensed milk and covered in melted chocolate. Brilliant! But I couldn't get the idea of honeycomb out of my head. So I began experimenting with homemade honeycomb, swapping out crackers for mini pretzels, and adding coconut chips and unsalted peanuts, two favorite candy bar ingredients I thought would work well in the mix. I consider the result the best of all possible worlds.

In a large, dry skillet over medium heat, gently toast the coconut chips, stirring frequently until they begin to brown and dry out, 3 to 5 minutes. Remove from the heat and allow to cool.

Line a rimmed baking sheet with parchment paper and lightly coat with cooking spray. Sprinkle the cooled toasted coconut, pretzels, and peanuts on top of the parchment in a mostly single layer and oval shape, leaving a 1½- to 2-inch border. Set the baking sheet on a wire rack.

In a small bowl, stir together the baking soda and salt. Clip a candy thermometer to the side of a 5- to 7-quart heavy bottomed saucepan so its base is submerged in the sugar mixture but not touching the bottom of the pan. Add the sugar, corn syrup, and ⅓ cup water and gently stir until all of the sugar is wet. Cook over medium-high heat without stirring until the mixture is light to medium amber in color and reaches 300°F on the candy thermometer (the hard-crack stage), about 10 minutes. Immediately remove the pan from the heat, and carefully whisk in the baking soda mixture (sugar mixture will foam up significantly), then quickly pour the mixture over the pretzel mix in an even layer. Let cool completely on the wire rack, about 30 minutes. (See Note about cleaning the pot.)

Meanwhile, in a medium microwaveable bowl, microwave the chopped chocolate in 20- to 30-second increments, stirring between each, until melted. Let cool to room temperature.

Recipe continues

Line another baking sheet or large cutting board with parchment paper. Break the hard candy into small pieces, about 2 inches each. Dip the candy, one piece at a time, into the melted chocolate, allowing excess to drip back into the bowl, then set on the lined baking sheet or board. Once all of the candy has been dipped, chill it in the refrigerator until set, 15 to 20 minutes. Transfer to an airtight container and keep chilled (for up to 5 days) until ready to serve.

CHOCOLATE-DIPPED, DULCE DE LECHE–FILLED SANDWICH COOKIES with Sea Salt

1 (14-ounce) can sweetened condensed milk (see Note)

¾ cup (1½ sticks) unsalted butter, cubed, at room temperature

¾ cup granulated sugar

2 large eggs

1½ teaspoons pure vanilla extract

2 cups unbleached all-purpose flour, plus more for dusting

¼ teaspoon kosher salt

½ teaspoon baking powder

8 ounces bittersweet chocolate (70%), coarsely chopped (about 1½ cups)

Flaky sea salt (such as Maldon) for sprinkling

Note: A 14- to 16-ounce jar of store-bought dulce de leche can be used in place of making your own (See Kitchen Wisdan, page 206).

I was introduced to Doug Quint and Bryan Petroff, the guys behind Big Gay Ice Cream, by friend and food TV host Andrew Zimmern in the fall of 2012. We were at an event together when he rushed me through a long line and pushed a cone of chocolate-dipped soft serve ice cream into my hand, claiming that this modern take on the ice cream truck of our youth was about to take over the world. The cone was their signature Salty Pimp: vanilla soft serve, injected with dulce de leche, then dipped in dark chocolate and sprinkled with sea salt. I took one bite and immediately fell in love with both the creamy frozen concoction and the guys behind it. These cookies are a love letter to my trailblazing buddies and their dazzling dairy dessert.

Remove any labels from the can of sweetened condensed milk and place on the bottom of a large stockpot. Fill the pot with water, covering the can by 4 to 6 inches, then bring the water just to a boil over high heat. Reduce the heat to low, cover the pot, and continue boiling, frequently checking the water level, for 3 hours. (The can should be covered by at least 1 inch of water throughout the cooking process or it could explode.) Remove the can from the water and allow it to cool at room temperature. Chill until firm enough to spread, at least 45 minutes, or, if unopened, up to 1 week. Opened, it can be kept refrigerated in an airtight container for up to 1 week.

In the bowl of an electric mixer fitted with the paddle attachment, beat together the soft butter and sugar on medium speed until light and fluffy, about 3 minutes. Beat in the eggs, one at a time, until fully incorporated, then beat in the vanilla.

In a small bowl, whisk together the flour, salt, and baking powder. With the mixer on low, add the flour mixture to the butter mixture, a little at a time, until evenly combined (the dough will be sticky). Turn out the dough onto a lightly flour-dusted work surface. Using flour-dusted hands, divide it in half, then roll each piece into a log 1¾ to 2 inches in diameter. Wrap the logs in parchment paper, covering completely, including at the ends. Refrigerate until firm, at least 90 minutes (or overnight), or freeze for 30 minutes (or up to 3 weeks).

Heat the oven to 350°F with racks on upper and lower thirds. Line two baking sheets with parchment paper.

Recipe continues

If your dough is fully frozen (i.e., for longer than 30 minutes), let it stand at room temperature until soft enough to slice, 15 to 30 minutes. Slice the dough into ¼-inch-thick rounds (if dough becomes too soft to cleanly slice, chill again until firm). Place slices about 1 inch apart on the prepared baking sheets. Bake, rotating the sheets halfway through, until golden around the edges, 10 to 12 minutes. Let cool on the baking sheets for a few minutes, then transfer to a wire rack to cool completely; reserve one parchment-lined baking sheet.

Meanwhile, in a small microwave-safe bowl, microwave the chocolate in 30-second intervals, stirring between each, until melted.

Using a small spoon or offset spatula, spread 2 teaspoons of the chilled dulce de leche over the flat side of half of the cookies. Sandwich with the remaining cookies, flat sides together.

Dip half of each sandwich into the melted chocolate, then place on the reserved lined baking sheet and sprinkle the chocolate with a generous pinch of flaky sea salt. Refrigerate until the chocolate is set, about 15 minutes.

The cookies can be kept in an airtight container in the refrigerator for up to 1 week. Let them stand at room temperature for a few minutes before serving.

SOURCES

◆

Asian Products

Hoisin sauce, fish sauce, rice vinegar, sesame oil, soba noodles, udon noodles, vermicelli rice noodles, mung bean sprouts, and edamame can be found at most well-stocked supermarkets, and at Asian supermarkets such as Hmart (nj.hmart.com). Look for dry goods and pantry items in the Asian section, and fresh vegetables, like mung bean sprouts and edamame in produce. Edamame is also sold frozen.

Flours and Sugars

High-quality white, whole-wheat, and other flours, as well as alternative flours and sugars like rice flour, buckwheat flour, and maple and turbinado sugar, can be found in most well-stocked supermarkets or ordered online. Good brands to look for include King Arthur Flour (KingArthurFlour.com), Bob's Red Mill (BobsRedMill.com) and Wholesome (WholesomeSweet.com).

Harissa

Harissa can be found in the ethnic section at most well-stocked supermarkets, or ordered from Kalustyan's (Kalustyans.com), Sahadi's (Sahadis.com), and Amazon.com.

Licorice and Licorice Root Powder

Australian soft black licorice is widely available at well-stocked supermarkets and stores like Target and Walmart, and can also be purchased from Amazon.com and via the specialty candy shop Licorice International (LicoriceInternational.com), where you can also find *dubbel zout* (double salt) licorice. Look for licorice root powder at health food stores, or order from Kalustyans.com.

Matzo Meal

Look for matzo meal in the kosher section of well-stocked supermarkets, or order from Amazon.com.

Nuts and Seeds

Find chia seeds, pepitas, pine nuts, and other nuts and seeds at health food markets and well-stocked supermarkets, or order from TheNutBox.com and Amazon.com.

Peppers and Dried and Fresh Chilies

Look for whole dried chilies, such as anchos, as well as fresh chilies and peppers like Thai chilies, Scotch bonnets, and shishitos, at Latin markets and well-stocked supermarkets. Dried chilies can also be ordered from La Tienda (tienda.com), Kalustyans.com, Sahadis.com, and Amazon.com.

Pickapeppa Sauce

Pickapeppa Sauce can be found at Caribbean grocery stores and in the ethnic section of well-stocked supermarkets, or order from Pickapeppa.com, Kalustyans.com, or Amazon.com.

Pomegranate Molasses

Pomegranate molasses can be found in the ethnic section of well-stocked supermarkets, or ordered from Kalustyans.com, Sahadis.com, and Amazon.com.

Salts

Kosher salt and flaky sea salts like Maldon are widely available at most well-stocked supermarkets. Specialty salts, like smoked sea salt and a variety of other sorts, can be ordered from TheMeadow.com.

Schmaltz

Many good butcher shops, Jewish delis, and health food stores stock schmaltz, which can also be ordered from Fatworks (fatworksfoods.com).

Specialty Produce

Farmers' markets and good supermarkets are the best places to find high-quality produce, including a wide variety of greens (like dandelion), root vegetables (like jicama and celery root), and, when they're in season, less widely available fruits and vegetables like cucamelons. The Chef's Garden (chefs-garden.com) and Melissa's Produce (melissas.com) are both good online sources for high-quality produce, including hard-to-find items.

Spices

High-quality spices like Aleppo pepper, sumac, whole cumin seeds, za'atar, and more can be ordered from Kalustyans .com, Sahadis.com, and La Boîte (laboiteny.com).

Tahini

Tahini is widely available in the nut butter or ethnic section of most good supermarkets. My favorite brand, Seed + Mill, can be ordered online from seedandmill.com.

ACKNOWLEDGMENTS

◆

I am infinitely grateful to countless individuals, without whom this book simply wouldn't exist.

Mindy Fox, trusted friend of almost twenty years, partner in crime, detail detective, consummate cheerleader, and cooking mastermind, who made every day of work on this book, both in the kitchen and staring at the blank page, an adventure and a joy.

Teresia Precht, my chief *everything* officer, who tested each recipe, tirelessly managed every element (of this book and my life), and kept so many balls in the air with ease, even when I threatened to drop them.

Andy McNicol, my patient and sagacious literary agent at WME.

My editor, Karen Murgolo, who encouraged and guided me with calm, gracious enthusiasm, and her thoughtful, hard-working team at Grand Central Life & Style, including Matthew Ballast, Lisa Forde, Morgan Hedden, Tareth Mitch, Amanda Pritzker, Anne Twomey, Deri Reed, and their publisher, Ben Sevier.

Laura Palese, book designer extraordinaire and all-around awesome human.

Mindy and I together would like to thank Sadie Gelb for her positive and passionate help with so many crucial aspects of this project.

The visual dream team, who brought my recipes to life:

Photographer Johnny Miller
Food stylist Rebecca Jurkevich
Prop stylist Bette Blau

Photography and food and prop stylist assistants: Justin Conly, Judy Mancini, and Stephanie Becker

Glam Squad from Heaven: Jessie Riley and Charlotte Rose Coleman

The brilliant artisans and long-adored brands whose props I was honored to have grace these pages:

Keith Kreeger
www.keithkreeger.com

Margaret Braun
www.margaretbraun.com

Elephant Ceramics & Michele Michael
www.elephantceramics.com

Henry Street Studio & Aliza Simons
www.henrystreetstudio.com

Notary Ceramics & Sarah Van Raden
www.notaryceramics.com

Canvas Home Store
www.canvashomestore.com

Le Creuset
www.lecreuset.com

Staub
www.staubusa.com

Jeff Googel and Josh Bider at WME, and Kenny Slotnick at AGI Lifestyle, my trusted agents and professional spirit guides.

Elise Freimuth and Mary Wagstaff at Wagstaff Worldwide, and Sara Fuller, Joey Monroe, and Marcel Pariseau at True Public Relations for their endless energy, loyalty, and savvy media navigation.

The nomadic tribes I've been lucky enough to join through my many serendipitous adventures at *Food & Wine*, Bravo, and Magical Elves, including my cherished *Top Chef* crew.

A special thanks to Tom Colicchio, mentor, friend, and poet, for his thoughtful foreword, endless hours together at the dinner table, and his all-around kindness.

Thank you to the countless generous, whip-smart, insatiable friends who contributed to this book in ways both large and small, including but not limited to: Rena Ali, Mia Brown, Brandon Creed, Hallie Delaney, BJ Denis, Sue Devor, Melanie Dunea, Shana Faust, Matthew Gaudet, Seth Gold, Jessica Goldberg, Stacey Grill, Samantha Hanks, Cameron Kane, Peter Lindberg, Nilou Motamed, Sarah Rosenberg, Seton Rossini, Katherine Yang, Sonia Zala, and Amy Zavatto.

My beloved, wondrous, and supportive family: Renée and Ivor, Alan, Eric, Kim, Tyler, Elle, and Brooke Simmons, and Noreen, Herb, and Jodie Abrams.

And finally, my greatest loves, Jeremy and Dahlia Rae Abrams, who are, respectively, the reason I accomplish anything at all, and my single greatest accomplishment.

—**Gail Simmons**

A huge thanks to Gail Simmons: Making this book with you was an honor, as well as a lovely, fun, and extremely tasty adventure. My deepest gratitude also goes to David Black and Sarah Smith at David Black Agency; my husband, Steve Hoffman; Neil, Phyllis, and Jason Fox, and my extended Northeast, Midwest, and Southern families; and the many friends and colleagues who continue to cheer on the work that I do and love so much, and (very lucky me!) are far too numerous to list here.

—**Mindy Fox**

INDEX

◆

ABOUT THE AUTHORS

◆

Gail Simmons is a trained culinary expert, the special projects director at *Food & Wine*, and a judge on Bravo's Emmy-winning series *Top Chef* since its inception in 2006. Simmons makes frequent television appearances on *Today*, *Good Morning America*, *The Chew* and *The Talk*, and has been featured in *New York* magazine, *Travel + Leisure*, *GQ*, and *People*, among others. Her first book, a memoir titled *Talking with My Mouth Full: My Life as a Professional Eater*, was published in 2012. She lives in Brooklyn with her husband and daughter.

Mindy Fox is a writer, editor, producer, and former restaurant cook, who has authored and coauthored many cookbooks, including *Salads: Beyond the Bowl* and *The Perfectly Roasted Chicken*. A former editor at *Saveur* and *La Cucina Italiana*, her work has also appeared in *Food & Wine*, *Fine Cooking*, *In Style*, *Epicurious*, *The London Times*, and more. She lives in New York City with her husband and her beloved lab-hound.